Assessing Writing

THE CAMBRIDGE LANGUAGE ASSESSMENT SERIES

*Series editors*: J. Charles Alderson and Lyle F. Bachman

In this series:

**Assessing Vocabulary** by John Read
**Assessing Reading** by J. Charles Alderson
**Assessing Languages for Specific Purposes** by Dan Douglas
**Assessing Listening** by Gary Buck
**Assessing Writing** by Sara Cushing Weigle

# Assessing Writing

*Sara Cushing Weigle*

CAMBRIDGE
UNIVERSITY PRESS

PUBLISHED BY THE PRESS SYNDICATE OF THE UNIVERSITY OF CAMBRIDGE
The Pitt Building, Trumpington Street, Cambridge, United Kingdom

CAMBRIDGE UNIVERSITY PRESS
The Edinburgh Building, Cambridge CB2 2RU, UK
40 West 20th Street, New York, NY 10011–4211, USA
477 Williamstown Road, Port Melbourne, VIC 3207, Australia
Ruiz de Alarcón 13, 28014 Madrid, Spain
Dock House, The Waterfront, Cape Town, 8001, South Africa

http://www.cambridge.org

First published 2002

Printed in the United Kingdom at the University Press, Cambridge

*Typeface* 9.5/13pt Utopia   [CE]

*A catalogue record for this book is available from the British Library*

ISBN 0 521 78027 6 hardback
ISBN 0 521 78446 8 paperback

To my family: Clarke, Tommy, and James

# Contents

# Series Editors' Preface

Writing, which was once considered the domain of the elite and well-educated, has become an essential tool for people of all walks of life in today's global community. Whether used in reporting analyses of current events for newspapers or web pages, composing academic essays, business reports, letters, or e-mail messages, the ability to write effectively allows individuals from different cultures and backgrounds to communicate. Furthermore, it is now widely recognized that writing plays a vital role not only in conveying information, but also in transforming knowledge to create new knowledge. It is thus of central importance to students in academic and second language programs throughout the world. In many of these settings, the assessment of writing ability is of critical importance. Employers, academic instructors and writing teachers need to make decisions about potential employees and students, based on how well they can communicate in writing. But while the history of writing assessment goes back for centuries, it continues to be one of the most problematic areas of language use to assess. This is partly because of the vast diversity of writing purposes, styles, and genres, but primarily because of the subjectivity of the judgements involved in assessing samples of writing.

The author of this book, Dr. Sara Cushing Weigle, has extensive experience in teaching and assessing writing, and has conducted seminal research in this area. Her doctoral dissertation on writing assessment was awarded the TOEFL Award for Outstanding Doctoral Dissertation in Second/Foreign Language Testing in 1996, and she has since published numerous research studies in this area. Furthermore, her experience as a teacher has enabled her to present the complexities of writing assessment research and practice in a way that is readily accessible to practitioners and researchers alike.

This book provides a coverage of writing assessment that is both broad and in-depth, discussing the relevant research and theory, and addressing practical considerations in the design, development and use of writing assessments. Beginning with a discussion of the nature of writing as both a social and cognitive activity, the author offers a thorough and critical review of the relevant research and theories of writing ability that provides the grounding for the rest of the book. She then proposes a conceptual framework for designing and developing writing assessments. In subsequent chapters, the author provides detailed discussions of procedures for designing writing assessment tasks and of scoring procedures, in the contexts of both large-scale and classroom assessment, illustrating her main points throughout with examples from a wide range of writing assessments. She devotes an entire chapter to an approach to assessment – portfolio assessment – that is both controversial and widely used, not only for writing assessment, but also for large-scale assessment of educational achievement. In her final chapter, the author looks ahead to examine the effects of technology on writing itself, and on writing pedagogy, as well as the potential contributions of new technologies to writing assessment. She also considers the politics of writing assessment, and the on-going tensions among different stakeholders about the nature of writing assessment, the ways in which these should be scored and interpreted, and the kinds of evidence that need to be provided to support the validity of the inferences and uses we make of the results of writing assessments.

In summary, this book provides a thorough discussion of practical issues and procedures in the design, development and use of writing assessments that is solidly grounded in research and theory. It thus has much to offer to both the test developer and the classroom teacher.

J. Charles Alderson
Lyle F. Bachman

# Acknowledgements

In the summer of 1996, at the Language Testing Research Colloquium in Tampere, Finland, Lyle Bachman and Charles Alderson asked me if I would be interested in contributing a book on writing assessment to the new CUP series on language testing. In the ensuing five years I gave birth to my second child, moved with my family from Los Angeles to Atlanta to start a new job, bought a house, rejoiced with my much-loved father when he found and married the woman of his dreams, and mourned with my new stepmother a year later when Dad was diagnosed with pancreatic cancer and passed away. All the while Lyle and Charles, along with Mickey Bonin of Cambridge University Press, waited patiently for me to complete this manuscript and never gave up hope that I would eventually complete it. Now that it is finally finished, I need first of all to thank Lyle, Charles, and Mickey for their patience and unwavering support. I am also grateful for their guidance and feedback at every stage of the process. Lyle in particular has been willing to read and comment in detail on many drafts of each chapter, and I would like to acknowledge his many contributions to the book.

I am grateful for the support and encouragement of my colleagues at Georgia State University. In particular, I would like to thank my past and current department chairs, Joan Carson, Gayle Nelson, and Pat Byrd, for their support of this project in various ways. In addition, Gayle Nelson and Pat Dunkel have used drafts of several chapters of this book in their courses, and the feedback of their students has been helpful in improving the final product.

Two semesters of students in my Issues in Second Language Writing class have read and commented on drafts of several chapters of the book, and their comments have been quite insightful. In particular, I would like to thank Maria Ines Valsecchi and John Bunting for their comments and especially for their enthusiasm about the book at a time when I was having my doubts about ever finishing it. My research assistant, Gerry Landers, was a tremendous help in getting the list of references and tables together. I would also like to thank Cindy Lutenbacher for giving me coffee, beer, and a shoulder to cry on, and Jim Purpura for lending humor and support from afar.

Finally, I would like to thank my family for their support. My husband Clarke has given me time and space for writing, listened to my complaints and suffered patiently through my temper tantrums, and supported me in a hundred other small ways that I am only now beginning to appreciate. My sons Tommy and James, simply by being their own delightful selves, have kept me mindful of the truly important things in life. A written acknowledgement could never sufficiently convey my gratitude to them, but I hope that a trip to the ice cream store will be a good start.

The publishers and I are grateful to the authors, publishers and others who have given permission for the use of copyright material identified in the text. It has not been possible to identify, or trace, sources of all the materials used and in such cases the publishers would welcome information from copyright owners.

*Research in the teaching of English* by AC Purves, A Soter, AS Takala & A Vahapassi. Copyright 1984 by the National Council of Teachers of English, *Primary trait scoring* by R Lloyd-Jones, CR Cooper & L Odell from *Evaluating Writing.* Copyright 1977 by the National Council of Teachers of English. Reprinted with permission. An overview of writing assessment: *Theory, research and practice* by W Wolcott (with SM Legg), Copyright 1998 by the National Council of Teachers of English. *Criterion-referenced language test development* by BK Lynch and F Davidson, reprinted with permission of Yale University Press. Extracts from *Test development plan with specifications for placement instruments anchored to the model standards* by FA Butler, SC Weigle, AB Kahn & EY Sato, CSE UCLA 1996. *Proficiency sample project* by M Apodaco, 1990. Test of English as a Foreign Language 2000. TOEFL materials are reprinted by permission of Educational Testing Service, the copyright owner; however, the test questions and any other testing information are provided in their entirety by Cambridge University Press. No endorsement of this publication by Educational Testing Service should be inferred. *Testing ESL composition* by H Jacobs, S Zinkgraf, D Wormuth, V Hartfiel & J Hughey (1981). Extract from *Communicative language testing* by CJ Weir, 1990. Extract from scoring procedures for ESL contexts in *Assessing second language writing in academic contexts* by L Hamp-Lyons. Copyright © 1991 L Hamp-Lyons. Reproduced with permission of Greenwood Publishing Group, Inc., Westport, CT. *Language testing in practice* by Lyle F Bachman & Adrian S Palmer © Lyle F Bachman & Adrian S Palmer 1996, reproduced by permission of Oxford University Press. Extracts from *First Certificate in English*: a handbook UCLES. Extracts from *IELTS specimen Materials 1995*, and *IELTS Handbook 2002*, UCLES. Extracts from *Contextualized Writing Assessment* (CARLA 2001). *Designing and assessing effective classroom writing assignments for NES & ESL students*, reprinted from *Journal of second language writing*, Vol 4 no 1 pp 17–41, J Reid and B Kroll, copyright 1995, with permission from Elsevier Science. *Assessing the portfolio* by L Hamp-Lyons and W Condon (2000), reprinted with the permission of Hampton Press, Inc. Checklist for portfolio contents from Portfolio plus: *a critical guide to alternative assessment* p169 by L Mabry copyright 1999, reprinted by permission of Sage Publications, Inc.*Writing assessment* by G Summer and E Spalding, University of Kentucky 1998. The development of large-scale placement assessment at the University of Michigan by M Willard-Traub, E Decker, R Reed & J Johnston, 1992–1998. *Toward a new theory of writing assessment. College Composition and Communication*, by B Huot. Copyright 1996 by the National Council of Teachers of English.

Atlanta, September 2001

........................................................................................................

# CHAPTER ONE

# Introduction

The ability to write effectively is becoming increasingly important in our global community, and instruction in writing is thus assuming an increasing role in both second- and foreign-language education. As advances in transportation and technology allow people from nations and cultures throughout the world to interact with each other, communication across languages becomes ever more essential. As a result, the ability to speak and write a second language is becoming widely recognized as an important skill for educational, business, and personal reasons. Writing has also become more important as tenets of communicative language teaching – that is, teaching language as a system of communication rather than as an object of study – have taken hold in both second- and foreign-language settings. The traditional view in language classes that writing functions primarily to support and reinforce patterns of oral language use, grammar, and vocabulary, is being supplanted by the notion that writing in a second language is a worthwhile enterprise in and of itself.

Wherever the acquisition of a specific language skill is seen as important, it becomes equally important to test that skill, and writing is no exception. Thus, as the role of writing in second-language education increases, there is an ever greater demand for valid and reliable ways to test writing ability, both for classroom use and as a predictor of future professional or academic success.

What does it mean to test writing ability? A common-sense answer to this question is that "the best way to test people's writing ability is to get them to write" (Hughes, 1989: 75). If we agree with this statement, it follows that a test of writing involves at least two basic components: one or more writing tasks, or instructions that tell test takers what to write, and a means of evaluating the writing samples that test takers produce. However, as we shall see, designing a good test of writing involves much more than simply thinking of a topic for test takers to write about and then using our own judgement to rank order the resulting writing samples. Before we can make decisions about designing assessment tasks or scoring procedures, we need to consider a number of key questions. These questions include the following:

- What are we trying to test? That is, how are we defining writing ability for the purposes of the test – are we interested primarily in whether test takers can form grammatical sentences, or do we want to know how well they can use writing for a specific communicative function?

- Why do we want to test writing ability? What will we do with the information that we get from the test?

- Who are our test takers? What do we need to know about them in order to design tasks that allow test takers to perform at their highest ability?

- Who will score the tests, and what criteria or standards will be used? How can we ensure that raters apply the scoring standards consistently?

- Who will use the information that our test provides? In what form will the information be the most useful?

- What are the constraints (of time, materials, money, and labor) that limit the amount and kind of information we can collect about test takers' writing ability?

- What do we need to know about testing to make our test valid and reliable?

This book attempts to outline answers to these questions, and is organized in the following way. The rest of Chapter 1 provides an introduction to writing assessment by considering, first of all, the reasons why people use writing in second-language contexts, and second, the types of writing texts people are likely to need to write in a second language, both inside and outside the language classroom. The introduction is followed by an overview of writing assessment in both first and second languages, comprising two chapters. Chapter 2, The Nature of Writing Ability, reviews literature from the fields of composition, applied linguistics, and psychology to discuss the nature of writing ability and the connections between writing and other language skills, particularly speaking and reading. Chapter 3, Basic Considerations in Assessing Writing, reviews the purposes for testing writing in a variety of settings for various populations, and discusses principles for evaluating test usefulness (Bachman and Palmer, 1996).

Chapters 4 through 7 deal with what has been traditionally called direct testing of writing, particularly for large-scale assessment: timed writing on a topic not known to test takers in advance. Chapter 4 reviews a large body of research on writing assessment, looking at writing tasks, rating scales, raters, and texts. Chapter 5 presents information and advice on designing tasks for writing assessment, and Chapter 6 discusses scoring procedures. Chapter 7 provides an in-depth discussion of a number of writing tests for a variety of contexts.

The final three chapters deal with topics in writing assessment that go beyond the traditional timed impromptu writing test. Chapter 8 discusses classroom evaluation of writing, looking at options for responding to and evaluating student writing at various stages of the writing process, from pre-writing through to a polished, final text. Chapter 9 discusses portfolio assessment, or the assessment of writing ability by collecting and evaluating a number of texts written at different times and for different audiences and purposes. Finally, Chapter 10 looks towards the future, discussing unresolved issues and future directions in second-language writing assessment.

## Writing in first- and second-language contexts

Before we can discuss how to test writing, we must start by attempting to define what we mean by **writing ability**. As we will see, however, this is not a simple task, since, as researchers in both first- and second-language writing have pointed out, the uses to which writing is put by different people in different situations are so varied that no single definition can cover all situations (Purves, 1992; Camp, 1993; White, 1995). For example, the ability to write down exactly what someone else says (an important skill for a stenographer) is quite different from the ability to write a persuasive argument. For second-language learners, learning to write may mean anything from attempting to master the most commonly used Chinese characters to being able to write a dissertation for a Ph.D. Instead of attempting an all-encompassing definition, then, it may be more useful to begin by delineating the situations in which people learn and use second languages in general and second-language writing in particular, and the types of writing that are likely to be relevant for second-language writers.

Perhaps the best way to begin to appreciate the complexities in L2 writing is to contrast it with L1 writing. As Vähäpässi (1982), Leki (1992) and others have pointed out, first language writing is inextricably linked to formal education. While virtually all children are able to speak their native language when they begin school, writing must be explicitly taught. Furthermore, in comparison to speaking, listening, and reading, writing outside of school settings is relatively rare, and extensive public writing (that is, writing beyond the sentence or paragraph level and intended for an audience other than oneself or one's close associates) is reserved for those employed in specialized careers such as education, law, or journalism.

In first-language settings, the ability to write well has a very close relationship to academic and professional success. Grabowski (1996) notes that:

> Writing, as compared to speaking, can be seen as a more standardized system which must be acquired through special instruction. Mastery of this standard system is an important prerequisite of cultural and educational participation and the maintenance of one's rights and duties . . . The fact that writing is more standardized than speaking allows for a higher degree of sanctions when people deviate from that standard.
>
> (Grabowski, 1996: 75)

Thus, in first-language education, learning to write involves learning a specialized version of a language already known to students. This specialized language differs in important ways from spoken language, both in form and in use, as we shall see in Chapter 2, but builds upon linguistic resources that students already possess. The ultimate goal of learning to write is, for most students, to be able to participate fully in many aspects of society beyond school, and for some, to pursue careers that involve extensive writing.

The value of being able to write effectively increases as students progress through compulsory education on to higher education. At the university level in particular, writing is seen not just as a standard-ized system of communication but also as an essential tool for learning. At least in the English-speaking world, one of the main functions of writing at higher levels of education is to expand one's own knowledge through reflection rather than simply to communi-cate information (Bereiter and Scardamalia, 1987; Purves *et al.*, 1984). Writing and critical thinking are seen as closely linked, and expertise in writing is seen as an indication that students have mastered the cognitive skills required for university work. Or, to phrase it somewhat more negatively, a perceived lack of writing expertise is frequently seen as a sign that students do not possess the appropriate thinking and reasoning skills that they need to succeed. In first-language writing instruction, therefore, particularly in higher education, a great deal of emphasis is placed on originality of thought, the development of ideas, and the soundness of the writer's logic. Conventions of language (voice, tone, style, accuracy, mechanics) are important as well, but frequently these are seen as secondary matters, to be ad-dressed after matters of content and organization.

While the specific goals of writing instruction may vary from culture to culture (see Saari and Purves, 1992, for an overview of mother-tongue and language education internationally), it is clear that writing is an important part of the curriculum in schools from the earliest grades onward, and that most children in countries that have a formal education system will learn to write, at least at a basic level, in that setting. In this sense, we can say that first language writing instruction is relatively standardized within a particular culture.

In contrast, the same cannot be said of second-language writing because of the wide variety of situations in which people learn and use second languages, both as children and as adults, in schools and in other settings. We can distinguish between at least five main groups of second-language learners, as shown in Table 1.1 (adapted from Bernhardt, 1991). The first group consists of children from a minority language group receiving their education in the majority language. These children need to learn to read and write in a language that is not spoken in their home in order to succeed in school and ultimately in the workplace. A second group of children are majority language speakers in immersion programs or otherwise learning a second language in school. In this case, mastery of the second language enhances their education but is not critical to ultimate

Table 1.1 *Groups of second language learners (adapted from Bernhardt, 1991)*

|  | Learners | Needs | Purpose |
|---|---|---|---|
| Children | minority group members; e.g. in bilingual programs | academic 'school' writing skills | for survival |
|  | majority group members; e.g. in immersion programs |  | for enhancement |
| Adults | minority group members, immigrant status | immediate functional literacy skills | for survival in the workplace |
|  | quasi-temporary academic status |  | for advanced subject matter degrees |
|  | majority language group members; e.g. traditional foreign-language learners | academic 'educated' language skills | for educational and/or job enhancement and/or interest |

educational success, in contrast to the first group. A common factor for both groups of children is that their first language is still developing, and that, like first-language writers, writing is very much a school-based and school-oriented activity.

There are also three distinct groups of adult second-language learners. The first group consists of immigrants to a new country, who are frequently from a lower-prestige language background and may or may not be literate in their first language. For these learners, writing at a basic functional level is essential for survival in the workplace. In marked contrast to this group is a second group of adults: those who have left their home countries to seek an advanced university degree. These adults are already highly educated and literate in their first language, and their writing needs are very sophisticated. Finally, there is a third group of L2 learners: majority language group members who are learning a second language for personal interest and/or career or educational enhancement. Like the second group, this third group is generally well educated; unlike the second group, however, they may not have as great a need to write in their second language, and certainly the writing that they will do is less complex and demanding than that of the second group.

To summarize, then, groups of second-language learners can be distinguished by age, by level of education and first-language literacy, and by the real-world need for writing outside of the classroom. In addition to these factors, the ability and opportunity to write in a second language are also determined by other considerations. One important factor is the stage or level of acquisition of the second language. This factor will be discussed in detail in Chapter 2; for the present, we will simply note that one cannot write in a second language without knowing at least something about the grammar and vocabulary of that language. An additional factor is the relative similarity or difference between the two languages: writing in a language that is closely related to one's native language in terms of grammar, vocabulary, and writing system is clearly easier than writing in a language that is vastly different. Finally, an important consideration, which is related to the real-world need for writing discussed above, is the role of the second language as a language of wider communication: someone learning English as a foreign language will probably have more realistic needs for writing in that language than someone learning Russian, for example.

As this discussion has shown, then, the differences between first and second-language writing are considerable, and in particular the variety of backgrounds, experience, needs, and purposes for writing is much greater for second-language writers than for first-language writers. As we shall see later on in this book, this variety has important implications for the testing of writing, both in terms of designing appropriate writing tasks and in terms of evaluating writing.

## Classification of written text types

One important implication of the variety of background, experience, and needs of second-language writers is that the types of writing produced by these different groups vary considerably as well. To continue our discussion of what is meant by writing ability, then, we will now turn to another question: What do people write, and under what circumstances? As discussed above, writing can be understood as meaning anything from forming letters to writing extended discourse. What kinds of writing are relevant for which groups of second-

Table 1.2 *General model of writing discourse (Vähäpässi, 1982)*

| Cognitive Processing / Primary Audience | Primary Content | I REPRODUCE | II ORGANIZE/REORGANIZE | | III INVENT/GENERATE | |
|---|---|---|---|---|---|---|
| | | Linguistically precoded/ Predetermined Information | Known | | New or Alternative | |
| | | | Spatial/ Temporal | Phenomena, Concepts or Mental States | Spatial/ Temporal | Phenomena, Concepts or Mental States |
| **Dominant Intention/ Purpose** | | | | | | |
| 1. To learn (metalingual mathetic) — Self | | Copying Taking dictation | Retell a story (heard or read) | Note Resume Summary Outline Paraphrasing | | Comments on book margins Metaphors Analogies |
| 2. To convey emotions, feelings (emotive) — Self / Others | | Stream of consciousness | Personal story Personal diary Personal letter | Portrayal | Reflective writing – Personal essays | |
| 3. To inform (referential) — Others | | Quote Fill in a form | Narrative report News Instruction Telegram Announcement Circular | Directions Description Technical description Biography Science report/ experiment | Expository writing – Definition – Academic essay/article – Book review – Commentary | |

The traditional literary genre and modes can be placed

| Purpose | | | | | |
|---|---|---|---|---|---|
| 4. To convince, persuade (conative) | Others | Citation from authority/expert | Letter of application<br>Statement of personal views, opinions | Advertisement<br>Letter or advice | Argumentative/ persuasive writing<br>– Editorial<br>– Critical essay/article | under one<br><br>or more |
| 5. To entertain, delight, please (poetic) | Others | Quotation of poetry and prose | Given an ending –<br>create a story;<br>Create an ending<br>Retell a story | Word portrait or sketch<br>Causerie | Entertainment writing<br>– Parody<br>– Rhymes | of these four<br><br>purposes. |
| 6. To keep in touch (phatic) | Others | Postcards | Postcards, letters | | | |
| | DOCUMENTATIVE DISCOURSE | | REPORTORIAL DISCOURSE | | EXPLORATORY DISCOURSE | |

language writers? If we are going to have a generalized model of second language writing that covers all five groups of second-language writers, it is important to have a system for describing and categorizing writing text types in terms of their most important characteristics.

One useful model of writing discourse was originally laid out by Vähäpässi (1982) for an international study of school writing. This model is reproduced here as Table 1.2.

As the table shows, text types can be categorized along two major dimensions: cognitive processing, and dominant intention or purpose. Along the horizontal axis, three fundamental levels of cognitive processing can be distinguished. The least demanding task is to reproduce information that has already been linguistically encoded or determined (Type I). Examples of writing at this level would be taking dictation or filling in a form. The next level of cognitive processing, organizing, involves arranging or organizing information that is known to the writer (Type II). An example of this type of writing would be a laboratory report. Finally, the most demanding level of cognitive processing involves inventing or generating new ideas or information, as in expository writing (Type III). It is this third type of writing – writing for knowledge transforming – that is seen as most critical in academic writing for first-language writers, and for second-language writers in academic settings, as discussed above.

Along the vertical axis, Vähäpässi lists six different dominant intentions or purposes, following a scheme originally proposed by Jakobson (1960). These purposes are to learn, to convey emotions, to inform, to convince or persuade, to entertain/delight, and to keep in touch. Note that, unlike the cognitive demands, there is no implied hierarchy among these purposes – that is, the ability to achieve one of these functions does not depend on the ability to do others, even though it may be argued that persuading is more difficult that informing, for example. Along with these purposes, there is also consideration of the primary audience, either self or others. Written texts can thus be placed into the grid created by the intersection of these two axes.

While this categorization was intended originally for school writing, it may be useful to return to the five groups of second-language writers described above and map their typical writing needs onto this grid (see Table 1.3). The first two groups – children being schooled in their second language – will need any or all of these writing types, depending on their level of schooling and the specific demands of the

Table 1.3 *Groups of second-language writers and types of writing (adapted from Bernhardt, 1991)*

| | Learners | Needs | Purpose | Type of writing |
|---|---|---|---|---|
| Children | minority group members; e.g. in bilingual programs | academic 'school' writing skills | for survival | I, II, III |
| | majority group members; e.g. in immersion programs | | for enhancement | I, II, III |
| Adults | minority group members, immigrant status | immediate literacy skills | for survival in the workplace | I, II |
| | quasi-temporary academic status | academic 'educated' language skills | for advanced subject matter degrees | I, II, III |
| | majority language group members, e.g. traditional foreign-language learners | | for educational and/or job enhancement and/or interest | I, II |

curriculum. For students nearing the end of compulsory education and intending to go on to higher education, Type III writing takes on greater importance. Similarly, those who are pursuing advanced degrees in a second-language environment will also need to write across all three levels of cognitive processing, with writing to inform and writing to persuade of particular importance for this group of second-language writers.

On the other hand, for the other two groups of adult second-language learners – minority language group members writing for survival, and majority language group members writing for personal enhancement – the need for writing will be much more restricted, both inside and outside the classroom. Looking first at the language classroom, the predominant use of writing for both groups tends to be Type I writing, with the dominant function of learning. As mentioned previously, the traditional role of writing in a language classroom, especially for those near or at the beginning of their language studies, is to support and reinforce the learning of oral communication of knowledge about the structure and vocabulary of the language. This is particularly the case for foreign-language learners; second-language learners in the first group have a greater and more immediate need for basic writing, and instruction for these students thus tends to include more writing earlier on of the 'survival' type, such as writing one's name and address and filling out basic forms. Within the language classroom, other types of writing may be used, although for most second-language learners in these two categories these will be restricted to the first two levels of cognitive demands.

Looking beyond the language classroom to the real-world writing needs of these two groups, it is easy to imagine that the first group – immigrants in an L2 environment – may have some use for informational (referential) writing – for example, filling in forms, writing a narrative report of a workplace accident, or writing instructions. One might also imagine some use for connative (persuasive) writing; for example, writing a letter of application for a job. For the second group, foreign-language learners, there may be even less necessity for real-world writing, depending on their personal and professional goals, and on the usefulness of the second language as an international means of communication. For an English speaker learning a language such as Italian, for example, it may be satisfying to be able to write to a hotel in Rome for reservations, yet one could easily accomplish the same goal by writing in English. For the native speaker of Italian learning English, on the other hand, it is much more likely that knowing how to write in English will be practically useful in a real-life situation.

To summarize, it is clear from the above discussion that the writing needs of different groups of second-language learners are quite varied in terms of both cognitive demands and communicative function. In developing appropriate writing tests for these different populations, then, it will be important to keep these differences in mind.

## Summary

In this chapter, we have begun thinking about writing assessment by looking at different groups of second-language learners and the role that writing plays in their second language. In the next chapter, we will take a closer look at the various ways in which writing can be conceptualized – as a linguistic, cognitive, social, and cultural phenomenon – so that, by defining the phenomenon we are interested in, we will have a strong foundation in determining how to test it.

....................................................................................................

# CHAPTER TWO

# The nature of writing ability

## Introduction

In Chapter 1, the role of writing in second-language learning was explored. In this chapter, we turn to a consideration of the nature of writing ability. Defining the skill that we want to test is a critical starting point in designing a test, and, as we shall see, the definition of writing ability for a particular context will depend in large measure on the considerations discussed in Chapter 1: that is, the specific group of second-language writers and the type of writing that these writers are likely to engage in.

This chapter looks at the nature of writing ability from several perspectives: first, in comparison with the other so-called productive skill of speaking, next as a social and cultural phenomenon, then as a cognitive activity. Finally, the relationship between writing and second-language proficiency is discussed.

## The relationship between writing and speaking

It is traditional in language teaching and testing to categorize in-stances of language use into four skills: reading, writing, listening, and speaking, using channel (aural versus visual) and mode (productive versus receptive). The extent to which these different skills actually involve different cognitive mechanisms or are simply various socio-culturally mediated manifestations of a more general language ability is a matter of some controversy. While a full treatment of this issue is beyond the scope of this volume, in coming up with a definition of writing that can be useful for assessment it may be worthwhile spending some time considering the relationship between writing and the two skills most closely related to it: speaking (the other productive skill) and reading (the other visual skill). The role of reading in writing is dealt with later on in this chapter; in this section, I will summarize how recent scholars have conceptualized writing and speaking relationships.

The relationship between writing and speaking is important for language testing, among other reasons, because of the question to what extent writing can be seen as a special case of L2 language use and to what extent writing represents a distinctly different ability from speaking, drawing on many of the same linguistic resources but also relying on distinctly different mental processes. A good deal of literature in both first- and second-language studies has addressed the differences between speaking and writing from a number of different perspectives. As Grabe and Kaplan (1996) point out, linguists and educational researchers have historically held contradictory positions about the relationship between writing and speaking: traditional linguistic inquiry has held that speech is primary and written language is merely a reflection of spoken language, while educational research has taken the stance that the written form of the language is more 'correct' and therefore should be more highly valued than oral language. However, in recent years a consensus has been emerging to reconcile these two positions: neither oral nor written language is inherently superior to the other, but oral and written texts do vary across a number of dimensions, including (but not limited to) textual features, sociocultural norms and patterns of use, and the cognitive processes involved in text production and comprehension.

A useful summary of some of the differences between speaking and writing can be found in Brown (1994). Brown provides the following list of the characteristics that ordinarily differentiate written language from spoken language:

- **Permanence:** oral language is transitory and must be processed in real time, while written language is permanent and can be read and reread as often as one likes;
- **Production time:** writers generally have more time to plan, review, and revise their words before they are finalized, while speakers

must plan, formulate, and deliver their utterances within a few moments if they are to maintain a conversation;

- **Distance** between the writer and the reader in both time and space, which eliminates much of the shared context that is present between speaker and listener in ordinary face-to-face contact and thus necessitates greater explicitness on the part of the writer;

- **Orthography**, which carries a limited amount of information compared to the richness of devices available to speakers to enhance a message (e.g. stress, intonation, pitch, volume, pausing, etc.);

- **Complexity**: written language tends to be characterized by longer clauses and more subordinators, while spoken language tends to have shorter clauses connected by coordinators, as well as more redundancy (e.g. repetition of nouns and verbs);

- **Formality**: because of the social and cultural uses to which writing is ordinarily put, writing tends to be more formal than speaking;

- **Vocabulary:** written texts tend to contain a wider variety of words, and more lower-frequency words, than oral texts.

While Brown's list is a valuable, if somewhat oversimplified, starting point for discussing speaking/writing differences, the fact that the differences between speaking and writing go far beyond these surface textual features is becoming widely recognized. In particular, speaking and writing are frequently used in different settings, for different reasons, and to meet different communicative goals. Furthermore, the cognitive processes involved in writing differ in important ways from those used in speaking. The remainder of this section deals briefly with these issues.

As Grabowski (1996) notes, very few of the surface differences between speaking and writing result from the inherent properties of speaking and writing under ordinary circumstances. In fact, only the first two items on Brown's list (permanence and production time) can be seen as fundamental in this sense: writing ordinarily leaves a physical trace, which can later be referred to either by the writer or by the reader, while speaking, unless it is recorded, does not, and the physical act of writing takes longer than the physical act of speaking. All other differences between spoken and written texts either arise from these two fundamental differences, or can be ascribed to the fact that writing and speaking are for the most part used in different contexts and for different purposes. Grabowski lists a number of conditions under which writing tends to be chosen over speaking, noting that while the choice is frequently based on social or conventional norms, other factors such as the costs and benefits of one mode of communication vis-à-vis the other also play a role. For example, it may be less costly to send an e-mail message than to make a long-distance phone call; on the other hand, if the message is urgent the advantage of speed may be more important than a saving of money.

In an extensive review of the literature on speaking/writing connections, Sperling (1996) concludes that:

> to talk of written and spoken language differences is to consider the range of communicative purposes to which either writing or speaking is put. In this sense, broader characteristics – such as what gets said and what remains implicit, what is foregrounded and what is backgrounded, and what is stated by whom and under what circumstances – implicate the norms and expectations of the range of contexts in which both writing and speaking are produced. (Sperling, 1996: 56)

In other words, even though features such as vocabulary and formality do frequently differ across speaking and writing, it may ultimately be more important to consider the wider social and cultural context in which speaking and writing are used. One of the most important distinctions between writing and speaking in this regard is the fact that, as discussed in Chapter 1, writing is highly valued in educational settings, and the standardization of writing means that accuracy in writing is frequently more important than accuracy in speaking. The importance of correctness in writing as opposed to speaking is particularly relevant for writing in academic contexts, where writing is frequently seen as a key to entry into the 'academic discourse community' (Spack, 1988; Swales, 1990). This issue is discussed in detail later in this chapter.

In addition to the social and cultural influences on writing as opposed to speaking, it is important to consider cognitive differences. To what extent does writing differ from speaking in terms of its demands on cognitive resources? Of all the differences between speaking and writing that have been discussed, it is the fact that the addressee is not generally present during the writing process that seems to have the most important cognitive implications. On the one hand, unlike a speaker, a writer does not need to devote cognitive resources to strategies for maintaining the flow of conversation such as avoiding long pauses or filling pauses with turn-keeping signals

(Sacks *et al.*, 1974; Grabowski, 1996). In writing, then, more time and energy can be spent on cognitive activities such as planning and information retrieval, as there is less communicative pressure to continuously produce utterances (Grabowski, 1996). On the other hand, the absence of an addressee presents a challenge to writers that speakers do not face: while speakers receive immediate feedback from listeners on how well a message is being communicated, writers must somehow construct a coherent message that attempts to take into account the existing knowledge, interests, and goals of the addressee without such feedback. Thus, a writer must devote a considerable amount of cognitive energy simultaneously managing several different kinds of information: information about the writing topic, information about the audience, and information about acceptable forms of written texts. In fact, it is this ability to anticipate the audience and shape a message appropriately in the absence of a conversation partner that distinguishes expert from inexpert writers. This point is brought up again later in this chapter.

It should be noted here that the discussion about speaking and writing has oversimplified somewhat the distinctions between these two modes of communication to emphasize the differences between the interactional nature of ordinary speech (i.e. conversation) and the solitary nature of ordinary writing (i.e. writing various kinds of texts consisting of at least several connected sentences). In the real world, of course, there are plenty of examples of speech that exhibit characteristics of written language (sermons and lectures, for example) and many examples of written language that resemble speech (for example, e-mail communication, informal notes, or screenplays). Furthermore, current instructional practices, at least in the US, emphasize collaborative writing, peer response, and other forms of interaction to mitigate many of the challenges of writing discussed above (Sperling, 1996). As Bachman and Palmer (1996) point out, what have traditionally been called separate skills (such as speaking and writing) are more properly seen as different 'combination[s] of language abilities and task characteristics' (p. 76); that is, it is the nature of the specific task that determines which areas of language ability are engaged. For the purposes of language testing, Bachman and Palmer's perspective helps clarify the distinction between speaking and writing because these are seen not as fundamentally different abilities *per se*, but as different types of language-use tasks. This is a useful distinction because we are frequently interested in people's ability to use language both for real-time interaction and for creating coherent texts without the aid of a conversation partner.

In summary, speech and written discourse draw on many of the same linguistic resources and can be used in many cases to meet the same communicative goals. However, writing differs from speech in a number of important ways, both in terms of textual qualities and in terms of the factors that govern the uses of each modality. Written language is not merely spoken language put on paper; rather, it is a distinct mode of communication, involving among other things very different sociocultural norms and cognitive processes. The next sections of this chapter discuss these aspects of writing in more detail.

## Writing as a social and cultural phenomenon

### Social aspects of writing

The physical act of writing is sometimes thought of as mainly the result of cognitive effort on the part of an individual writer. Indeed, the traditional approach to writing assessment has been to focus primarily on the cognitive aspects of writing, and these aspects will be discussed in detail below. However, it is important to view writing not solely as the product of an individual, but as a social and cultural act. Writing is 'an act that takes place within a context, that accomplishes a particular purpose, and that is appropriately shaped for its intended audience' (Hamp-Lyons and Kroll, 1997: 8). In a similar vein, Sperling (1996: 55) notes that 'writing, like language in general, [is] a meaning-making activity that is socially and culturally shaped and individually and socially purposeful.' Expanding on the social nature of writing, Hayes (1996) states:

> [Writing] is also social because it is a social artifact and is carried out in a social setting. What we write, how we write, and who we write to is shaped by social convention and by our history of social interaction . . . The genres in which we write were invented by other writers and the phrases we write often reflect phrases earlier writers have written.                        (Hayes, 1996: 5)

Much of the current literature on academic writing in a second language (specifically in English) emphasizes the social aspects of writing, referring to the process of learning to write in academic contexts as one of 'initiating ESL students into the academic discourse community' (Spack, 1988; see also Swales, 1990). From this perspective, learning to write involves much more than simply learning the grammar and vocabulary of the language, or even the rhetorical forms common to academic writing. Writing may involve, for each discipline, 'examining the kinds of issues a discipline considers important, why certain methods of inquiry and not others are sanctioned, how the conventions of a discipline shape text in that discipline, how individual writers represent themselves in a text, how texts are read and disseminated within the discipline, and how one text influences subsequent texts' (Spack, 1988: 38). There is some controversy over whether it is important, or even possible, for teachers of writing to be well versed in the discourse conventions of disciplines outside their own (Spack, 1988), and also to what extent there exists a single 'academic discourse' that is shared across the academy and can thus be taught to ESL students (see Johns, 1990; Raimes, 1991; and Grabe and Kaplan, 1996, for summaries of these issues). While these controversies will not be solved in a volume on writing assessment, they serve as an illustration of the kinds of social issues that are involved in second-language writing research. For the purposes of this book, it is important to be aware of these issues because the social context of writing influences, among other things, the choice of genre and task in writing assessment. These issues will be addressed again in Chapter 5.

## Cultural aspects of writing

The cultural aspects of writing have also been the subject of some controversy. The notion of contrastive rhetoric was first introduced by Kaplan (1966), who analyzed a large number of ESL essays and pointed out distinctive differences in the written discourse of students from different cultures, which he symbolized in clear, simple diagrams. English writing was described as a straight line, while 'Oriental' discourse was symbolized by an inward-pointing spiral, for example. While Kaplan's original thesis has been subjected to a number of criticisms (see Brown, 1994, and Leki, 1992, for summaries of these criticisms), the idea of contrastive rhetoric has recently regained respectability, as it has become clear to researchers that many aspects of writing are influenced by culture. Leki (1992) and Grabe and Kaplan (1989, 1996) provide useful introductions to some of the cultural influences on writing. They point out that variation in writing in different cultures does not reflect inherent differences in thought patterns but rather 'cultural preferences which make greater use of certain options among the linguistic possibilities' (Grabe and Kaplan 1996: 184). These variations are learned primarily through the educational system, either directly (as in English, where certain rhetorical patterns are explicitly taught) or indirectly through extensive exposure to culture-specific patterns of discourse. Thus, these variations can be seen to some extent as reflections of cultural values as promoted through education.

In recent years, a number of investigators have explored variations in writing patterns that can be at least partially attributed to cultural influences. For example, Arabic prose is frequently said to use more coordination and parallelism, unlike the subordination and hierarchical organization preferred by writers of English (Ostler, 1987; Yorkey, 1977; Kaplan, 1966; all cited in Leki, 1992). Spanish writers prefer lengthy introductions, and instead of focusing narrowly on the main ideas of an essay, as in English, Spanish writers make use of digressions and asides to show their breadth of knowledge on the topic (Collado, 1981; cited in Leki, 1992). In Chinese, writers tend to provide a series of examples without stating the main point of the example or tying them together through a generalization, in contrast to the English preference for transparent, explicit connections in prose (Matalene, 1985; cited in Leki, 1992).

Investigation into contrastive rhetoric has demonstrated that cultural expectations can have a consequence for the coherence of texts – that is, the organization of a text into a meaningful whole. Coherence, as Leki (1992) notes, is not an inherent quality of the text itself, but rather comes from the accuracy of the writer's assessment of what the reader will be able to infer from the text. Because readers of a text bring their own background knowledge and expectations to the reading (Carrel and Eisterhold, 1983), misreadings of the author's intended message are possible, if not likely, if the writer has not gauged the needs and expectations of the reader correctly. For example, native speakers of English expect writing to be hierarchically organized, with explicit connections between ideas and direct statements, and with original content (Leki, 1992). English has also been called a 'writer-responsible' language (Hinds, 1987), meaning that the writer makes explicit the connections between propositions and ideas in the text so that readers do not need to infer these connections on their own. In a reader-responsible language, in contrast, the writer leaves many things implicit and it is the reader's job to make appropriate inferences to ferret out the writer's intended meaning. As long as there is a match between the expectations of the reader and those of the writer, the reader will be able to make a coherent interpretation of the text. However, if the writer comes from a 'reader-responsible' language or a culture where the expectations differ in other ways, an English-speaking reader is apt to find the writing difficult to read, poorly organized, or excessively vague. As Hayes (1996) points out, readers form a representation, not just of the text itself, but of the writer's persona as well; thus, it is a short step from perceiving a text as incoherent to perceiving the writer as somehow being deficient (stupid, illogical, etc.) as well. The role of reader expectations has important implications for the scoring of writing tasks and will be discussed again in Chapter 4.

To summarize, writing is both a social and a cultural activity, in that acts of writing cannot be looked at in isolation but must be seen in their social and cultural contexts. The implication for the testing of writing is that writing ability cannot be validly abstracted from the contexts in which writing takes place. To some extent, the ability to write indicates the ability to function as a literate member of a particular segment of society or discourse community, or to use language to demonstrate one's membership in that community.

## Writing as a cognitive activity

### Writing expertise

Before discussing the cognitive aspects of writing in detail, it may be useful to review the literature on writing expertise. A good deal of literature has looked at the process of writing, most frequently by using retrospective interviews or think-aloud protocols (for example, Hayes and Flower, 1980; Flower and Hayes, 1980; Perl, 1979; Sommer, 1980; Zamel, 1983; Raimes, 1985). In think-aloud protocols, writers say aloud their thoughts as they write, allowing the researcher to gain insight into the mental activity and decision-making processes of the writer as he or she carries out a writing task (see Ericsson and Simon, 1980, for a thorough account of this methodological approach). This line of research indicates that good writers spend more time planning and revising their work than novice writers, and tend to edit their writing for content and organization rather than simply making surface changes to the text. Expert writers also take into account their audience, by considering among other things what a potential reader is likely to know about the subject, how much needs to be explained and what can be left implicit, and what sorts of evidence the reader will likely find persuasive.

## Models of the writing process

In attempting to capture the differences between expert and novice writers and to describe the various influences on the writing process, a number of researchers have proposed models of the writing process. While models of complex cognitive activities such as writing can never be completely accurate (or proven), they are useful for considering the various factors that influence the process. Some of the questions addressed by these models include the following. What are the cognitive processes, or mental activities, involved in writing? What sources of knowledge does the writer draw upon in writing? What other factors influence the writing process? These are important issues to consider when developing or using a test of writing for several reasons: they help define the skill(s) being tested more clearly by describing the processes involved as accurately and precisely as current knowledge allows; they point out possible areas where individual differences in skill may be found, thus providing useful information about the differences between skilled and unskilled writers; and they make explicit other influences that may affect writing but that are not related to skills being assessed.

### Hayes and Flower (1980)
An early and influential model of the writing process was that of Hayes and Flower (1980). Hayes and Flower described the writing process in terms of the task environment, which included the writing assignment and the text produced so far, the writer's long-term memory, including knowledge of topic, knowledge of audience, and stored writing plans, and a number of cognitive processes, including planning, translating thought into text, and revising (see Figure 2.1). One of the important insights brought out in the Hayes–Flower model is the fact that writing is a recursive and not a linear process: thus instruction in the writing process may be more effective than

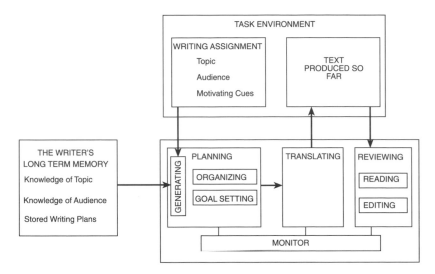

Figure 2.1  The Hayes–Flower (1980) writing model

providing models of particular rhetorical forms and asking students to follow these models in their own writing.

While a number of other researchers have proposed models of writing since the Hayes–Flower model was first introduced, I will focus on only two of them: that of Hayes (1996), itself an updated version of the Hayes–Flower model, and that of Bereiter and Scardamalia (1987). These two models complement each other, as they focus on different issues in writing. The Hayes model attempts to outline the various influences on the writing process, particularly those internal to the writer, while the Bereiter and Scardamalia model addresses the different processes followed by expert versus novice writers. While both of these models are based on first-language writing, they have important implications for second-language writing as well, and provide useful background to discussions later in this chapter and in the book about the development of writing ability, the differences between skilled and unskilled writers, and the special challenges in second-language writing assessment.

### *Hayes (1996)*

Hayes' (1996) model of writing sees the writing process as consisting of two main parts: the task environment and the individual (see Figure 2.2). The task environment can be divided into the social environment and the physical environment. The social environment consists of the audience (real or imagined) for one's writing, as well as any collaborators in the writing process. The physical environment includes the text written so far, which influences and shapes the writer's further efforts, and the composing medium, e.g. handwriting or word processing. The latter has been included in the model in part because of the profound influence technological innovations have had on both the cognitive and social aspects of writing. For example, some studies have found differences in the planning and editing processes of writers using word processors as opposed to pen and paper (Gould and Grischkowsky, 1984; Haas, 1987). Technological issues will be discussed again in Chapter 10. The central focus of the Hayes model is the individual, rather than the task environment. Individual aspects of writing involve interactions among four components: working memory, motivation and affect, cognitive processes, and long-term memory. Hayes' model of working memory is based upon a well-known conception of working memory developed by Baddeley (1986), with some modifications. Hayes conceptualizes working memory as being composed of three components: phonological memory, which stores auditory/verbal information (i.e. speech), the visual–spatial sketchpad, which stores visually or spatially coded information (for example, written words or graphs), and a semantic memory, which stores conceptual information.

Hayes' model recognizes the important roles that motivation and affect play in writing. Specifically, a writer's goals, predispositions, beliefs and attitudes, and cost/benefit estimates may influence the way a writer goes about the task of writing and the effort that will be put into the writing task. For example, Hayes cites research by Dweck (1986) and Palmquist and Young (1992) suggesting that students' beliefs about the causes of successful performance influence the amount of effort they are willing to exert: if writing ability is seen as an inherent and relatively unchangeable talent, students tend to be more anxious and to think less of themselves as writers. Similarly, students who experience failure tend to work harder if they believe that success is due to effort, while they tend to give up and work less if they believe that success is due to innate abilities.

The cognitive processes in the Hayes model include text interpretation, reflection, and text production. Text interpretation, which includes listening, reading, and scanning graphics, is the process by which internal representations are created from linguistic and graphic

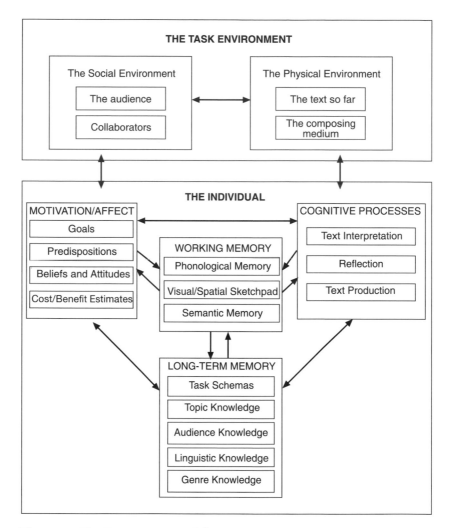

Figure 2.2  The Hayes (1996) model

input. Reflection is a process by which new internal representations are created from existing internal representations. Finally, in text production, new linguistic (written or spoken) or graphic output is produced from internal representations. These three processes are involved not only in drafting a piece of writing but in revising one's writing as well.

Hayes emphasizes the importance of reading as a central process in writing, and discusses three types of reading that are essential in

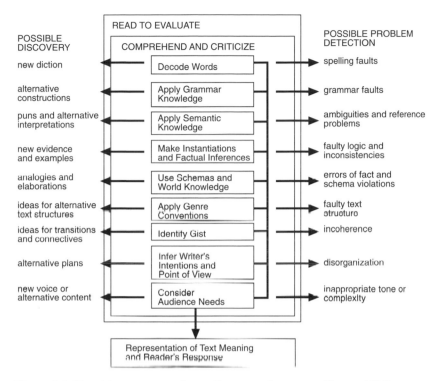

Figure 2.3 Cognitive processes in reading to evaluate text (Hayes, 1996)

writing. The first of these is **reading to evaluate**, in which the writer reads his or her text critically to detect possible problems and to discover potential improvements. A model for reading to evaluate is found in Figure 2.3, which shows the cognitive processes involved in reading, such as decoding words, applying grammar knowledge, and so on, and the possible problems and discoveries that reading to evaluate can lead to. As mentioned above, it has been demonstrated that inexpert writers tend to revise local (i.e. sentence-level) errors but not global errors (i.e. errors of content and organization). Hayes proposes three reasons why writers may fail to revise on a global level. First, writers may not be able to detect global problems because of poor reading skills. Second, writers may not have adequate working memory to attend to both global and local errors. Finally, writers may not have an adequately developed task schema for revision: that is, they may not be aware of the need to pay attention to global errors.

Two other kinds of reading that are involved in writing are **reading**

**source texts** and **reading instructions**. Since writing tasks are frequently based on source texts, there is an obvious relationship between the ability to understand the source text and the ability to use information from the text in one's writing. Similarly, if writers define their writing task based on a misunderstanding of the task instructions (e.g. 'define X,' 'argue for or against Y') they may not be able to address the task appropriately.

The fourth individual component in Hayes' model is long-term memory, in which information and knowledge relevant to the writing task is stored. Long-term memory includes such things as task schemas, topic knowledge, audience knowledge, genre knowledge, and linguistic knowledge. Task schemas are defined as 'packages of information stored in long-term memory that specify how to carry out a particular task' (p. 24). Task schemas include information about task goals, the processes necessary for accomplishing the task, how to sequence the processes, and how to evaluate the success of the task. An example of a task schema is a schema for revision, as mentioned above. Topic knowledge is, of course, essential for writing, as one must have something to write about. Knowledge of the audience includes consideration of many of the social and cultural issues discussed above. Similarly, genre knowledge includes knowledge about the socially and culturally appropriate forms that writing takes in a given situation for a given purpose. (See Swales, 1990, for a thorough discussion of genres, particularly in academic writing.) Finally, linguistic knowledge includes knowledge about the language resources that are brought to bear in the writing process.

The Hayes model, while complete in many respects, has two shortcomings with respect to second-language writing. The first is a lack of specificity in defining the situational variables involved in writing. To describe these variables more completely, we can turn to another model of writing: that of Grabe and Kaplan (1996), an adaptation of a model of communicative language use for academic purposes by Chapelle *et al.* (1993). While Hayes merely notes that writing is a social act and lists the audience and collaborators as factors, Grabe and Kaplan frame the task environment in terms of *participants, setting, task, text,* and *topic.* They also provide a detailed taxonomy listing examples of the variables of setting, task, text, and topic for academic writing. For example, settings include such places as classrooms, libraries, computer centers, etc., and tasks include such things as lecture notes, letters, essays, and laboratory reports. These notions are essential to consider in describing the writing situation fully and in developing tasks for writing assessment, and will be discussed in more detail in Chapter 5.

Another shortcoming of the Hayes model, especially in terms of its usefulness for second-language writing assessment, is the lack of attention paid to linguistic knowledge. Again, the Grabe and Kaplan (1996) model can be used to fill in this gap. Grabe and Kaplan, following a well-established line of research in applied linguistics, provide a detailed list of the components of language knowledge relevant to writing (see Table 2.1). This view of language knowledge, building on the work of Hymes (1972), Canale and Swain (1980), and Bachman (1990), divides language knowledge into three types: **linguistic knowledge**, **discourse knowledge** and **sociolinguistic knowledge**. Linguistic knowledge includes knowledge of the basic structural elements of the language, sociolinguistic knowledge includes knowledge of the ways in which language is used appropriately in a variety of social settings, and discourse knowledge refers to knowledge of the ways in which cohesive text is constructed. More recent formulations of the components of language ability are discussed in Chapter 3; for the purposes of this chapter, however, Table 2.1 provides an overview of the different aspects of language competence and may be useful in outlining considerations for the designing and scoring of writing tasks for assessment.

It should be noted that much of what is considered language knowledge in this model is contained in the Hayes model under 'task schemas' and 'genre knowledge,' although clearly not in as much detail. However one chooses to conceptualize these various areas of knowledge, the main point is that linguistic or grammatical knowledge, discourse knowledge, and sociolinguistic knowledge are all essential for writing and none should be slighted in testing writing.

To sum up, the Hayes model is significant because of its thoroughness in describing the various factors that influence writing, particularly in terms of motivation/affect, cognitive processes, and long-term memory. When supplemented by factors discussed by Grabe and Kaplan, the Hayes model has particular implications for second-language writers, discussed later in this chapter.

### Bereiter and Scardamalia (1987)

Another influential model of writing is that of Bereiter and Scardamalia (1987). Bereiter and Scardamalia propose a two-model

Table 2.1 *Taxonomy of language knowledge (adapted from Grabe and Kaplan, 1996: 220–1)*

I. *Linguistic knowledge*
   A. Knowledge of the written code
      1. Orthography
      2. Spelling
      3. Punctuation
      4. Formatting conventions (margins, paragraphing, spacing, etc.)
   B. Knowledge of phonology and morphology
      1. Sound/letter correspondences
      2. Syllables (onset, rhyme/rhythm, coda)
      3. Morpheme structure (word-part knowledge)
   C. Vocabulary
      1. Interpersonal words and phrases
      2. Academic and pedagogical words and phrases
      3. Formal and technical words and phrases
      4. Topic-specific words and phrases
      5. Non-literal and metaphoric language
   D. Syntactic/structural knowledge
      1. Basic syntactic patterns
      2. Preferred formal writing structures (appropriate style)
      3. Tropes and figures of expression
      4. Metaphors/similes
   E. Awareness of differences across languages
   F. Awareness of relative proficiency in different languages and registers

II. *Discourse knowledge*
   A. Knowledge of intrasentential and intersentential marking devices (cohesion, syntactic parallelism)
   B. Knowledge of informational structuring (topic/comment, given/new, theme/rheme, adjacency pairs)
   C. Knowledge of semantic relations across clauses
   D. Knowledge of recognizing main topics
   E. Knowledge of genre structure and genre constraints
   F. Knowledge of organizing schemes (top-level discourse structure)
   G. Knowledge of inferencing (bridging, elaborating)
   H. Knowledge of differences in features of discourse structuring across languages and cultures
   I. Awareness of different proficiency levels of discourse skills in different languages

III. *Sociolinguistic knowledge*
   A. Functional uses of written language
   B. Application and interpretable violation of Gricean maxims (Grice, 1975)
   C. Register and situational parameters
      1. Age of writer

2.  Language used by writer (L1, L2, . . .)
3.  Proficiency in language used
4.  Audience considerations
5.  Relative status of interactants (power/politeness)
6.  Degree of formality (deference/solidarity)
7.  Degree of distance (detachment/involvement)
8.  Topic of interaction
9.  Means of writing (pen/pencil, computer, dictation, shorthand)
10. Means of transmission (single page/book/read aloud/printed)

D.  Awareness of sociolinguistic differences across languages and cultures
E.  Self-awareness of roles of register and situational parameters

description of writing that addresses an apparent paradox in writing: the fact that, on the one hand, virtually everyone in a literate society can learn to write as well as they can speak, while on the other hand, expertise in writing involves a difficult, labor-intensive process that only some people master. To resolve this apparent contradiction, Bereiter and Scardamalia propose a distinction between **knowledge telling** and **knowledge transforming**. Knowledge telling is similar to impromptu speaking in that it involves very little planning or revision. This is the kind of writing that Bereiter and Scardamalia call 'natural' or 'unproblematic,' as it can be done by any fluent speaker of a language who has a grasp of the writing system. The writing of most children and adolescents falls into this category. It is a process that can be used to solve one of the fundamental problems of writing, which is to generate content without the benefit of a conversation partner, as discussed earlier in this chapter. Bereiter and Scardamalia stress the importance of the interactive elements in conversation that are absent in writing:

> when people converse they help each other in numerous, mostly unintentional ways. They provide each other with a continual source of cues – cues to proceed, cues to stop, cues to elaborate, cues to shift topic, and a great variety of cues that stir memory. They serve as text grammarians for one another, raising questions when some needed element of a discourse has been omitted.
>
> (Bereiter and Scardamalia, 1987: 55)

Because these aspects of interaction are missing in writing and must be supplied by the writer him- or herself, generating content in the absence of a partner is a formidable obstacle in learning to write. To overcome this obstacle, beginning writers generally rely on three sources of input to help them come up with appropriate content. The first is the topic (or the assignment, in a school setting) and the second is the writer's discourse schema, or his or her knowledge about the forms of writing, including what elements need to be included to fulfill the task and how they should be arranged. For example, an assignment to write an opinion essay might cue a student to provide a statement of opinion and one or more facts in support of the opinion. The third source of input is the text written so far, which can be used as a cue for generating additional content. These three sources of information are easy for a novice writer to access and are sufficient to generate an adequate response to a writing assignment. Thus, knowledge telling follows the straight-ahead form of ordinary speech production and does not require any greater amount of planning or goal setting than does everyday conversation (pp. 9–10).

The process of knowledge telling is represented graphically in Figure 2.4. As the figure shows, the writer uses a mental representation of the writing assignment to call up both content knowledge (what is known about the topic) and a schema for the type of discourse required by the assignment (e.g. an opinion essay or a process description). Content and discourse cues (called topic and genre identifiers) in the assignment are used to search one's memory for relevant content items. These content items (ideas) are subjected to a test of appropriateness (e.g. Does this sound right? Does it support my argument?) and, if accepted, are written down. Now the cycle repeats itself, but this time using the text written so far, rather than the original mental representation of the assignment, as a source for additional memory probes. The writing process ends when the memory probes fail to find additional appropriate content. Bereiter and Scardamalia supply a quote from a 12-year-old that describes this process quite aptly:

> I have a whole bunch of ideas and write down until my supply of ideas is exhausted. Then I might try to think of more ideas up to the point when you can't get any more ideas that are worth putting down on paper and then I would end it.
>
> (Bereiter and Scardamalia, 1987: 9)

In contrast to the 'natural and efficient' process of knowledge telling, knowledge transformation involves much more effort and skill, and is not achieved without a great deal of practice. In knowledge transformation, the process of writing involves not only putting one's

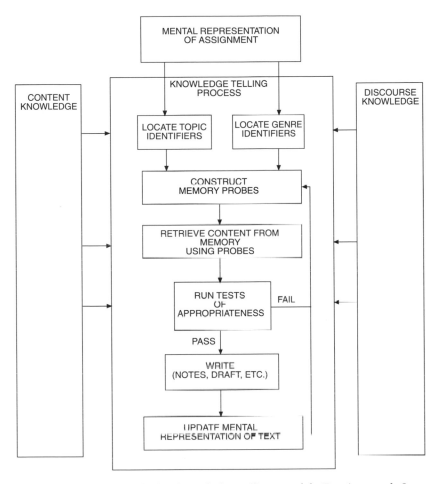

Figure 2.4 Structure of the knowledge-telling model (Bereiter and Scardamalia, 1987)

thoughts to paper as they occur, but actually using writing to create new knowledge: in this kind of writing the process of writing itself frequently leads to new knowledge and may change a writer's view of what he or she is trying to communicate. Bereiter and Scardamalia's model of knowledge transformation is found in Figure 2.5. As the figure shows, the first step in the process of knowledge transformation involves problem analysis and goal setting, which lead to problem-solving activities in two domains, called the content problem space and the rhetorical problem space. In the content problem space,

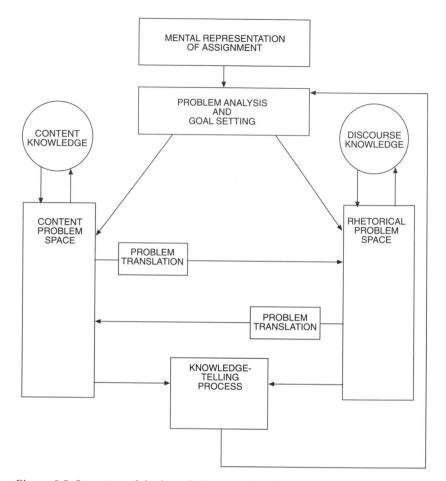

Figure 2.5 Structure of the knowledge-transforming model (Bereiter and Scardamalia, 1987)

issues of belief and knowledge are dealt with, while in the rhetorical problem space, the writer works on how to best achieve the goals of the writing assignment. An attempt to find a solution to a content problem may lead the writer to a rhetorical problem, and vice versa. In the words of Bereiter and Scardamalia, there is 'a two-way interaction between continuously developing knowledge and continuously developing text' (p. 12). The solutions to the rhetorical and content problems become the input for the knowledge-telling process, during which the actual written text is produced.

As Grabe and Kaplan (1996) note, Bereiter and Scardamalia's two-model process has much to recommend it. It provides an explanation for the differences between skilled and unskilled writers: that is, skilled writers use writing strategies that are substantially different, not just more refined, from those of unskilled writers. It also provides an account for why writing tasks differ in difficulty, even for skilled writers: if the information demands of a task are great and the writer is inexperienced with a particular genre, the task will require more cognitive effort to resolve issues in both the content and rhetorical problem spaces. Although the model has limitations (for example, the model does not provide an explanation for how one makes the transition from knowledge telling to knowledge transformation; see also Grabe and Kaplan [1996: 127–8]), the distinction between knowledge telling and knowledge transformation is a useful notion for both writing pedagogy and assessment. In particular, it highlights some important issues in setting tasks for writing assessment, such as the role of genre familiarity in determining task difficulty, as mentioned above. Writing tasks that are familiar and can be addressed satisfactorily through a knowledge-telling process may be accessible to inexperienced writers but may not distinguish between better and poorer writers as well as tasks that are complex enough to elicit a knowledge-transforming strategy from better writers. On the other hand, if the task involves a genre that is unfamiliar to writers, some writers who are otherwise skilled may not be able to perform well. These issues will be addressed in more detail in Chapter 5.

## Second-language writing

In this section, issues specific to second-language writing are discussed. Over the past several years a consensus has emerged among researchers that second-language proficiency – defined as control over the linguistic elements of a second language – and expertise in writing are different, although not unrelated abilities (Cumming, 1989; Kroll, 1990; Krapels, 1990), that is, second-language writers use many of the same writing processes in their second language as in their first, and expertise in writing can transfer from the first to the second language, given at least a certain level of language proficiency. However, because of the constraints of limited second-language knowledge, writing in a second language may be hampered because of the need to focus on language rather than content. Silva (1993), in a review of differences between first and second-language writing, found that writing in a second language tends to be 'more constrained, more difficult, and less effective' (p. 668) than writing in a first language: second-language writers plan less, revise for content less, and write less fluently and accurately than first-language writers.

The discussions earlier in this chapter provide some insights into what areas of knowledge may be implicated in these differences. The necessity of devoting cognitive resources to issues of language may mean that not as much attention can be given to higher-order issues of content and organization, since the capacity of working memory is limited. In addition, the cognitive processes outlined in Hayes' (1996) model – in particular text interpretation and text generation – may be more difficult for second-language writers because of limited language proficiency. Text interpretation, it will be recalled, is used in reading (or listening to) source texts, reading (or listening to) task instructions, and reading one's own writing, either to evaluate it or to use it as a cue for generating additional content. A faulty understanding of the source text or task instructions may adversely affect one's ability to perform well on a writing task. In addition, poor reading comprehension skills may limit one's ability to evaluate one's own writing, as mentioned previously in this chapter.

The process of text generation, or encoding internal representations (ideas) into written text, may be disrupted by the need for lengthy searches for appropriate lexical and syntactic choices. Consequently, the written product may not match the writer's original intention. This result may be either because of limited linguistic knowledge or because the effort required for text generation may tax the writer's resources so completely that the idea is lost from working memory before it can be put down on paper. Given that the text written so far is an important source of input to the writer, it becomes clear that the writer is at a further disadvantage if the text so far is incomplete or inaccurate and cannot provide the appropriate memory cues to the writer.

In addition to limited linguistic resources, second-language writers may be disadvantaged by social and cultural factors: they may not have awareness of the social and cultural uses of writing in the second language, the appropriate ways in which various functions can be expressed in writing, or the expectations of readers from a different culture. Motivational and affective factors play a role as well. There is a lengthy literature on the role of affect and motivation in second-language learning, and many of the research findings in this area are applicable to second-language writing. The relationship between one's desire to integrate into the new culture and one's success in learning a second language has been explored by researchers such as Gardner and Lambert (1972), Schumann (1978), and, more recently, Peirce (1995), who notes that investment in the target culture may depend on a belief that there will eventually be a return on that investment. Shen speaks of the necessity of changing one's own identity in order to write well in a second language:

> In order to write good English, I knew that I had to be myself, which actually meant not to be my Chinese self. It meant that I had to create an English self and be *that* self.    (Shen, 1988: 461)

For many second-language writers, the motivation to invest in the new language and culture may not be as pressing. Graduate students in science and engineering, for example, may wish to return to their countries after completing their studies and may not see the need to adapt to the second-language environment beyond what is necessary for their education. Similarly, foreign-language learners who are studying language for their own personal enrichment may be equally unmotivated to invest in the language, and this may influence the amount of energy and time they are willing to devote to learning how to write well in that language.

Other motivations besides the desire to integrate into the culture may influence writing as well. Grabe and Kaplan (1996) provide the following list of possible motivators: grades, higher proficiency, learn[ing] new information, future job/promotion, impress[ing] teacher/other students (p. 219).

In terms of other affective variables, perhaps the most salient is writing anxiety, or writing apprehension (Daly and Miller, 1975). Some research has demonstrated a difference in the quality of writing produced by apprehensive versus non-apprehensive L1 writers when time constraints are involved (Kean *et al.*, 1987, cited in Madigan *et al.*, 1996) or when the task involves personal narrative (Faigley *et al.*, 1981, cited in Madigan *et al.*, 1996). While little, if any, research has addressed the relationship between writing apprehension and writing quality in second-language contexts, it may well be that writing apprehension is an equal or greater issue for these writers than for L1 writers. In particular, the issue of time constraints is salient for second-language writers, because they are unable to write as fluently and quickly as their native speaker peers.

## Summary

While writing in a first language is a challenging, complex task, it is more so in a second language. The review of literature presented in this chapter outlines some of the complexities involved in defining writing, the differences between speaking and listening, and some of the ways in which writing has been conceptualized as a social, cultural, and cognitive phenomenon and presents some of the particular challenges faced by second-language writers. Many of these challenges will be raised again in later chapters as issues surrounding the development of writing tasks and scoring systems are discussed.

........................................................................................................

# CHAPTER THREE

# Basic considerations in assessing writing

In Chapters 1 and 2, the nature of writing ability and the use of writing by different groups of language learners were considered. In this chapter, I will focus more specifically on issues related to the assessment of language in general, and writing in particular. As noted earlier, the models of the writing process presented in Chapter 2 were developed primarily with first-language writers in mind; thus, they are not concerned specifically with the development of language ability as expressed through writing, but assume a more or less stable language system and focus on the development of cognitive and meta-cognitive strategies that are involved in generating coherent texts for specific audiences and purposes. In this chapter I will discuss writing assessment from the point of view of language testing, which has traditionally concerned itself with defining what is meant by language ability in general, as an underlying cognitive ability and as manifested through the traditional skills of speaking, listening, reading, and writing. For the purposes of this chapter I will therefore be looking at writing tests as a specific type of language test, keeping in mind, however, that the degree to which a writing test is specifically measuring language as opposed to measuring other cognitive skills is not always clear-cut.

The framework for much of the discussion in this chapter comes from Bachman and Palmer's (1996) volume on language testing. The chapter is organized as follows. First, various test purposes are described. Next, the relationship between language performance, or actual language use, and the abilities and personal characteristics that

underlie language performance is discussed, and the notion of performance assessment is introduced. Finally, a model of test usefulness is
presented, which provides a systematic approach to considering
various aspects of tests that make them more or less useful for a given
situation.

## Test purpose: making inferences and making decisions

In choosing or designing a writing test, the logical place to begin is by
considering what we plan to use the test for. In other words, why are
we interested in testing writing ability – what is our purpose?
Bachman and Palmer (1996) discuss two main purposes for language
tests, of which we can consider writing tests to be a subset. The
primary purpose is to make inferences about language ability, and the
secondary purpose is to make decisions based on those inferences.
That is, since we cannot directly observe a person's language ability,
we use his or her responses to test items as data from which we make
inferences about the ability that underlies the test performance.
These inferences are then used as data for making a variety of decisions at an individual, classroom, or program level.

For example, let us consider three types of inferences that we can
make on the basis of a language test: proficiency, diagnosis, and
achievement. Leaving aside for the moment a precise definition of
language proficiency, we use inferences about general language proficiency to make decisions such as admission to academic programs,
placement into different levels of a language program, exemption
from certain coursework, or selection for a particular job. Inferences
about diagnosis – that is, the strengths and weaknesses of individual
students – are used primarily by teachers to tailor their instruction to
meet their students' needs. Inferences about achievement – or the
degree to which individuals or groups of students have met specific
instructional goals – are used to make decisions about grading and
promotion on the individual level, and about modification of instruction on the classroom level. Inferences about achievement are also
used on a program-wide or even state or national levels to make
decisions about curriculum and funding for programs.

As Bachman and Palmer (1996) note, an important aspect of decisions made on the basis of inferences about language ability is
whether they are high-stakes or low-stakes decisions. High-stakes

decisions have a significant impact on the lives of individuals or on programs, and are not easily reversed, so that errors in these decisions can be difficult to correct. Examples of high-stakes decisions are college admissions or the awarding of funding to schools based on test results. Low-stakes decisions, on the other hand, have a relatively minor impact on individuals and programs, and errors in these decisions tend to have less drastic consequences. For example, placement into one of a series of language courses in an Intensive English Program is a relatively low-stakes decision, particularly if students can be moved to a different level after the first few days of class.

## Language use and language test performance

As mentioned above, the primary purpose of a language test is to make inferences about language ability. It is therefore essential, for a particular test, that we clearly specify what is meant by language ability. That is, we need to be clear about how this ability – however we define it – is manifested in non-test (i.e. real-world) language use, on the one hand, and in a language test, on the other. We refer to the ability that we want to test as a **construct**, and defining the construct is one of the most fundamental concerns in developing a test. For a language test, the key to defining the construct of interest is in determining what factors are involved in real-world language use, and which of those factors are essential to what we want to measure and what we do not. To take an example, suppose a student chooses to write an essay comparing and contrasting the works of Mozart and Beethoven, a writing task that would require a certain amount of knowledge about music. In a composition course, we may be interested in knowing whether students are able to organize a comparison/contrast essay, and thus the students' knowledge about music would not be part of the construct we are trying to measure. On the other hand, if a student chose this task for a music history course, the instructor would most likely be interested in knowing about the students' ability to write about music, and thus would include this knowledge as part of his or her construct definition. It is important to remember, as Alderson notes, that constructs are not so much 'psychologically real entities that exist in our heads,' (2000: 118) but abstractions that we define for a particular assessment purpose. In other words, there is no one single definition of language ability that will be applicable for all situations. Rather, for each testing situation, a definition of the ability, or construct, of interest must be developed that takes into account the test takers, the purpose of the test, and the target language use situation.

In Chapter 2, reference was made to various formulations of the components of language ability in applied linguistics research, beginning with the work of Hymes (1972). Current scholarship in the field seems to have arrived at a consensus position that communicative language ability – or the ability to use language to achieve genuine communicative function – consists of interactions between aspects of **language knowledge**, on the one hand, and **strategic competence**, on the other, as set forth by Bachman (1990) and modified by Bachman and Palmer (1996). (See, for example, McNamara, 1996, and Douglas, 2000, for thoughtful discussions of the Bachman and Palmer model of communicative language ability.) The specifics of what constitutes language knowledge and strategic competence have been reformulated by a number of scholars (e.g. Chapelle *et al.*, 1993; Douglas, 2000). For the purposes of this discussion, I am following Douglas (2000), whose formulation is a slight modification of the Bachman and Palmer (1996) framework. The essential components of language knowledge and strategic competence are summarized in Table 3.1.

As opposed to the Grabe and Kaplan taxonomy of language knowledge specifically relevant to writing, the more general taxonomy of components of language ability put forth by Bachman and Palmer (1996) and Douglas (2000) consists of **grammatical knowledge**, or knowledge of the fundamental building blocks of language, **textual knowledge**, or knowledge of how these building blocks are put together to form coherent texts, **functional knowledge**, or knowledge about how language is used to achieve a variety of communicative functions, and **sociolinguistic knowledge**, or knowledge about how to use language appropriately in different social settings.

Strategic competence is defined by Bachman and Palmer as 'a set of metacognitive components, or strategies, which can be thought of as higher order executive processes that provide a cognitive management function in language use, as well as in other cognitive activities' (1996: 70). Strategic competence is thus considered to be a general (i.e. non-language-specific) ability that allows one to make use of one's language knowledge in appropriate ways to meet one's communicative goals. Specifically, strategic competence provides the link between one's language knowledge and the external situation, and

Table 3.1 *Components of communicative language ability (adapted from Douglas, 2000: 35)*

---

**Language knowledge**

Grammatical knowledge
- Knowledge of vocabulary
- Knowledge of morphology and syntax
- Knowledge of phonology

Textual knowledge
- Knowledge of cohesion
- Knowledge of rhetorical or conversational organization

Functional knowledge
- Knowledge of ideational functions
- Knowledge of manipulative functions
- Knowledge of heuristic functions
- Knowledge of imaginative functions

Sociolinguistic knowledge
- Knowledge of dialects/varieties
- Knowledge of registers
- Knowledge of idiomatic expressions
- Knowledge of cultural references

**Strategic competence**

Assessment
- Evaluating communicative situation or test task and engaging an appropriate discourse domain
- Evaluating the correctness or appropriateness of the response

Goal setting
- Deciding how (and whether) to respond to the communicative situation

Planning
- Deciding what elements of language knowledge and background knowledge are required to reach the established goal

Control of execution
- Retrieving and organizing the appropriate elements of language knowledge to carry out the plan

---

also between one's language knowledge and other individual characteristics, especially topical knowledge (Bachman & Palmer, 1996).

Bachman and Palmer (1996) conceptualize strategic competence as having three main components: **goal setting**, **assessment**, and **planning** (discussed in detail below). Douglas (2000), building upon the

Bachman and Palmer framework, also sees strategic competence as including **control of execution**, or organizing the required elements of language knowledge and topical knowledge to carry out a communicative plan. As an example of how these strategies are used in writing, take the case of writing a letter to the editor of a newspaper in order to influence public opinion on a specific issue. Goal setting involves deciding to write the letter, to accomplish this purpose. Assessment involves taking stock of what is needed to write the letter – for example, knowledge about the topic, the form of such letters, the appropriate level of formality, and so on – as well as one's own linguistic resources for writing the letter. A plan is then generated to write the letter, and the plan is executed to greater or lesser degrees of success, depending on the writer's control of execution. Assessment is used again to evaluate the letter before it is sent.

As defined by Bachman and Palmer, strategic competence is a problem-solving ability that is not specific to language use in general or to writing in particular. However, it can also be argued that there are specific metacognitive strategies involved in writing, particularly when a writing task involves 'knowledge transformation' rather than 'knowledge telling,' as discussed in Chapter 2. Furthermore, it is these writing-specific strategies that distinguish novice writers from expert writers, given equivalent degrees of linguistic knowledge and general strategic competence. Thus, when we speak of strategic competence in writing, we mean not just general problem-solving abilities, but the abilities described in the models of writing presented in Chapter 2: for example, the process of reflection in the Hayes (1996) model, or the problem-solving processes in the content problem and rhetorical problem spaces in the Bereiter and Scardamalia (1987) models. Just as chess players develop problem-solving strategies specific to the game of chess that are not necessarily transferable to other cognitive activities, so writers through practice and experience develop strategies that are specific to writing.

Bachman and Palmer point out that, in addition to language knowledge and strategic competence, actual language use in genuine communicative situations involves other considerations: specifically, topical knowledge, personality factors, and affect or emotional factors. As an example, we can return to the example of writing a letter to the editor. Accomplishing this task requires a number of factors other than language knowledge. To begin with, one would need knowledge of the subject under discussion (topical knowledge), and one would need to feel strongly enough about the topic to write about it (affect). Furthermore, one's personal characteristics (e.g. experience with letters to the editor, degree of extroversion) may influence the choice of content and language, as well as whether one actually follows through with the plan to write the letter.

In a language test (and I am still considering writing tests to be a subset of language tests for the purposes of this discussion), we are primarily interested in language ability, not the other components of language use that are involved in actual communication. Nevertheless, we need to think about these components when we are designing tests so that we can specify as explicitly as possible the role that they play in the successful completion of the test tasks. In some cases they may be included in the definition of the ability we are interested in testing, whereas in others, we may want to reduce their effect on test takers' performance and thus on their test scores. For example, if we want to include knowledge about classical music as part of the construct 'writing about music' we will design tasks that depend on this knowledge, whereas if we are interested in a more general definition of writing ability we would avoid tasks that depend on specific background knowledge.

Thus, topical knowledge may or may not be specifically assessed in a writing test and thus may or may not be part of the construct being measured. Bachman and Palmer (1996: 121) note that there are three basic options for defining the construct with respect to topical knowledge: specifically excluding topical knowledge from the construct, including both language ability and topical knowledge in the construct definition, and defining language ability and topical knowledge as separate constructs. The option chosen will depend on the specific purpose of the test. For example, Hughes (1989) argues that in general language proficiency testing, writing tasks that require examinees to use their own content knowledge should not be used, stating that 'in language testing, we are not normally interested in knowing whether students are creative, imaginative, or even intelligent, have wide general knowledge, or have good reasons for the opinions they happen to hold. For that reason we should not set tasks which measure those abilities' (p. 82). On the other hand, as Douglas (2000) points out, one of the distinctive features of language for specific purposes (LSP) testing is the role that topical knowledge plays in defining the construct. Since an LSP test by definition requires test takers to engage in tasks that are related to the target language use situation, relevant background knowledge will always be part of the construct to a greater or lesser degree (p. 39).

While topical knowledge is sometimes included in a construct definition, personal characteristics and affect are usually explicitly excluded from the construct, and we try to avoid inadvertently measuring these factors in a language test. However, it is important to know something about characteristics such as age, sex, and educational background so that we can develop tasks that are appropriate for the specific test takers and to avoid biasing test tasks either in favor of or against test takers who have certain characteristics. Similarly, the role of affect in communication is important to consider in designing a test, not because we are interested in measuring affect, but because affect is involved in any language use situation and must therefore be accounted for. In other words, affect can have a facilitating or a debilitating effect on language performance, and if we want test takers to perform at their best, it is important to gauge the likely affective response of examinees to test tasks. This issue will be raised again in Chapter 5.

## Writing as performance assessment

One way to bring Bachman and Palmer's conceptualization of language use and language ability into clearer focus for writing assessment is to introduce the notion of performance assessment. The term performance assessment is used to describe any assessment procedure that involves either the observation of behavior in the real world or a simulation of a real-life activity – i.e. a performance of the ability being assessed, and the evaluation of the performance by raters. Performance assessments thus differ from traditional paper-and-pencil tests in the degree to which they represent or simulate behavior in the real world. In this sense, any writing test that involves actual writing, as opposed to completing multiple-choice items, for example, can be considered a performance test, since the written product represents a performance of writing.

McNamara (1996) provides a useful distinction between a strong sense and a weak sense of performance assessment in language testing. In the strong sense of the term, the focus of a performance assessment is on the successful completion of a given task that requires language use, and not on the language use itself. For example, if the task is to write a persuasive essay, the writer is successful if the reader is persuaded; or, if the task is to write a letter of apology, the writer is successful if the reader is willing to forgive the writer, regardless of the linguistic accuracy of the writing. Of course, as McNamara points out, if the writing is done in a testing situation, the writer will not be genuinely motivated to apologize to the reader, any more than the reader will be genuinely moved to forgiveness – the closest we can hope for as readers is to imagine that we would feel satisfied with the apology if we in fact had been offended in this specific way by the writer.

In a performance test in the strong sense of the term, language ability, and more specifically, language knowledge, in Bachman and Palmer's terms, may be only partly responsible for successful task completion, and extra-linguistic factors may compensate for weaknesses in language knowledge. For example, imagine that test takers were asked to write out directions to a party. If a test taker drew a simple map rather than writing verbal instructions, but the directions were clear and accurate, the task has been fulfilled successfully, but clearly, abilities other than language knowledge were involved in completing the task. Performance tests in this sense – where the sole criterion is real-world success, regardless of the means used to achieve it – can generally not be considered language tests, as McNamara points out.

In the weak sense of performance assessment, on the other hand, the focus of the assessment is on the language used, not on the fulfillment of the task *per se*. Tasks used to elicit language may resemble real-world writing tasks, but the purpose is to display language proficiency, not the ability to persuade or apologize. In other words, the readers who score the writing are interested more in the linguistic aspects of the writing than in whether they feel persuaded or ready to forgive the writer.

As McNamara notes, most language tests fall somewhere in between these two ends of the continuum. In terms of writing tests, both the specific test tasks and the scoring criteria may vary in the extent to which factors other than language ability are involved. Writing tasks at the weak end of the continuum tend to focus on a limited range of areas of language ability, and are thus highly controlled in content and language and/or limited in their correspondence to real-life writing tasks. An example of such a task would be a sentence-completion task or a task requiring examinees to change a paragraph from the present tense to the past tense. In contrast, tasks that allow for a high degree of individual variation in factors, such as topical knowledge and affect, correspond more closely to real-world writing tasks, for example essays written in response to a reading passage in an academic language course. Tasks such as these are all on the strong end of the continuum. Similarly, scoring criteria that focus on discrete aspects of language – use of vocabulary, organization, and so on – would tend to make a test fall at the weaker end of the continuum as opposed to criteria that focus on successful completion of the task.

## Test usefulness

Bachman and Palmer (1996: 17) maintain that 'the most important consideration in designing and developing a language test is the use for which it is intended, so that the most important quality of a test is its usefulness.' They define test usefulness in terms of six qualities, defined below: reliability, construct validity, authenticity, interactiveness, impact, and practicality. While these qualities are all important, it must be emphasized that it is virtually impossible to maximize all of them. In particular, practicality, or the amount of available resources, is a limiting factor, and requires prioritization among the other qualities (Lyle Bachman, personal communication, 2000). Therefore, instead of attempting to maximize each quality of usefulness, the task of the test developer is to determine an appropriate balance among the qualities for the specific situation. Bachman and Palmer present the following three guiding principles for considering the qualities of usefulness in test construction and selection:

> *Principle 1:* It is the overall usefulness of the test that is to be maximized, rather than the individual qualities that affect usefulness.
> *Principle 2:* The individual test qualities cannot be evaluated independently, but must be evaluated in terms of their combined effect on the overall usefulness of the test.
> *Principle 3:* Test usefulness and the appropriate balance among the different qualities cannot be prescribed in general, but must be determined for each specific testing situation.
> (Bachman and Palmer, 1996: 18)

In other words, since every assessment context is different, the relative importance of these six qualities of usefulness will vary from situation to situation, and test developers must strive to maximize overall usefulness given the constraints of the particular situation, rather than trying to maximize all six qualities.

I will now define the six qualities of usefulness, particularly as they relate to writing assessment.

**Reliability** can be defined as consistency of measurement across different characteristics or facets of a testing situation, such as different prompts and different raters. A test is said to be reliable if individuals receive the same score from one prompt or rater to the next, and if a group of examinees is rank-ordered in the same way on different occasions, different versions of a test, or by different raters. Reliability is an essential consideration in testing and is a prerequisite for test validity. That is, if we cannot feel confident that our test gives consistent results, we cannot be sure that the inferences and decisions we make on the basis of test results will be appropriate and fair. At the same time, just because our results are consistent, we cannot necessarily be sure that they reflect the ability we want to test.

Reliability in a test of writing can be affected by several factors, including variables related to the writing task itself (e.g. the topic, the expected discourse mode of the response, the number of discrete writing samples a candidate is asked to provide) and by variables related to the scoring process (e.g. the background and experience of the raters, the nature of the rating scale, and the training given to raters). These issues are discussed in detail in Chapters 4 and 6.

**Construct validity** refers to 'the meaningfulness and appropriateness of the interpretations that we make on the basis of test scores' (Bachman and Palmer, 1996: 21). **Construct validation** refers to the process of determining whether a test is actually measuring what it is intended to measure. In order for decisions based on test results to be fair, it is important to understand as precisely as possible what ability the test is attempting to measure, and to what extent the test is actually measuring that ability and not some other ability. Furthermore, it is important to be clear about the domain of writing to which the test is intended to generalize. For example, in a test of business writing, if our test tasks comprise only letters and memoranda we would be on very shaky ground if we wanted to generalize our test results to other genres of business writing, such as reports and executive summaries. Thus, construct validation is specific to each test and depends crucially on the definition of the ability of interest for a particular testing context. Depending on the context and the purpose of a writing test, the ability of interest may be defined in a number of different ways, e.g. 'the ability to generate well formed sentences' or 'the ability to persuade an audience through the selection of appropriate evidence, tone, and rhetorical strategies.'

The construct validation process will include both collection of empirical evidence and a theoretical rationale (Messick, 1989). While a variety of kinds of evidence can be used to demonstrate construct validity, perhaps the most common are the five discussed by Chapelle (1998: 51): (1) content analysis, (2) empirical item investigation, (3) task analysis, (4) relationships between test scores and other measures, and (5) experimental research identifying performance differences over time, across groups and settings, and in response to experimental interventions. I will discuss each of these types of evidence briefly.

Content analysis usually consists of the judgements of subject-matter experts to determine the adequacy and representativeness of the test content vis-à-vis the domain to which test results are intended to generalize. For example, content analysis of a writing test used for placing students into composition courses might involve asking instructors to judge the test tasks in terms of their degree of correspondence to the writing tasks that are used in the courses. Empirical item investigation involves the identification of factors that affect item difficulty and discrimination (Carroll, 1989, cited in Chapelle, 1998) – that is, how easy or difficult it is to receive a high score on a particular test item or task, and how well the item or task discriminates among high-ability and low-ability test takers. In terms of writing tasks, factors that affect task difficulty involve factors within the test takers themselves, factors within the prompt, and factors within the scoring procedures. These factors are discussed at length in Chapter 4; for the purposes of the present discussion, the essential point is that construct validity is enhanced when the factors that contribute to difficulty are those that are included in the definition of the construct. To put it somewhat more negatively, if the factors that contribute to difficulty are unrelated to the construct – for example, if the task is worded in such a way that some better writers are confused by the task instructions, or if successful completion of the task requires background knowledge that only some test takers possess – construct validity of our interpretations will be diminished.

Empirical task analysis involves documenting the strategies that test takers use to complete test tasks, such as the use of think-aloud protocols to investigate the writing process, as discussed in Chapter 2. These strategies are then compared to the strategies that would be predicted based on a theoretical definition of the construct.

Investigating relationships between test scores and other measures, frequently referred to as criterion-related validity evidence, involves calculating correlations between the test of interest and other measures of the same construct, such as another test or teacher judgements of student ability. Finally, experimental evidence of construct validity can be gathered by generating and testing hypotheses about how various characteristics of the test taker or the testing situation might be related to test performance. For example, if a test is intended to measure achievement in writing following instruction, experimental evidence of construct validity could consist of a comparison of test results before and after instruction. Higher test scores following instruction could be considered evidence of construct validity of the test, particularly if a control group who was not given instruction showed no improvement on the test during the same time period. As another example, imagine that test takers are allowed to hand-write or type their essays on a writing test. If it turned out that hand-written essays received significantly higher scores than typed essays, this would be considered evidence against construct validity, as transcription mode is not part of the definition of the construct.

In testing writing, construct validity must be demonstrated in at least three ways: (1) the task must elicit the type of writing that we want to test (see discussion of authenticity below); (2) the scoring criteria must take into account those components of writing that are included in the definition of the construct; and (3) the readers must actually adhere to those criteria when scoring writing samples. These issues are discussed in detail in Chapters 4, 5, and 6.

The next quality of usefulness discussed by Bachman and Palmer is **authenticity**, defined as 'the degree of correspondence of the characteristics of a given language test task to the features of a target language use (TLU) task' (Bachman and Palmer, 1996: 23). That is, the test task – in our case, a writing task – must be representative of the type of writing that examinees will need in the world beyond the test. In some cases, this is relatively unproblematic. For example, in a general-purpose English test for EFL learners, writing tasks that simulate the type of writing that these learners might be expected to accomplish can be fairly easily identified: a letter to a tourist agency requesting travel information or a written response to a job advertisement. In other cases, authenticity is a bit more problematic. For English-speaking learners of foreign languages, who may have little real need to write in that language outside the language classroom, it may be more difficult to find an appropriate writing task that represents an authentic TLU situation. In this case, the test developers may decide that authenticity is less of a consideration than other aspects of usefulness such as reliability.

Another problematic area in terms of authenticity is English for academic purposes, one of the most common arenas for testing writing. A typical writing test – in which examinees must write a timed impromptu essay on a topic about which they have no advance knowledge – is relatively inauthentic in at least four ways. First, academic writing outside of a testing situation typically involves the use of source materials as input, in the form of assigned readings, lectures, and class discussions. As a result, students have generally dealt with the topic through reading, speaking, and listening before writing about it and are thus (in theory) well equipped in terms of background knowledge and schemata to write about it. Second, except in the case of timed examinations, most academic writing is not timed or speeded, and writers can take as much time as their schedules and inclinations allow to reflect on the topic, refer to outside sources, and revise and edit their writing before turning it in for a grade. Third, while writing tests are frequently scored by raters who are unknown to the examinees (and vice versa), the audience for most academic writing is the students' instructor. Students thus have the advantage of knowing what that reader is likely to expect in terms of task demands, level of formality, content, and so on, and can shape their written text more appropriately to their perceptions of their instructors' expectations. Finally, most academic writing (with the possible exception of instruction in composition and/or creative writing) is judged primarily on accuracy of content, rather than on the appropriateness of the organization or the use of language. While an essay examination is more authentic for these writers than, say, a multiple-choice test of grammar and usage, it is clear from this discussion that authenticity will be an issue when designing tasks for testing academic writing. In fact, these considerations of authenticity have been in the forefront of arguments in favor of using portfolio assessment and other alternatives to timed impromptu essays, particularly for classroom writing assessment. This issue is addressed again in Chapters 8 and 9.

Bachman and Palmer (1996) define **interactiveness** as 'the extent and type of involvement of the test taker's individual characteristics in accomplishing a test task' (p. 25). As discussed above, the relevant characteristics for language testing include language knowledge (i.e. knowledge of the linguistic code), strategic competence (i.e. strategies for effectively managing cognitive and linguistic resources to complete a task), topical knowledge, and affective schemata, or how examinees respond emotionally to test tasks. Interactiveness is important in language testing because these characteristics are all engaged in actual language use. Thus an assessment task that only involves language knowledge but not the other characteristics may give us some idea of how much a test taker knows about the language, but not about how well he or she can use the language.

An example of a relatively non-interactive writing task would be a task that required examinees to change all the verbs in a paragraph from present tense to past tense. In this task, examinees must demonstrate their knowledge of English grammar, but their need for metacognitive strategies is limited, nor do they necessarily need to know anything about the topic of the passage. Such a task is limited in its affective appeal as well, as it is fairly mechanical and may not engage test takers' interests as much as a more interactive task.

On the other hand, a highly interactive writing task would involve not just linguistic competence but strategic competence as well. The metacognitive strategies involved in an interactive writing task would include, in Bachman and Palmer's framework discussed above, **goal setting** (what am I trying to accomplish with this piece of writing?), **assessment** of various facets of the task, including the rhetorical situation (who is the reader, and what will he or she expect?), one's own linguistic resources for completing the task, and eventually one's success in completing the task, and **planning** how to complete the task. In terms of topical knowledge, the writer must already know something about the topic or must be given the information as part of the task instructions – otherwise, test takers who know more about the topic will be at an unfair advantage over those who do not. Finally, an interactive task should engage the writer's interest so that he or she is able to perform at an optimal level. The role of content knowledge and emotional engagement as they affect writing task design are discussed in more detail in Chapter 5.

**Impact** can be defined as the effect that tests have on individuals (particularly test takers and teachers) and on larger systems, from a particular educational system to the society at large. As Bachman and Palmer note, tests are never administered in a vacuum, but reflect and represent societal goals and values, and the uses of test scores have consequences for individuals and groups that must be considered carefully in making decisions regarding the administration and use of tests.

One area of impact that has received increased attention in recent years is the impact of tests on curricula and instruction, frequently referred to as **washback**. As with any consequence, washback can be positive or negative. Positive washback can be defined as any effect of a testing procedure that encourages teachers to adopt practices that are in line with the current best thinking in the field with respect to pedagogy. Negative washback is any effect of testing that leads teachers to practices which they feel are counterproductive, in terms of student learning, or which do not reflect the current thinking in the field. A good example of positive washback as it relates to writing can be seen in the TOEFL examination. Until recently, the TOEFL examination did not include a writing sample as part of the standard examination; it was only included in the optional Test of Written English. When the computer-based TOEFL was introduced operationally, it included a 30-minute writing sample that was factored into the structure score and also reported as a separate score to test users. As a result, many language schools that offer TOEFL preparation courses are focusing on essay writing rather than just on grammar recognition. Presumably, this may have the salutary effect of better preparing potential international students to study at North American universities, where writing is seen as essential to academic success.

It should be noted, however, that washback is a complex phenomenon, and that the relationship between a test and subsequent changes in instructional practices is not straightforward. It has been suggested that beneficial washback depends in part upon factors such as the importance of the test, the status of the language being tested, and the purpose and format of the test (Shohamy *et al.*, 1996). Positive washback is more likely to occur as a result of adding a writing component to a high-stakes test such as the TOEFL than, for example, as a result of adding a similar writing component to a low-stakes foreign language test that is being used primarily to evaluate a language program. Furthermore, changes in the instructional practices of individual teachers may be mediated by such influences as the teacher's personal beliefs, institutional requirements, prevailing social, political, and economic issues (Wall, 1996), along with student expectations and the availability of appropriate instructional materials (Alderson and Hamp-Lyons, 1996).

Because of the variety of factors outside the test that may affect washback, the design of the test itself cannot guarantee positive washback. However, test developers can take steps to promote positive washback in a number of ways. Bailey (1996) suggests that beneficial washback is more likely to occur when test takers, teachers, and administrators understand the purpose of the test and find the results informative and believable; when the test is based on clearly articulated goals and objectives that are related to what is being taught; when test tasks are clearly related to real-world language tasks, and when test takers have an investment in the assessment process, for example through self-assessment. These considerations have been central in the growing movement towards portfolio assessment in writing, discussed in Chapter 9.

Bachman and Palmer note that test takers themselves can be affected by three aspects of testing procedures: the experience of preparing for and taking the test, the feedback that they receive about their performance, and the decisions that are made on the basis of their test results. In order to maximize positive impact in these three areas, it is important to consider how test takers perceive the test, how accurate and informative the feedback they receive is, and how to maximize the accuracy of test scores so that decisions are fair and appropriate.

Tests, particularly large-scale, high-stakes tests, can also have an impact on society as a whole, so it is crucial to consider the value systems that a given test may be promoting. For example, the type of writing that is elicited on a statewide assessment may be considered an indication of the type of writing that society values. As was discussed in Chapter 2, in some societies, personal writing may be highly valued, while in others, writing is used to pay homage to existing scholarship rather than to present one's own point of view. The very fact that writing is currently a part of many large-scale educational assessments in the US is an acknowledgement of the importance that society places on writing in academic contexts. Thus, we need to consider carefully the impact that a test will have on larger systems as well as on individuals.

**Practicality** is defined as the relationship between the resources that will be required for test development and administration and the resources that are available for these activities. To state this somewhat more simply, a test is only practical if the resources available for test-related activities meet or exceed the resources required to develop and/or administer the test. Resources can be described in terms of human resources, material resources, and time for designing tasks, administering tests, scoring and score reporting. Practicality is a key limitation for writing assessment for two important reasons. First, while in an ideal world we would want to collect as many different writing samples as possible from test takers to sample the domain adequately, the nature of writing limits the number of tasks that can be accomplished in a limited time. Second, the scoring of writing tasks is time-consuming and labor intensive, and practicality concerns may make certain scoring procedures unfeasible. When designing a test of writing, therefore, it is critical to make sure that sufficient resources are available to make the test viable. In addition, it is also important to consider the allocation of resources for various development and administrative activities. For example, hiring writing instructors to write multiple-choice test items so that one does not need to hire raters to score essays would be a questionable allocation of available resources (Lyle Bachman, personal communication).

The cost and time required to test writing on a very large scale, as in national and international assessments, has led to the somewhat controversial movement towards scoring writing tests by computer. This issue will be revisited in more detail in Chapter 10.

To summarize, in designing a test of writing, it is important to consider the six qualities of usefulness proposed by Bachman and Palmer – construct validity, reliability, interactiveness, authenticity, impact, and practicality. While it may not be possible to maximize each quality, test developers should strive to maximize overall usefulness of a test by giving careful consideration to the qualities of usefulness and determining for each testing situation an appropriate balance among them.

## Summary

This chapter has provided an introduction to writing assessment by considering test purposes, the abilities and other individual factors underlying language use, particularly in writing, and considerations of test usefulness. As we have seen, designing a test of writing involves defining the ability we are interested in testing for a given test purpose. This in turn requires identifying the factors other than the ability we are intending to test that may be engaged by the test task, so that we can attempt to control them to ensure that the inferences about language ability we make on the basis of test results are valid. Furthermore, for a test to be useful for a given purpose, the test designer needs to take into consideration the various aspects of test usefulness, deciding on a minimally acceptable level for each aspect, based on the specifics of the situation. With these considerations in mind, we now turn to a discussion of research related to large-scale writing assessment in Chapter 4, and then to the two key components in designing writing tests: designing writing tasks in Chapter 5, and developing scoring procedures in Chapter 6.

......................................................................................................................

# CHAPTER FOUR

# Research in large-scale writing assessment

## Introduction

This section of the book provides guidance for developing large-scale writing tests; that is, tests of writing beyond the level of the classroom. Chapter 4 presents an overview of research in what is often referred to as 'direct' writing assessment, while Chapters 5 and 6 build on the theoretical underpinnings of Chapter 4 to provide practical guidance in developing tasks for writing assessment (Chapter 5) and scoring procedures (Chapter 6).

An assessment task in which test takers actually produce a sample of writing, often referred to as a 'direct' test of writing, is probably the most common method for testing writing in both first- and second-language contexts. Hamp-Lyons (1991a: 5) gives five characteristics of a so-called 'direct' test of writing. Candidates must write at least one piece of continuous text (here Hamp-Lyons suggests a minimum number of 100 words, but this minimum presupposes a fairly high level of language proficiency and may not be appropriate for low-proficiency learners); test takers are given a set of instructions (or 'prompt') but have considerable leeway in responding to the prompt; each text is read by at least one, and normally two or more, trained raters; judgements are tied to a common yardstick, such as a set of sample responses or one or more rating scales; and judgements are expressed as numbers, rather than or in addition to verbal descriptions. Two additional characteristics of most such writing tests are the fact that texts are written in a limited time frame, generally between thirty minutes and two hours, and that the topic is unknown to test takers in advance.

The term 'direct' is commonly used to contrast this type of test with so-called 'indirect' tests of writing – most often, multiple-choice tests of grammar and usage. However, the term 'direct' is somewhat problematic, since any test is at best an indirect indicator of an underlying ability (Messick, 1994). I will therefore use the term 'timed impromptu writing test' (occasionally shortened to 'writing test') throughout to refer to this approach to assessing writing.

This description of a timed impromptu writing test distinguishes it from its two chief rivals in large-scale assessment: so-called indirect tests of writing, as mentioned above, on the one hand, and portfolio assessment, or the evaluation of a number of texts written in non-testing situations over an extended time period, on the other. It also distinguishes a timed impromptu writing test from other classroom-based evaluations of student writing.

Of all forms of writing assessment, the timed impromptu writing test is probably the best researched. For a number of years, particularly in the United States, the focus of this research was on establishing acceptable levels of interrater reliability, that is, consistency of ratings among different raters. As Camp (1993), White (1994, 1995), and others have noted, this research was essential in order for this form of writing assessment to be accepted by educational institutions and large testing bodies, such as Educational Testing Service, as a satisfactory alternative to more 'objective' measures that could be machine scored. Both research and practical experience gave rise to a set of procedures that, when followed closely, increased the efficiency and reliability of writing tests. These procedures included designing and pre-testing prompts carefully to make them accessible to all test takers, selecting and training raters, double-marking of essays, ensuring the independence of scores so that one rater is not influenced by the scores that another rater gives, and using a scoring rubric along with model essays that instantiate the criteria outlined in the rubric. Most large-scale writing assessments of both first- and second-language writers in the United States and other countries now use some variant of these procedures. Beginning in the early 1980s, however, questions began to be raised about the validity of this method of testing writing, and it is validity that is the central concern of researchers at present. In particular, questions have been raised about whether the procedures that lead to scoring reliability actually detract from validity (Charney, 1984; Huot, 1990a, 1996).

Any investigation of validity is an on-going enterprise involving numerous sources of information and approaches to data analysis. It may be useful to begin the discussion of validity by considering the various factors that affect test scores. These factors, represented in Figure 4.1 (adapted from McNamara, 1996, and Kenyon, 1992), include the writing task, the written text itself, the scale being used, characteristics of the raters, characteristics of the writers other than their writing ability, and various contextual factors. Contextual factors include the immediate context of the assessment itself (i.e. the physical conditions under which the test is administered) and the particular social milieu in which the assessment takes place (i.e. the school or institutional setting), which determines the goals of the assessment and the broader social and cultural context and relates to cultural norms about writing, assessment, and so on. While it may not be possible to measure the effects of all of these factors, their inclusion serves as a reminder that any assessment takes place in a given social and cultural context and may not be generalizable outside of that context. The figure opposite provides a framework for reviewing research in writing tests in both first- and second-language contexts. As the discussion below makes clear, the variables interact with each other in complex ways; in the words of Purves (1992), 'different tasks present different problems, which are treated differently by students and judged differently by raters' (p. 112). However, for the sake of convenience, studies are grouped together under concerns of task, text, rater, scale, context, and writer, even though many, if not most, of the studies discussed here involve interactions between two or more of these factors.

## Task variables

In a typical writing test, test takers are asked to respond to a very small number of writing tasks, frequently only one or two. Despite an increased awareness of the limitations of using only a few tasks, in most cases practical considerations (i.e. test administration time and the cost of scoring) severely restrict the number of tasks that candidates can respond to. It is therefore crucial that the task be constructed very carefully to allow all candidates to perform to the best of

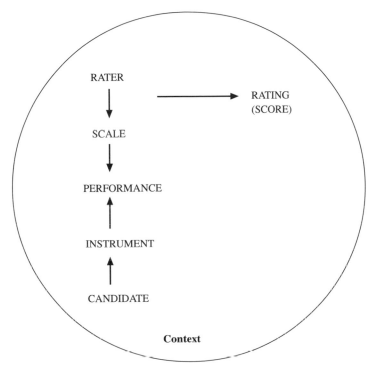

Figure 4.1 Factors in writing assessment (adapted from McNamara, 1996)

their abilities and to eliminate variations in scoring that can be attributed to the task rather than the candidates' abilities.

Some of the questions we might ask about writing tasks are the following. Most generally, on what dimensions do writing tasks vary, both 'in the real world' and in testing situations? This question has to do with content coverage, or 'construct representation,' (Messick, 1989): in a writing test we are interested in sampling from a specific domain of writing, so it is useful first of all to describe the domain. Second, of the many ways in which writing tasks can vary, which are associated with different levels of performance, and which are not? This question is relevant for a number of reasons. First, we want to minimize the amount of error in the test, both random and systematic, referred to as 'construct-irrelevant variance' (Messick, 1989). As far as possible, we want test takers to interpret the task in the same way so that their written efforts are comparable, and we want to reduce or eliminate any cause of confusion or difficulty in interpreting the task or in completing it within the allotted time. In addition, we frequently want to be able to compare performances on one occasion with those on another – for example, if we administer a placement test on different occasions, or if we want to measure growth in writing ability following a semester of study – or we may want to allow test takers to choose from a number of different writing prompts. In this case we need to know how much we can vary tasks or prompts and still get comparable results. Finally, if task dimensions are systematically related to differences in performance, it is useful to know wherein these differences lie – are task differences associated with observable differences in the grammatical, lexical, or rhetorical features of texts, or can differences in scores be mainly attributed to some aspect of the scoring method – that is, do raters use different criteria in assigning scores to different task types? Table 4.1, adapted from writing task classifications by Purves *et al.* (1984) and Hale *et al.* (1996), displays a number of dimensions across which assessment tasks tend to vary. Because different researchers in this area have used different terms for similar concepts, it may be helpful to give definitions of each of these dimensions before discussing the research. For the purposes of this discussion, the **task** is an overarching term that includes all relevant dimensions within the assessment, whether or not they are explicitly stated, while the **prompt** refers specifically to the written instructions to the test taker. Each of the dimensions is discussed briefly before the research related to these dimensions is presented.

**Subject matter** is simply the general content area that test takers are asked to write about, whether it be their families, a controversial issue in their academic field, or an abstract notion such as success. The **stimulus** refers to the material that forms the basis for generating writing content. For example, a task may involve describing a graph, evaluating information presented in a table or chart to make a choice, reading and responding to a short text, agreeing or disagreeing with a quotation, and so on. The **genre** refers to the expected form and communicative function of the written product; for example, a letter, an essay, or a laboratory report. The **rhetorical task** is broadly defined as one of the traditional discourse modes of narration, description, exposition, and argument/persuasion, as specified in the prompt, while the **pattern of exposition** (Hale *et al.*, 1996) refers to subcategories of exposition or specific instructions to the test taker to make comparisons, outline causes and effects, and so on. The cate-

Table 4.1 *Dimensions of tasks for direct writing assessment*

| Dimension | Examples |
| --- | --- |
| Subject matter | self, family, school, technology, etc. |
| Stimulus | text, multiple texts, graph, table |
| Genre | essay, letter, informal note, advertisement |
| Rhetorical task | narration, description, exposition, argument |
| Pattern of exposition | process, comparison/contrast, cause/effect, classification, definition |
| Cognitive demands | reproduce facts/ideas, organize/reorganize information, apply/analyze/synthesize/evaluate |
| Specification of: | |
| –audience | –self, teacher, classmates, general public |
| –role | –self/detached observer, other/assumed persona |
| –tone, style | –formal, informal |
| Length | less than ½ page, ½ to 1 page, 2–5 pages |
| Time allowed | less than 30 minutes, 30–59 minutes, 1–2 hours |
| Prompt wording | question vs. statement, implicit vs. explicit, amount of context provided |
| Choice of prompts | choice vs. no choice |
| Transcription mode | handwritten vs. word-processed |
| Scoring criteria | primarily content and organization; primarily linguistic accuracy; unspecified |

Adapted from Purves *et al.* (1984: 397–8) and Hale *et al.* (1996)

gory of **cognitive demands** is based on Bloom's (1956) well-known taxonomy of educational objectives and refers to 'the level of thinking skills or intellectual functioning [presumed to be] required to accomplish certain tasks' (Hale *et al.*, 1996: 12), and ranges in writing assessment tasks from reproducing facts/ideas, as in copying or taking dictation, to organizing/reorganizing facts, events, or ideas, as in retelling stories, giving directions, or describing something, to inventing/generating ideas as in expository and argumentative prose (Purves *et al.*, 1984; see also Table 1.2).

Prompts vary in terms of the amount of **specification** about a number of factors, including the intended audience, the role that the writer is to take, the tone or style that the writer is asked to adopt, or the expected length of the response. Variations in the **wording of prompts** may also occur that can affect performance, such as the degree to which the rhetorical task or pattern of exposition is explicitly stated, the use of questions versus imperatives, and so on.

A controversial issue, particularly in second-language writing assessment, is whether or not to offer a **choice of prompts** to test takers and the implications for performance if a choice is or is not offered. Finally, with the increased use of computers for writing and for testing, the issue of **transcription mode** – handwriting or word processing essays – has become relevant. **Scoring procedures** are discussed extensively in Chapter 6; for the purposes of the present discussion it should be noted that tasks vary with respect to whether the instructions to the test taker make explicit the criteria that will be used to evaluate writing. This is an important consideration because, when scoring criteria are made known to test takers, it may well be the case that variations in scoring criteria affect the way test takers undertake the task and hence their performance on the test.

It should be noted that these categories are not necessarily mutually exclusive: in particular, there is a logical relationship between cognitive demands and rhetorical task, as different discourse modes may be more or less cognitively challenging. For example, narration and description as ends in themselves, i.e. without interpretation or analysis, involve reproducing or reorganizing information, while exposition and persuasion by definition involve more the complex cognitive functions of analysis and evaluation (Hale *et al.*, 1996). The category of specification also overlaps with the categories related to task purpose and form, as prompts vary in terms of the amount of guidance they give as to genre, rhetorical task, and pattern of exposition. It is thus difficult if not impossible to single out any particular variable as being in and of itself critical in terms of influencing test performance, and indeed few if any studies have been designed to address a single variable and control for all other task variables.

Rather than looking at the effects of single variables, then, it may be more useful to look at research in terms of how these variables tend to cluster and interact. In a review of the literature on L1 writing assessment, Huot (1990b) divides research on task variables into three categories: discourse mode, rhetorical specification, and wording and structure of writing prompts; Tedick and Mathison (1995), reviewing similar literature from a second-language perspective, follow the same classification, but add subject matter as a fourth category. In the following discussion, I will review the literature related to discourse mode, followed by considerations of content area, stimulus material, rhetorical specification, and prompt wording.

## Discourse mode

Discourse mode, in this categorization scheme, or 'the type of writing called for in a prompt' (Huot, 1990b: 240) subsumes the categories of genre, rhetorical task, pattern of exposition, and cognitive demands. Evaluating the role of discourse mode in writing assessment is a challenging task, involving as it does a consideration of a variety of dimensions, each of which may independently or together have an influence on the quality of writing. It is perhaps unsurprising that findings in this area have been inconsistent and inconclusive, as studies have tended to focus on one aspect without controlling for others or for the confounding effects of subject matter.

Nevertheless, the picture that emerges from studies in this area is that variables related to discourse mode or purpose do affect test scores under certain circumstances. In a study of 11th and 12th graders writing in their L1, Quellmalz *et al.* (1982) found that students generally performed better on expository tasks than narrative tasks. Hoetker (1982) also reported on the results of the California State University and Colleges Equivalency Examination, noting that scores in 1974 were much lower than those in 1973, and attributing the difference to the fact that the 1973 topic asked students to reflect on a personal experience and the 1974 topic required abstract reasoning.

On the other hand, in a study of L2 writers, Carlson *et al.* (1985) found that correlations of holistic scores – that is, single scores based on an overall impression of the writing – on the Test of Written English (TWE) across two topic types (compare/contrast versus interpreting a chart or graph) were as high as those within topic types, indicating that the two types were rank-ordering test takers similarly. Similar results are reported by Spaan (1993), using two writing prompts of very different parameters.

Whether these differences in scores (or lack thereof) are due to qualitative differences in the texts produced by test takers or to some aspect of the scoring is still an open question. Some researchers have found qualitative differences in the texts themselves. Crowhurst (1980) looked at L1 narratives and argumentative writing across three grade levels and found that argumentative essays elicited significantly longer T-units (i.e. independent clauses along with any dependent clauses) than narratives. Furthermore, for 10th and 12th graders, although not for 6th graders, length of T-unit was significantly related to holistic scores in the argument essays but not in the narratives.

Reid (1990) found significant differences between two TWE essay types in essay length and lexical variables such as word length and percentage of content words, but no syntactic differences.

On the other hand, evidence is mounting that the scoring process itself is an important mitigating variable that can influence whether test scores differ across different discourse modes. Hake (1986) found that L2 essays that were pure narratives of personal experience were misgraded much more frequently than were expository essays using personal narration to illustrate or support an assertion. Purves (1992), reporting on a large-scale international study of first-language school writing, notes that correlations across different functional essay types vary from country to country, and hypothesizes that these differences may be due to differences in raters rather than in actual student ability. Hamp-Lyons and Matthias (1994) found that L2 essay topics that were judged more difficult by composition specialists tended to get higher scores than those judged to be easier, and suggested that raters may be unconsciously rewarding test takers who choose the more difficult prompt or may have lower expectations for that topic.

Weigle (1994, 1999) compared the rating patterns of inexperienced and experienced raters of ESL compositions both before and after training across two prompt types: one that involved making and defending a choice based on information presented in a table or chart (the Choice prompt), and one that required test takers to describe trends in a graph and make predictions based on the information presented in the graph (the Graph prompt). While both groups of raters graded the Choice essays equally severely before training, the inexperienced untrained raters were significantly more severe in their rating of the Graph essays than the experienced raters. An analysis of raters' think-aloud protocols suggested several factors that might account for these results. The Choice prompt tended to elicit traditional five-paragraph essays that were similar in form to one another, while the Graph prompt could be approached from several rhetorical angles. Inexperienced raters found the scoring guide descriptors – which mentioned qualities of the introduction, body, and conclusion – easier to apply to the Choice essays and were thus able to apply the scoring criteria appropriately to these essays even without training. These raters tended to penalize the Graph essays for not following the traditional five-paragraph format. Experienced raters, on the other hand, tended to reward Graph essays that 'broke the mold' and approached the topic in more original ways, and at the same time tended not to use the top end of the scale for the Choice essays. This study in particular highlights the complex interrelationship between task variables (particularly discourse mode), rater variables, and scoring criteria, all of which can affect scores on writing tests.

## Content area

There has been surprisingly little research on the effects of writing in different subject or content areas, possibly because of the infinite number of subjects available to write on and the common-sense notion that topics must be as general as possible to be accessible to all test takers. The issue of content area is of particular interest in Language for Specific Purpose (LSP) programs, in which students need to learn the language of a particular profession (for example, air traffic control or hotel management) or academic discipline. Again, the results of the few studies in this area are mixed. Hamp-Lyons (1986, cited in Hamp-Lyons, 1990) found that there were no systematic differences in performance on the British Council's English Language Testing Service (ELTS) between general prompts and prompts in the writers' disciplines, while Tedick (1990) found that students performed better on a topic in their own discipline than on a more general topic. Other studies have found interactions between prompt type and subject matter (e.g. Brown *et al.*, 1991). In short, while it seems sensible to assume that test takers can perform better when they are writing about subjects they know and care about than when they are not, it is likely that the effects of content are mitigated by other task variables.

## Stimulus material

Another dimension of tasks that deserves a closer look, particularly as testing programs move towards writing tasks that are integrated with reading or listening tasks, is the nature of the stimulus for writing: to what extent do differences in the material provided for test takers as content lead to differences in performance? Of course, the nature and amount of material can vary infinitely, so it would be difficult to provide a definitive answer to this question. An L1 study by Smith *et al.* (1985) does address one aspect of task stimulus: they found that students generally performed better on a task that involved reading several short excerpts on a topic than when they read only one such excerpt. In a more recent study, Lewkowicz (1997) investigated differences in the quality of essays written by EFL learners in Hong Kong based on whether they were given a background reading or not. Lewkowicz found that providing a background text gave students ideas, but did not improve the quality of writing. Furthermore, that writers who were given a text tended to develop their ideas less than students who were not given a text, and also tended to rely heavily on the language of the source text. This is clearly an area where more research is needed.

### Rhetorical specification and prompt wording

Rhetorical specification, as defined by Brossell (1986), concerns the extent to which the writing prompt specifies for the writer the purpose, audience, speaker, and subject of a writing task. Brossell (1983), working with school-aged L1 writers, tested the hypothesis that writing prompts with full rhetorical specification would elicit higher quality essays than writing prompts with less specification. However, he found that prompts that had a medium level of information load produced higher quality compositions than those with either full specification or no specification. Brossell hypothesized that the moderate-load prompt helped to focus students more than the low-load prompt, but the high-load prompt repeated unnecessary information and may thus have wasted examinees' time that could have been spent writing.

The wording of essay prompts may also have an effect on test scores, but this too has not been conclusively demonstrated. Brossell and Ash (1984) and Hoetker and Brossell (1989) found no significant differences in scores due to differences in prompt wording. These studies were done with L1 writers; it may well be the case that differences in the wording of essay prompts have a greater effect on L2 writers, but this has not been demonstrated empirically, apart from anecdotes of ESL students misunderstanding culture-specific terms such as 'blind date' in writing prompts (Kroll and Reid, 1994).

## Summary of research on task variables

In short, although a good deal of research has been done on effects of task variation, the picture is not clear at this point in terms of which specific differences in writing prompts affect examinee performance and in what ways. What is clear, however, is that individuals use different cognitive, rhetorical and linguistic strategies when they are faced with tasks that vary according to topic, purpose, and audience, and that raters' responses across task types vary as well. If nothing else, the literature on task variability reinforces the limitations of using a single writing task as a measure of general writing ability.

## Text variables

An important question in writing assessment research has been the degree to which specific aspects of texts are related to test scores. There is a fair amount of research in both L1 and L2 that relates specific features of texts to test scores. This research has tended to take one of two forms. In several studies, various measures of linguistic features (e.g. number of words, number of T-units, vocabulary, spelling errors) have been computed and correlated with (usually) holistic ratings. In other studies, holistic ratings have been compared to analytic ratings of such features as quality of content, organization, and language.

A number of L1 studies have demonstrated that length, or quantity of text produced, is a significant predictor of holistic scores (Nold and Freedman, 1977; Stewart and Grobe, 1979; Grobe, 1981; Breland and Jones, 1984). Apart from length, a number of variables have been shown to be associated with scores. Grobe (1981), for example, found that measures of syntactic maturity, usage, mechanics, and vocabulary each made independent contributions to holistic scores, with vocabulary being the strongest predictor of scores. Other textual variables that have been found to correlate with test scores in L1 include the use of final free modifiers (Nold and Freedman, 1977), the use of indefinite noun phrases (Sullivan, 1987, cited in Huot, 1990b), and handwriting (Markham, 1976; Chase, 1968). In the L2 literature, Homburg (1984) found five variables that discriminated among three different levels of writing ability: moderately serious errors per T-unit, dependent clauses per composition, words per sentence, coordinating conjunctions per composition, and error-free T-units per composition. Tedick and Mathison (1995) found that effective rhetorical framing of an essay – that is, the degree to which the essay content fulfilled the expectations set up by the introduction – was an important variable in predicting holistic scores. Janopolous (1992) also found that readers recalled more propositions from higher scoring essays than from lower scoring ones.

While the studies described above have shown relationships between various text features and scores, these studies by themselves do not address the issue of what raters actually base their scores on when evaluating writing. To answer this question, we need to turn to studies of rater response to essays.

## Rater variables

The study of rater variables in writing assessment has taken two main foci: a consideration of what attributes of compositions raters focus on while evaluating writing, and the investigation of background rater characteristics and their effects of the process of reading compositions and ultimately on the scores that raters use.

In one line of research, verbal protocol analysis has been used to investigate the process of composition rating and to determine what aspects of writing are attended to by raters, frequently as a means of investigating differences between expert and novice raters. Huot (1988) found that both expert and novice raters attended primarily to content in rating L1 essays, although the expert raters had more coherent rating strategies than the novice raters. In studies of raters of L2 writing, both Cumming (1989) and Connor and Carrell (1993) reported similar findings; i.e. that raters tended to devote the majority of their attention to content, or gist.

Vaughan (1992), also looking at raters of L2 writing, tentatively identified several approaches to holistic assessment, such as the 'first impression dominates approach' or the 'grammar-oriented rater.' Vaughan suggests that, while raters can agree on many essays based on the guidelines for holistic assessment, they may fall back on their individual rating style for essays that do not clearly fit the descriptors of the scale. In a recent study of raters of L2 writing, Lumley (forthcoming) describes the problems that raters face in reconciling conflicts between scale descriptors and aspects of the texts they are evaluating, hypothesizing that the main function of rating scales and training is to help raters channel their diverse reactions to texts into narrower, more manageable statements that meet institutional requirements.

In recent years, researchers have also begun to focus on attributes of raters that may affect their ratings. Of these, composition teaching or rating experience are the variables that have received the most attention. Ruth and Murphy (1988) report on a study by Keech and McNelly (1982), who compared the holistic ratings of high school students, novice teachers, and expert teachers on 114 L1 student essays, and found that student ratings were significantly lower than expert teacher ratings, with novice teacher ratings in between the two groups. On the other hand, Sweedler-Brown (1985) found that rater trainers were harsher in their ratings of L2 writing than less experienced readers. Similar results are reported by Cumming (1990) in L2 and Breland and Jones (1984) in L1. Weigle (1994, 1999) found an interaction between rater groups and tasks, as discussed in the previous section.

In second-language writing, comparisons between ESL specialists and other raters (e.g. English faculty or other content-area faculty) have demonstrated that raters from different disciplines apply different criteria to non-native English writing (Mendelsohn and Cumming, 1987; Santos, 1988; Brown, 1991; Sweedler-Brown, 1993), highlighting the role of rater background experience in assigning scores to compositions.

Another relevant line of research is the cultural background of raters. Some studies have shown that raters who are familiar with common L1 rhetorical patterns tend to be more accepting of L2 essays with those patterns than are other raters (Kobayashi and Rinnert, 1999; Land and Whitley, 1989; Hinkel, 1994).

Rater training is another important variable that has been studied, particularly in L2 research. Shohamy *et al.* (1992) found that rater training was a more significant variable than experience in terms of rater reliability, although they did not report any differences in terms of relative severity. Weigle (1994, 1998) found that rater training improved the reliability of raters but did not completely erase individual tendencies to be severe or lenient in rating.

One aspect of rater behavior that has been shown to influence test scores is rater expectations. Stock and Robinson (1987) go so far as to say that expectations may be as important as the quality of the text itself in determining composition scores. Diederich (1974) found that raters gave higher scores to the same L1 essays when they were told that the essays were written by honors students than when they were told the essays were written by average students. Recent studies of L1 handwritten versus word-processed essays have demonstrated that raters tend to score handwritten essays higher, in part because the expectations of formatting, grammatical and spelling accuracy are higher in word-processed essays and errors are thus more noticeable and glaring in these essays (Powers *et al.*, 1994).

It is clear from this brief review that rater variables can be very influential in determining scores on writing tests. Raters bring their own backgrounds, experiences, and values to the assessment of writing, and while training can help bring raters to a temporary agreement on a set of common standards, research has consistently shown that raters will never be in complete agreement on writing scores. Furthermore, there appears to be a complex relationship between raters and tasks, in that raters base their judgements of writing on their expectations for a specific task as well as on the attributes of the specific texts they are judging.

## Rating scales

Another important element in writing assessment is the nature of the rating scale that is used. Since the rating scale represents the most concrete statement of the construct being measured, it is clearly important to understand how rating scales influence decisions made about test takers. Different types of rating scales are discussed in detail in Chapter 6; for the purposes of the present discussion I will simply note that most rating scales can be classified as either holistic (a single score is given to each writing sample) or analytic (separate scores are given to different aspects of writing, such as content, organization, language use, and so on).

While the literature is replete with arguments for or against various scale types for both L1 and L2 writers, there has been surprisingly little research on the effects of different scale types on outcomes. In other words, what are the ultimate implications if a holistic vs. an analytic scale is used? In one of very few studies in the L1 literature that address this issue, Freedman (1979) compared the holistic and analytic evaluations of college students and professional writers, and found that the professional writers were distinguished from the college writers on the analytic scale but not the holistic scale. Furthermore, college writers received approximately the same scores regardless of the scale used, while professional writers consistently scored higher on the analytic scale. In a more recent study, Carr (2000) investigated the effects of changing the rating scale for the composition subtest of a university ESL placement test from an analytic to a holistic scale. Carr found that changing the rating scale altered the emphasis of the entire test – consisting of listening, reading, and writing subtests – giving more weight to the productive modality than to the receptive modality, despite the fact that no other part of the test was changed.

Somewhat more is known about the relative reliability of different scale types. Weir (1990) reports on studies by Hartog *et al.* (1936) and Cast (1939), which indicated that analytic scores were more reliable than holistic scores, although there was no rater training involved in either of these studies. Bauer (1981) also found that analytic scoring was more reliable than holistic scoring, although the latter is more cost effective.

## Context variables

Variability within the rating context includes such factors as ordering of compositions, time of day of the rating session, whether the rating is done alone or in a group setting, and the type of training received.

A number of studies in L1 writing have demonstrated a contrast effect in ratings: a medium quality essay tends to receive a low score when it is preceded by a number of high quality essays, and tends to receive a higher score when it is preceded by a number of lower quality essays (Hales and Tokar, 1975; Hughes *et al.*, 1980; Daly and Dickson-Markman, 1982). Daly and Dickson-Markman concluded that the contrast effect can be reduced by presenting essays in a random order; however, Hughes and Keeling (1984) found that contrast effects were not eliminated by the use of model essays to guide raters and that contrast effects are 'an unavoidable concomitant of essay scoring' (p. 281).

Freedman (1981) studied the influence of a number of contextual variables, including day, rating session within days, and trainers, on holistic essay scores. She found that, next to the ability of the writers themselves, the largest source of variance came from the trainers. Looking back at the training data, Freedman concluded that subtle differences in the way the two trainers approached the training session led to differences in the rating sessions.

One factor related to the scoring context that deserves more attention is the social aspect of essay scoring. In many large-scale assessments, raters are brought together as a group for a period of up to several days to score essays. White (1994) argues that the sense of community that is engendered in such rating sessions is an essential aspect of essay scoring and helps to maintain reliability by enforcing the rating standards. However, in other settings, raters are provided with ample training and model essays but do the rating independently of other raters. This condition frequently prevails when essays are read for research purposes rather than for an operational examination or when writing tests are given on a small scale and only two raters are involved. To my knowledge no research has been done on the relative reliability of scoring under these two conditions. With the rise of computer-based testing and scoring via the Internet, this issue may be an important one to investigate in the future.

## Test-taker variables

While test takers are, in a very fundamental sense, the most important element of a writing test, surprisingly little research has been done on the responses of test takers to test tasks. As Ruth and Murphy (1984) note, a writing task as intended by test writers may not be the same task that is perceived and attempted by writers. However, little is known about how test takers read and decide how to respond to essay tests. Such information is important to gather to answer questions such as the optimal level of specification of a prompt or whether or not to give test takers a choice between two or more prompts.

Very few studies have looked at the writers as they encounter a writing test, but the few studies that have explored this area have highlighted the idiosyncratic nature of responding to writing tasks. Weaver (1973, cited in Hamp-Lyons, 1991d) found that writers need to transform a 'teacher-initiated' topic into a 'self-initiated' topic: that is, each writer must somehow make the task into something that he or she can respond to meaningfully. Hamp-Lyons (1991b) contrasts the strategies of L2 writers who, not feeling completely at home with the subject matter of the prompt, apologize for their lack of knowledge in their essays, with those who skillfully mount a challenge to the prompt, positioning themselves as authorities who through their own expertise could argue successfully that the prompt itself, rather than their own lack of knowledge, was problematic. Murphy and Ruth (1993) interviewed several high school students about their interpretation of a specific essay prompt and found numerous ways in which the prompt could plausibly be read, and as a result the authors recommend that unexpected but plausible interpretations of the task be honored by raters.

One specific area of test taker behavior that has been investigated is test takers' choice of prompts. In a study of prompt choice, Polio and Glew (1996) found that the most frequently cited reason for choosing a particular prompt was perceived familiarity with the topic. Other reasons given were the level of generality or specificity of the prompt, the perceived rhetorical structure elicited by the prompt, interest in the prompt, and knowledge of appropriate English vocabulary. Polio and Glew also found that students did not feel that choosing a topic took up an inordinate amount of time, and they overwhelmingly agreed that there should be a choice of topic on a writing test. Similar results were found by Weigle *et al.* (2000) in a study of prompt choice on a university writing test for non-native speakers of English. However, Weigle *et al.* also found that reasons for choosing specific prompts differed according to whether the prompts were personal or non-personal, with familiarity being more important for personal prompts and perceived ability to organize and develop a topic being more of a factor for non-personal prompts.

Beyond these few studies, there is a dearth of information about how writers interact with test tasks and respond to them. As Hamp-Lyons (1991b) notes:

> Without accompanying studies of students as they encounter written examinations . . . we shall remain unsure of what students do when they approach an essay test: How (indeed if) they read the prompt, how they establish salience for elements of the prompt, what makes them choose one prompt over another where a choice is given, [and] how they decide what persona to present to the reader.          (Hamp-Lyons, 1991b: 103)

This is an area of writing assessment that would be well worth additional investigation in the future.

## Summary

In this chapter, research related to essay tests of writing has been reviewed. It is clear from this review that there are many interrelated factors that must be taken into consideration when designing tasks and scoring procedures for writing assessment. It should also be noted here that the vast majority of research on writing assessment has dealt with a limited population of first- and second-language writers – primarily adults who are using writing for academic purposes. Research on writing assessment for other groups of language learners, such as foreign language learners, young language learners or immigrant/refugee groups is limited. Until such research is forthcoming, the reader is cautioned to take into account the important differences between the various populations of language learners before generalizing the research presented here to other learner groups. However, the research presented in this chapter can be useful as one of many complementary data sources for making decisions about assessing writing.

......................................................................................................

# CHAPTER FIVE

# Designing writing assessment tasks

This chapter presents principles of test design for large-scale writing assessment – that is, testing beyond the level of the individual classroom. The chapter is divided into two parts; the first part presents general considerations in test development, specifically the use and importance of test specifications and the importance of pre-testing; the second half of the chapter presents considerations for designing writing tasks, which take into account the research on assessment discussed in Chapter 4. Throughout the chapter, sample writing tasks are presented that illustrate the main points under discussion.

## The process of test development

General procedures for language test development can be found in numerous sources (e.g. Bachman and Palmer, 1996; Alderson *et al.*, 1995; Norris *et al.*, 1998; Davidson and Lynch, 2002). These sources emphasize that test development involves several stages, which do not proceed in a strictly sequential or linear fashion, but inform each other in an iterative fashion; that is, the feedback received at one stage of the process may make it necessary to return to a previous step to rectify a problem. One way to conceptualize the development process for a test of writing is to consider it as consisting of three stages: design, operationalization, and administration (Bachman and Palmer, 1996). The **design stage** involves gathering information about such things as the test purpose, characteristics of the target population and their real-world writing needs, and available resources. In this stage as well, the construct to be measured by the test is defined and decisions are made how to evaluate the qualities of usefulness throughout the test development process and how best to allocate and manage available resources. In the **operationalization stage**, information from the design stage is used to create **test specifications**, or blueprints for the development of specific test tasks and complete tests. From these specifications, test tasks and items are written, which are eventually compiled into a complete test. Finally, the **administration stage** involves both pre-testing the items and complete tests with representative samples from the target population, and administering the test operationally. I will discuss each of these stages briefly.

## Design stage

The design stage of test development involves gathering critical information and making decisions that will guide the entire test development process. The design stage ordinarily begins with consideration of the test purpose, which generally stems from a **mandate** (Lynch and Davidson, 1994). A mandate grows out of a perceived need on the part of various stakeholders, such as administrative bodies or teachers, to measure language ability for a particular purpose, such as to determine placement into language courses or to make decisions about job candidates. For example, the director of a language school might wish to test students' writing at the end of a general business English course to determine whether its curriculum is adequately preparing students for work in an English-speaking environment, or teachers in an Intensive English program may decide that the placement test they have been using for a number of years needs revision to reflect recent changes in the curriculum.

Lynch and Davidson (1994) point out that the mandate 'comes from a combination of curriculum philosophy and political reality' (p. 736); in other words, the political and philosophical context for any given test will influence the mandate and ultimately the test that is developed. This point is important to keep in mind in test development, as ultimately the test will only be successful in practical terms if it is seen to fulfill the mandate adequately.

Once the purpose for the test and the target population have been identified, the construct that the test is intended to measure needs to be defined. Construct definitions can be based on a course syllabus or on a theoretical definition of language ability more generally, or writing ability in particular (Bachman and Palmer, 1996). A construct definition based on instructional objectives in a course syllabus is useful when we want to know about specific areas of language ability. For example, in a beginners' language course we may want to know whether students have mastered particular grammar points that have been taught. In a technical writing course, we might be interested in whether students can write business letters or describe a process accurately and clearly.

Theory-based construct definitions are derived, not from the contents of a course syllabus, but from a theoretical model of the ability we are trying to test. Theory-based construct definitions are most useful in situations where test content cannot be based on a specific curriculum, as is often the case with selection and placement tests. Proficiency tests are, by definition, theory-based rather than curriculum-based. The model of language ability presented in Bachman and Palmer (1996), discussed in Chapter 3, or the similar model for writing proposed by Grabe and Kaplan (1996), discussed in Chapter 2, provide taxonomies of the areas of linguistic and textual knowledge that are involved in language use. A model such as this, along with information about the test takers, the testing context, and the purpose of the test, provides a useful starting point for defining the construct of interest. For instance, in a test of writing for low-proficiency foreign-language learners, we may decide that we are primarily interested in linguistic and textual knowledge, or knowledge about the grammar and vocabulary of the language and how sentences are organized into texts, rather than functional or sociolinguistic knowledge, or knowledge of how to use language to achieve a variety of communicative functions and how to vary language use appropriately in different settings. Functional and sociolinguistic knowledge may be more important in a test for academic purposes, as we may be interested in knowing whether students can write essays that fulfill a specific function, such as to evaluate or persuade, and whether they can choose language that meets the expectations of formality of an academic audience.

In addition to the components of language knowledge, the role of strategic competence and topical knowledge need to be specified in the construct definition. While strategic competence is engaged to a greater or lesser degree in virtually any writing task, the test developers may or may not wish to include strategic competence as part of the construct definition, and the tasks and scoring procedures will reflect this choice. To continue with the same examples, in a writing test for low-proficiency foreign-language learners, we may be primarily interested in whether students have mastered the grammar and vocabulary that has been taught in class. In this case, strategic competence would not play a large role in the construct definition, and we would want to design test tasks that do not depend heavily on strategic competence. In addition, the scoring procedures would, of course, focus primarily on the linguistic aspects of the written product. In contrast, in an academic setting, we may be interested in knowing whether students can write a persuasive essay, taking into account both sides of an argument and the likely biases of the audience. In this case strategic competence would play a major role, and may be emphasized more strongly than linguistic competence in both the task description and the scoring rubric.

Similarly, the role of topic knowledge in the construct definition needs to be spelled out, since writing by definition has to be about something. As discussed in Chapter 3, Bachman and Palmer (1996) give three options for construct definition with respect to topical knowledge: (a) exclude topical knowledge from the construct definition; (b) explicitly include topical knowledge as part of the construct definition; and (c) define topical knowledge and language ability as separate constructs. The first option, excluding topical knowledge from the construct definition, is appropriate in cases where test takers are not expected to have similar knowledge, and where decisions about individuals are intended to be based solely on language ability. A placement test for a language program is a good example of such a situation. Test designers may want to select the second option, explicitly including topical knowledge in the construct, in situations where test takers are expected to have similar topical knowledge, as in language for specific purposes (LSP) programs. (See also Douglas, 2000, Chapter 2, for an in-depth discussion of the role of topical knowledge in LSP tests.) Finally, test designers may be interested in measuring both topical knowledge and language ability as separate constructs. An example of such a situation would be an achievement test for a content-based language course, in which students are asked to display their understanding of the content through writing.

The final point to be made with respect to the design stage of test development is that it is important to consider all aspects of test usefulness (reliability, construct validity, authenticity, interactiveness, impact, and practicality) from the very beginning of the test development process. Bachman and Palmer (1996: 136) caution against two extreme positions that should be avoided: the notion that the highest level of all six aspects can or should be achieved (an impossible task due to practical limitations, as discussed in Chapter 3), and the idea that one or more of the aspects is so critical that it must be pursued at the expense of others. Bachman and Palmer suggest setting minimal acceptable levels for the various aspects of test usefulness and provide a list of questions that can be used to guide test developers in coming up with a plan to evaluate the usefulness of a test at various stages of development. For example, for the logical evaluation of construct validity, useful questions include: 'Is the language ability construct for this test clearly and unambiguously defined?' and 'To what extent does the test task reflect the construct definition?' (pp. 140–141). Test developers can use such questions to guide their test planning and to evaluate draft test tasks, instructions, and scoring procedures before they are used operationally. In addition, at the test design stage, test developers should devise a plan for collecting empirical evidence of the aspects of test usefulness. Specific types of evidence that are useful for writing assessment are discussed under 'operationalization' and 'administration' below.

One aspect of test usefulness that needs to be taken into particular consideration at the design stage is practicality, for the obvious reason that a test, no matter how well designed and theoretically well grounded, cannot be implemented without sufficient resources. For writing assessment, human resources are the most essential. Task writers are needed to draft and try out writing tasks in the development stage, and when the test is operational, and there need to be enough raters to score the tests in a timely fashion. Other resources to be considered include material resources, such as space, equipment, and supplies. Space needs might include a space for test administration, a room for raters, and storage space for future and past test forms. Equipment needs might include a word processor and a photocopy machine, and supplies include such things as paper and pencils. Time is another essential resource. Sufficient time is required at the development stage to ensure that tasks are clearly written and elicit responses that can be rated. Time is also essential for reading and scoring written responses. It is important for test developers to consider all of these resources at the design stage to avoid potential problems with the test at a later date.

As the outcome of the design stage, Bachman and Palmer (1996: 88) recommend the development of a **design statement**, which is a document containing the following information:

- a description of the test purpose(s),
- a description of the TLU domain and task types,
- a description of the target population,
- a definition of the construct,
- a plan for evaluating the qualities of usefulness, and
- an inventory of required and available resources and a plan for their allocation and management.

Other testing specialists (e.g. Alderson *et al.*, 1995; Douglas, 2000) include this information as part of the test specifications, discussed below. One advantage of producing a design statement before writing test specifications is that this approach provides an explicit structure for making sure that the aspects of test usefulness are taken into consideration throughout the test development process. On the other hand, as test specifications may have different audiences (see discussion below), it is sometimes helpful to have information such as the test purpose, description of the target population, and construct definition within the specifications themselves. Whether to have a design statement that is separate from test specifications is a matter of individual preference; ultimately the format of the documents that guide the test development process is less important than their utility in developing a good test.

## Operationalization stage

Operationalization is the process of moving from a general plan or design statement to detailed test specifications and an actual test. The importance of specifications, both at the level of the entire test and at the level of the individual test task, cannot be overemphasized. Bachman and Palmer (1996) give four reasons why specifications are useful: (1) they are useful for creating parallel forms of a test, or different tests with the same characteristics; (2) they allow an independent means for evaluating the intentions of the test developer;

(3) they provide a means for evaluating the finished test against the specifications; (4) they provide a means for evaluating the authenticity of the test. Lynch and Davidson (1994) also note that the process of developing test specifications allows test developers to come to a consensus about test objectives and to discover potential mismatches between tests and curricular goals. For these reasons care must be taken to write specifications as completely and in as much detail as possible.

Alderson *et al.* (1995) point out that test specifications are useful for a variety of audiences besides test writers, and that specifications may take different forms, depending on the particular audience. For example, people involved in test validation may need detailed specifications, while teachers whose students have been placed into their class on the basis of a particular test may only need to know general information about the content of the test (pp. 10–11).

A number of formats for specifications at the level of the whole test have been suggested by various scholars (Hughes, 1989; Bachman and Palmer, 1996; Alderson *et al.*, 1995; Norris *et al.*, 1998). In addition to the information contained in the design statement, if it is separate from the test specifications, specifications should contain, at a minimum, the following elements:

- a description of the test content, including the organization of the test, a description of the number and type of test tasks, time allotment for each task, and specifications for each test task/item type,
- the criteria for correctness,
- sample tasks/items.                              (Douglas, 2000: 110–113)

There are many possible ways of writing specifications that cover these essential elements; see in particular Bachman and Palmer (1996) and Alderson *et al.* (1995) for different approaches to developing specifications. Turning to the level of the individual task, rather than the entire test, it is here that the most complex and important decisions in test development are made. Later in this chapter, the issues involved in designing specific writing tasks will be discussed in detail. First, however, I will present a general format for specifications that I have found to be useful in my own experience as a test developer. This particular format was originally developed by Popham (1978) and is discussed in detail with reference to language testing by Lynch and Davidson (1994), and Davidson and Lynch (2002). Figure 5.1, adapted from Davidson and Lynch (2002), shows the components

---

**Specification Number:** provide a short index number.

**Title of Specification:** a short title should be given that generally characterizes each specification. The title is a good way to outline skills across several specifications.

**Related Specification(s)** if any: List the numbers and/or titles of specifications related to this one, if any. For example, if a writing task is based on a reading passage, separate specifications would be given for the passage and for each item.

**(1) General Description (GD):** a brief general statement of the type of writing being tested.

**(2) Prompt Attributes (PA):** a complete and detailed description of what the test taker will encounter. Depending on the circumstances, the description may include the following information:

(a) description of the writing task in terms of audience, purpose/communicative function, genre or form, and source of informational content;

(b) specific information about any text or visual that serves as the source of informational content;

(c) the linguistic characteristics of the prompt;

(d) a description of the space provided for the response.

**(3) Response Attributes (RA):** a complete and detailed description of the way the test taker will provide the answer; that is, a complete and detailed description of what the test taker will do in response to the prompt and what will constitute a failure or a success, including the criteria for evaluating or rating the response.

**(4) Sample Item (SI):** an illustrative item or task that reflects the specification; that is, the sort of item or task the specification will generate. A model response to the task should be included as well.

**(5) Specification Supplement (SS):** a detailed explanation of any additional information needed to construct items for a given specification.

---

Figure 5.1 Writing task specification format (adapted from Davidson and Lynch, 2002: 14)

of a test task specification. This type of specification includes a description of the skill or construct being measured, specific information about the prompt, or instructions to the test taker, the attributes of the expected response, a sample item, and other information that will be useful for test writers.

As Davidson and Lynch note, specifications are intended to be a flexible tool to help a team of test developers create a bank of appro-

SPEC #: FA36/QL12
TITLE: Composition: Multi-paragraph Writing (Personal Topics)
LEVEL: Beginning Adult Learners

**General Description (GD):** Students will demonstrate their ability to express their ideas, thoughts, and/or opinions within paragraphs while completing tasks on an assigned topic. In so doing, students will:

- Address the writing task
- Present clear organization and development of paragraphs
- Use details and/or examples to support a thesis or illustrate an idea
- Display facility in the use of language
- Exhibit grammatical accuracy in the area taught

**Sample Item (SI):** Describe your life in the United States now and your life in your country before. Tell which life you liker better and why.

**Prompt Attributes (PA):** Students will be assigned a writing task on a specific topic related to their own lives. Requirements for the selection of a topic and tasks include the following characteristics:

- A topic that is meaningful, relevant, and motivating to written communication
- A topic that does not require specific background information such as knowledge of current events
- A task that is authentic and conducive to academic writing
- A task that requires comprehension of and/or response to a specific assigned topic
- A task that requires the integration of rhetorical strategies common in academic writing

Directions to students will read as follows: Write two to three paragraphs on the assigned topic.

**Response Attributes (RA):** Students will write their essays on the assigned topic. Essays will be graded on content, organization, and correct use of grammar points covered in class.

**Specification Supplement (SS):** See the instructor handbook for sample topics and model responses, scoring rubric, and grammar points to be covered at this level.

Figure 5.2 Writing multi-paragraph essays (adapted from Davidson and Lynch, 2002: 28–9)

priate items, and thus the format may be adapted to meet the particular needs of a given situation. Figures 5.2 and 5.3 show examples of writing task specifications and illustrate how the basic specification format can be adapted in different ways. Figure 5.2, adapted from Davidson and Lynch (2002), is a specification for writing multi-paragraph essays. Note that the authors of the specification found it useful to include the sample item after the general description instead of following the response attributes. While additional information, such as the scoring rubric and model responses, could be included in the specification supplement, in this particular case the specification supplement refers test writers to separate documentation for this information.

A slightly different approach to the Popham model was taken by Butler *et al.* (1996), in a test development project for adult ESL students in California. In the writing test specifications, an introductory page is included which contains a general description that is applicable to all subsequent tasks. The general description reads as follows:

> The test taker will generate a written response of a paragraph or more in length to a prompt of two to four sentences that explicitly specifies the elements of the writing task including audience, purpose, form, and source of informational content.

In addition to this general description, the terms audience, purpose, form, and informational content are defined, and other information regarding the parameters of the task is provided. Each specific writing task type is then presented in a specification, with the following categories: test level (i.e. intended for higher- or lower-level students), stimulus attributes, response attributes, a prototype task, with explanatory notes demonstrating how the task matches the specification, and a model response. Figure 5.3 illustrates one such specification. Specifications such as those in Figures 5.2 and 5.3 have several advantages: they provide a framework for articulating explicitly and in specific detail many of the key features of the writing task, they provide guidance for item writers, and they can be used to communicate to various constituencies the goals of the test and how those goals are implemented.

It should be emphasized here, as in all aspects of test development, that the process of task specification and item writing go hand-in-hand rather than in a strictly sequential fashion. Sample test tasks can be written and tried out on a small-scale basis based on draft specifications, and the process of developing and trying out the tasks will inform further development of the specifications. It should also be noted, as Lynch and Davidson (1994) point out, that test specifications are intended to be dynamic rather than fixed and unchangeable, and are themselves subject to revision and improvement.

**Task Type GNI**

**Test level**

Level A

**Stimulus attributes**

The task is to write either a personal or institutional note to fulfill a basic social function using specific information provided in the prompt.

The primary text is a display or a paragraph appropriate for Level A test takers.

The language of the writing prompt is simple and clear using structures and vocabulary appropriate for students entering beginning high.

A facsimile of a ruled note pad containing six to ten lines is provided for the test taker's response.

**Response attributes**

The test taker must generate an appropriate response to the writing task in the space provided. The responses are scored by trained raters using a clearly articulated scoring rubric.

The model response is a series of related sentences that form one or more paragraphs and fulfill all the task requirements. The model response demonstrates adequate control over simple structures although there may be some errors. Complex structures may be attempted. The model response may include a few words or phrases directly copied from the primary text or the prompt but these are usually incorporated into the test taker's own language.

**Prototype task**

The Department of Parks and Recreation

is sponsoring free Saturday evening concerts

**July 9, 16 and 23**.

Concerts will begin at 7 p.m. and will last about two hours.

They will be held in the new outdoor amphitheater.

Call 555-8632 for more information.

adapted from Elk Grove Adult School ESL Placement Test

Your friend saw the announcement above and asked you to go to the concert on July 16th. You can't go that evening. Write a note explaining the problem and ask your friend to go with you on the 23rd.                    (*ctd.*)

| Just a note . . . |
| --- |
|  |
|  |
|  |
|  |
|  |
|  |
|  |

***Prototype task notes***

The audience is personal (a friend) and the purpose is to explain a problem and make a suggestion.

The test taker does not need to use the information from the test per se in the response, although he or she may use language from the prompt. If language from the prompt is used, it must be transformed from the second person to the first person.

***Model response***

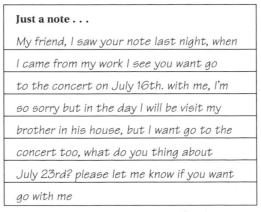

| Just a note . . . |
| --- |
| My friend, I saw your note last night, when |
| I came from my work I see you want go |
| to the concert on July 16th. with me, I'm |
| so sorry but in the day I will be visit my |
| brother in his house, but I want go to the |
| concert too, what do you thing about |
| July 23rd? please let me know if you want |
| go with me |

                           *Thanks*

Figure 5.3  Sample test specification for adult ESL placement test (Butler *et al.*, 1996)

## Administration stage

The third stage in the test development process is the administration of test tasks to examinees, both on a trial basis and operationally, and the concurrent collection and analysis of test data and other relevant information about the test procedures. An important point to note is that the administration phase overlaps significantly with the operationalization phase in the sense that test tasks need to be tried out before a test can be administered operationally, that is, to its intended test takers and for its intended use. In trying out test tasks, a distinction can be made between pre-testing and pilot testing (Butler *et al.*, 1996). In pre-testing, various tasks are tried out on a very small sample of test takers to get preliminary information about various aspects of the task such as whether the instructions are clear, how long it takes test takers to accomplish the task, and so on. Pilot testing, on the other hand, involves administering a complete version of a test to a larger sample in order to get statistical information. While both stages may not be feasible in every situation, it is important to conduct at least some pre-testing to make sure that the task is clear and understandable and elicits scoreable samples.

An illustration of how pre-testing can provide useful information to test developers comes from Kroll and Reid (1994: 245). The authors describe the pre-testing of the following prompt for the Test of Written English (TWE):

> Some people believe that life offers them an endless choice of opportunities. Others think that life is a series of one problem after another. Compare these two ways of looking at life. Which idea do you agree with? Give reasons to support your choice.

While the prompt seemed appealing and test takers were able to generate lengthy texts in response to the prompt, the raters found that writers had difficulty identifying specific problems or opportunities to write about, and many of the essays lacked focus. In addition, there were so many different approaches to the topic that raters had a difficult time deciding whether writers had fulfilled the task successfully and using the scoring rubric consistently over the different approaches to the topic. As a result of the pre-testing, the prompt was not used in operational testing.

From this example, and there are many others that could be described here, it can be seen that pre-testing a prompt is a crucial part of writing test design. Both quantitative and qualitative information can be gathered from test takers and other interested parties (i.e. teachers or administrators) that can be extremely useful in determining whether a given task will be successful on an operational test. Qualitative information can include direct questions to test takers (e.g. 'Were there any words in the prompt that you didn't understand?') or opinion statements with which test takers can agree or disagree (e.g. 'It was easy to organize an essay on this topic.' 'This topic allowed me to display my best writing.') The essays themselves can also be viewed qualitatively in terms of the degree to which test takers interpret the prompt in the way that the test designers intended and any problems of task interpretation or fulfillment that arise. Quantitative feedback, primarily from pilot testing, generally involves an examination of the range of scores that are given to writing samples and an investigation of inter-rater reliability, discussed at length in Chapter 6.

I will now turn to the specifics of designing writing tasks, and numerous factors that should be considered in task design.

## Considerations in task design

White (1994) notes that most test developers consider at least the following four minimum requirements for writing tasks: clarity, validity, reliability, and interest. **Clarity** is essential so that test takers can understand what is required of them quickly and easily. **Validity** has been discussed extensively in previous chapters; in this instance, White is referring to the potential of the prompt for eliciting written products that span the range of the ability of interest among test takers. Skilled writers should receive higher scores than unskilled writers, and a good prompt should allow weaker writers to write at their own level while allowing better writers to demonstrate their best writing. **Reliability**, also discussed in Chapter 3, is essential in that the scoring criteria should be applied consistently to all responses, and similar if not identical scores should be given to the same papers by different readers. While the achievement of acceptable levels of reliability is frequently a function of rater training and the development of a clear and concise scoring rubric, elements of task design can affect reliability as well. That is, a writing prompt must allow enough flexibility that test takers of different abilities and backgrounds can find a point of entry into it and have something to say. At the same time, if the prompt allows too much flexibility, the responses may be so divergent that they cannot be compared to one another. This problem is exemplified by the TWE prompt discussed above (see page 89), which was ultimately rejected after pre-testing for this very reason (Kroll and Reid, 1994). Finally, the task must be **interesting**, both to the writers and to the readers. Writers must be engaged enough in the task to find something to say (cf. the discussion in Chapter 3 about interactivity), and at the same time raters must be interested enough to read possibly several hundred essays on a given topic.

Beyond these four minimum requirements, the test developer must consider a number of other issues, some of which are outlined here. It should be kept in mind that the following are intended as guidelines, rather than as perfect answers. In any testing situation one must always balance the different aspects of test usefulness to find the most acceptable solution from among the available options. To illustrate how one might find an appropriate solution, I will provide examples from several different testing contexts.

## Subject matter

At issue here is the question of what topic (content area) test takers should write about, and what topics should be avoided. Perhaps the most important consideration here is accessibility to all test takers, since everyone needs to have an equal chance of success. For test takers of similar backgrounds, it is not difficult to find topics that nearly everyone will have something to say about and that are relevant for the purposes of the test. As an example of potential topics for general EFL studies, the IELTS (International English Language Testing System) Handbook (1999) provides the following list of topics for the general training writing module of the test, in which test takers must write both a letter in response to a given situation and an essay or report on a general topic:

- Travel
- Accommodation
- Current affairs
- Shops and services
- Health and welfare

- Occupational health and safety
- Recreation
- Social and physical environment

This list gives an idea of the range of situations that test takers may use when writing in their second language, and one can easily think of writing tasks that could be appropriate for some of these settings (for example, writing to a hotel to ask for a reservation).

In academic writing, in which test takers need to demonstrate the ability to write a well-organized essay, an area of controversy has been the choice between topics relying on personal experience and more general topics. Wolcott (1998) provides a thorough discussion of the advantages and disadvantages of these two general categories of topics. Personal topics, in which test takers write about their own experiences, have the advantage that test takers will become more engaged in the topic and may thus perform better than they otherwise would. Personal topics also do not require any specialized background knowledge and are thus accessible to most, if not all, test takers. In addition, personal topics tend to elicit a great variety of responses, which may help to sustain raters' interest – an important consideration, particularly in large-scale testing when raters may be asked to read large numbers of essays.

On the other hand, some students, particularly those from cultures in which self-expression is not valued in writing, may have difficulties with personal topics. Another disadvantage is that test takers may become overly emotionally involved in responding to personal topics, which can result in the writing becoming more of a release of strong emotion and a reliving of experience, with the writing process itself becoming of secondary importance. By the same token, scoring essays on personal topics can become problematic if students reveal painful personal details. Perhaps the most serious problem with personal topics in terms of construct validity, however, is the fact that personal writing is of limited relevance in many TLU situations, such as vocational and professional settings.

General (i.e. non-personal) topics may be problematic as well, even if they avoid some of the pitfalls of personal topics. Since these topics require test takers to write about something other than their own experience, there is a danger that test takers may not have the appropriate background knowledge to write with confidence on some topics. However, if the topic is sufficiently general for all test takers to have relevant knowledge, the responses may be stilted or mechanical, and raters may have a difficult time distinguishing between essays that are similar in form and content. Topics that are controversial, such as capital punishment or abortion, may arouse strong emotions that can interfere with the writing process, while the avoidance of controversial topics may have the effect of restricting topic choice to the most banal and prosaic of subject matter, with which both writers and readers may easily become bored.

A particularly problematic case for determining appropriate topics is that of international students beginning graduate study in an English-speaking country, as these students come from a wide variety of different countries and may be studying any number of disciplines, from music to business to astrophysics. As Horowitz (1991) has argued, there is a vast difference between tasks on writing tests and the writing tasks that students will need to face in their academic disciplines. These differences can be found in 'the length of the text, the role of the writer's background knowledge in producing that text, and the relation of the text produced to other texts within the discipline' (pp. 74–75). Another serious problem with assessing academic writing is the fact that outside of a writing test such writing is ordinarily judged by content-area specialists, and the usual raters of writing tests (writing or language teachers) may not have the background knowledge to judge writing in specialized areas.

While the limitations of providing appropriate writing tasks for academic writers in particular are great, they are not insurmountable, as long as one keeps in mind that any test of writing is limited in its ability to test the range of writing skills students will need in their academic careers. One possible solution for this population is to set different tasks for students in different content areas, although this solution has not always met with success. As noted in Chapter 4, Hamp-Lyons (1986, cited in Hamp-Lyons 1990) did not find systematic differences in the performance of students on a discipline-specific prompt and on a general prompt. On the other hand, Tedick (1990) found that students performed better on a flexible 'discipline-specific' prompt than on a more general prompt, lending support to the notion that students will perform better on a task that is personally relevant to them and on which they have appropriate background knowledge.

In short, there are numerous considerations in determining the actual topic or subject matter of a writing task. Foremost among these is the role of topical knowledge in the construct definition, as discussed above. In addition, these considerations include the relative homogeneity or heterogeneity of the test taker population, in terms of identifying topics that will be accessible to the largest number of test takers, the purpose of the assessment (in particular, whether general writing or academic writing is of concern), and striking an appropriate balance between topics that engage test takers' interest and abilities without eliciting strong emotional responses that interfere with the writing or the rating process.

## Stimulus material

A writing prompt can include source materials, such as a reading passage, a brief quotation, or a drawing, that provide content for test takers to write about, or it can simply nominate a topic without any additional stimulus material. There are valid reasons for either providing or not providing stimulus material, and ultimately the choice depends on the definition of the construct and the considerations outlined in the previous section. For example, if we are strictly interested in language ability and want to explicitly exclude topical knowledge from the construct, stimulus material such as a visual may be appropriate. In a foreign-language class, for instance, one might provide a series of pictures that tell a story and ask test takers to write the story that the pictures tell. Providing stimulus material of this sort provides the content for test takers to write about, allowing them to focus primarily on the linguistic aspects of the task. Providing the content to write about may be a particularly appropriate strategy for testing low-proficiency learners, as the cognitive demands of both having to generate appropriate content and having to find appropriate linguistic means of expressing that content may go beyond the capabilities of such learners.

On the other hand, if we are interested in testing such facets of writing as genre knowledge and the ability to construct an argument that takes into account the background knowledge and biases of the audience (which involves strategic competence as well as language ability), a prompt that provides a quotation and asks the writer to agree or disagree with the view expressed would be appropriate. Such a prompt requires the writer to generate both the ideas and the language and is thus more challenging than a prompt in which the content is provided by stimulus material.

In post-secondary academic writing, a strong case can be made for writing both to be based on a reading and to require students to provide appropriate and relevant support for ideas. University writing is virtually always based on some prior reading, if not also listening and speaking, and graded written products at the university in almost all cases must refer to written sources, whether it is an assigned text-book or independent research. As Horowitz (1991) points out, an essential feature of academic writing in such central genres as research papers is the relationship of the text one is writing to other texts that have been written. Arrington (1988) notes that 'citing the work of others connects, supports, and justifies our own ideas, or, by contrast, illustrates our own originality, or shows where we locate ourselves within the plurality of voices/texts conversing about our subject' (p. 191). While it is impossible to simulate this degree of interaction with other texts in a writing assessment, certainly an important aspect of academic writing is the degree to which a writer can position one's own ideas in relation to the ideas put forth by another writer. The contrast between writing on a test and writing in academic settings will be brought up again in Chapter 8.

Another argument for using a reading text as a basis for writing is to provide a common basis of information for all test takers to draw upon so that they are not hindered by trying to come up with what to say, and to avoid content bias, by giving everyone the same information to work with. Providing even a short reading on a topic may serve to activate the writer's background knowledge or schemata and make it easier for them to find something to say. Some research suggests that several short readings on a related topic may be even more effective than a single, longer reading (Smith *et al.*, 1985). This is the approach taken by the Michigan undergraduate writing assessment described in Feak and Dobson (1996).

On the other hand, using reading as a basis for writing can sometimes be problematic. Poor readers may be penalized if they misinterpret the reading passage, irrespective of their writing ability, and a poorly constructed task may allow some writers to borrow so extensively from the language of the input text that their own writing ability cannot be determined. As noted in Chapter 4, Lewkowicz (1997) found that providing background reading did not improve students' writing, and students tended to borrow heavily from the source text. It is sometimes possible to avoid these problems by having the writing task be related to, but not absolutely dependent on, a reading passage, particularly in a language test that tests both reading and writing. For example, in the placement test for an Intensive English Program in the US, students read a passage from an anthropology textbook that discusses the concept of beauty in various cultures, and then write an essay in which they describe how beauty is defined in their own culture. In their essay students can compare their definition of beauty with the examples presented in the text, but they are not obligated to do so.

Another way to avoid the problem of using the language of the reading passage is to construct the task in such a way that test takers are forced to transform the language to complete the task, as in Figure 5.4, taken from Butler *et al.* (1996). In this task, intended for adult immigrant ESL students, test takers are asked to retell a narrative in the first person. The narrative in the original reading passage is not told in chronological order, so test takers are forced to reconstruct the original narrative in order to create a coherent text. Tasks such as these are quite different from essay tests, and may be appropriate for use when the test developer wants to focus on specific elements of writing, or with beginning level writers. In summary, the issue of stimulus material depends in large measure upon the construct definition and the domain of writing to which one wants to generalize. There are valid arguments for and against using personal experience, a textual stimulus, or a non-verbal stimulus as prompts, and whatever type is used, care should be taken to ensure that test takers are not being tested on abilities that are not part of the construct as defined for the specific purposes of the test.

## Genre

Genre can be defined both in terms of the intended form and the intended function of the writing. By form is meant such written products as letter, laboratory report, or essay. Function can be thought of in terms of communicative functions, as is traditional in language teaching (e.g. describing, inviting, apologizing), or in terms of discourse mode, as is traditional in writing instruction (narration, description, exposition, argumentation). As with the other considerations we have discussed so far, the genre that the prompt is intended to elicit will depend in large measure on the universe of generalization, that is, what kind of writing, both in terms of form and function,

> **Strange True Stories**
>
> Police arrested James Haskell, seventeen, in March after he tried to buy beer at Wally's Mini-Mart by using a stolen driver's licence – that of Douglas Cleaver. The man behind the counter at Wally's knew it was stolen because he is Douglas Cleaver, who had had his license taken in a truck break-in two months earlier. Haskell fled when he heard Cleaver talking to police but left his wallet, which contained his real driver's license.

adapted from *The Los Angeles Reader*, 2 June 1994

Imagine you are Douglas Cleaver. Write a letter to a friend explaining the strange thing that happened to you at Wally's Mini-Mart. The letter has been started for you.

> Dear Chris,
>
> You won't believe what happened to me the other day!
>
> When I worked at Wally's Mini-Mart, someone tried to buy beer. I asked him to show me his driver's license. This driver's license wasn't real. Do you know why I could know it wasn't real? This driver's license was mine!! So, when I called the police, the guy heard I talking to the police and ran away.
>
> Fortunately the guy was arrested by police.   Be careful your wallet. Next person may be you!!

Figure 5.4  Writing task for adult immigrant students (Butler *et al.*, 1996)

**Write a note to your landlord asking him to fix a problem in your apartment. Tell him what the problem is. Write 3–4 sentences.**

_____

_____

_____

_____

_____

_____

_____

_____

Figure 5.5  Writing task for limited proficiency immigrants (CAL, 1984)

the test taker is going to have to do beyond the test? Thus authenticity, in Bachman and Palmer's (1996) terms, is a key consideration.

What constitutes an authentic writing task will differ greatly for different groups of language learners. For academic writing, an authentic task will most frequently be an essay of some sort, while for adult EFL writers the most logical sort of writing might be a letter asking for accommodation or some other practical writing task. Adult immigrants with limited literacy skills in their first language can be asked to write a short note to their landlord, as in Figure 5.5, from the BEST test (Basic English Skills Test; Center for Applied Linguistics, 1984). The most problematic case in terms of authenticity may in fact be that of foreign language learners, who may not ever have any genuine need to write in the FL outside of their classroom. An example of a possible solution to the problem of authenticity can be found in the Colorado Foreign Language Sample Proficiency Project (Apodaco, 1990), a set of instruments for assessing foreign-language achievement at the high school level. The writing assessment tasks are designed to simulate possible target language writing situations for students in this age group. Sample tasks are found in Figure 5.6. Chapter 7 also presents authentic tasks for foreign-language learners, from the Contextualized Writing Assessment (CoWA), a test for high school and college-aged students of French, German, and Spanish (CARLA, 2001). It should be noted that the test developer can only make reasonable

**Postcard 1**: Imagine that you are a target student who has just arrived in the United States for a year-long visit. Write a postcard to your parents at home telling about your American host family. You may use the other side of this paper for a rough draft. Write at least 50 words and no more than 150. You have 30 minutes.

**Postcard 2**: Write a postcard to your target pen-pal telling him/her that you are on your way to his/her town to visit or about a trip that you are on with your family. You may use the other side of this paper for your first draft. Write at least 50 words—no more than 150. You have 30 minutes.

**Note to parent 1**: You're an exchange student. Write a note for your target mom/dad telling her/him when you'll be home and why. You may use the other side of this paper for your first draft. Write at least 50 words—no more than 150. You have 30 minutes.

**Note to parent 2**: You're an exchange student. Write a note for your target mom/dad asking permission for an activity you want to do this weekend. You may use the other side of this paper for your first draft. Write at least 50 words—no more than 150. You have 30 minutes.

**Telephone message**: You're an exchange student. Write a message for your target big sister/brother telling her/him that a friend called. (You decide who.) Tell where, when, and why to meet this person. You may use the other side of this paper for your first draft. Write at least 50 words—no more than 150. You have 30 minutes.

**Situation 1: Hotel**: Write a letter to a hotel in target country. Give/ask for some of the following information: names, reservation, what you need in your room, whether you can pay with travelers'checks, if you want a private bath, the day you will arrive, if meals are included, etc. Write in target. You may use the other side of this paper for your first draft. Write at least 50 words—no more than 150. You have 30 minutes.

**Situation 2: Health**: The school nurse is not in her office. Write a note explaining why you need to see her as soon as she returns. Give specific information. Write in target. You may use the other side of this paper for your first draft. Write at least 50 words—no more than 150. You have 30 minutes.

**Situation 3: Invitation**: Write a letter inviting a friend somewhere. Include some of the following information: time, place, activity, prices (if appropriate), dress, means of transportation, etc. Write in target. You may use the other side of this paper for your first draft. Write at least 50 words—no more than 150. You have 30 minutes.

Figure 5.6    Writing task for secondary-level foreign-language learners (Apodaco, 1990)

guesses about what a given test taker or group of test takers will perceive to be an authentic task, because the test takers' perceptions of what is authentic may or may not match those of the test developers. An excellent example of a well-intentioned writing task that proved to be relatively inauthentic for particular groups of L1 students is provided by Keech (1982, cited in Murphy and Ruth, 1993). High school students were asked to write a letter to the principal of their school outlining a solution to a problem at the school. At one school the principal was seen as so distant and unresponsive that students were unable to conceive of writing him a letter. At another school with a particularly effective principal, students could not think of problems that they would want to bring up. For those particular schools, the prompt was unusable and had to be abandoned.

While authenticity is a key consideration in deciding on a form and discourse mode for a writing test, it is also important to bear in mind the effects of discourse mode on the actual writing performance and on scoring. As mentioned in Chapter 4, there is evidence that discourse mode makes a difference in performance – narrative and description are often seen as cognitively easier and lend themselves to less complex language than do exposition and argumentation. The language, that is elicited from these different discourse modes differs as well which is something that must be kept in mind, particularly for second-language writers who may not have mastered all elements of the linguistic code. Biber (1988) has categorized the language features of various communication types, and some of his findings are relevant here. For example, one of Biber's distinctions is between narrative and non-narrative discourse. The narrative discourse mode tends to involve past tense verbs, perfect aspect verbs, present participial clauses, and third person pronouns, while non-narrative discourse tends to use present tense verbs and longer, more elaborate noun phrases. Biber also notes that persuasive language tends to rely on modal auxiliaries and *if* and *unless* clauses. Thus, if linguistic competence – particularly in terms of range and accuracy of grammatical structures – is an important component of the construct being measured by a test, it is essential to consider the linguistic features that tend to co-occur in different text types. For more detailed discussions of how Biber's findings relate to second-language writing, particularly in academic settings, the reader is referred to Byrd (1998), and Reid and Byrd (1998).

The potential effect of discourse mode on scoring also needs to be considered. As was discussed in Chapter 4, there is some evidence that the expectations that raters bring to essays written in different discourse modes may affect the scores they give, for example, by rewarding test takers who choose seemingly more difficult topics with higher scores. The effects of discourse mode on scores is particularly important when a choice of topics is given to examinees, and efforts should be made to ensure that if a choice is given, the choices be as parallel as possible, particularly in terms of discourse mode. This issue will be touched on again under 'choice of tasks' below.

## Time allotment

Another important issue in writing assessment is deciding how much time test takers will be given to complete each task. One of the first considerations is whether writing is being tested as one skill within a larger battery of skills tests (as in a general language proficiency test) or as a skill on its own. In the former case, the amount of time devoted to writing will have to be considered with respect to the total testing time available and the degree of importance writing holds vis-à-vis other skills. For a test of business communication in English, writing will be an important component, while on a test for low-proficiency immigrants, writing may only receive minimal attention compared to oral communication and reading.

Particularly for tasks that require reflection and planning such as academic essays, a question of interest is the optimum time to provide test takers so they have enough time to plan, write, and (where necessary) revise their writing. Somewhat surprisingly, the research that has been conducted in this area does not necessarily bear out the common-sense notion that more time is better. Powers and Fowles (1996) report that students performed somewhat better on writing tasks for the Graduate Management Admissions Test (GMAT) when given 60 minutes than when they were given 40 minutes, but they note in their review of related literature that such effects have not been found uniformly in other research. Furthermore, Powers and Fowles' study suggests that time limits do not differentially benefit or disadvantage certain groups of students.

Another aspect to the problem of time limits is the cultural preferences and practices of the test takers. Purves (1992) notes that the amount of time students will take is largely dependent upon what they are used to. In an international study of school writing, it was found that in Finland and Italy, for example, students were routinely given 180 minutes to complete an in-class writing assignment and were expected to produce a polished draft, while students in the United States were generally given only 45 minutes to write an in-class assignment and were only expected to produce a first draft. In the performance data collected by Purves and his colleagues, students were allowed 60 minutes to write their essays; however, students from the US frequently finished in 35 or 40 minutes and did not know what to do with the extra time, as they were unused to having time to complete two or three drafts at a single sitting.

The issue of time allotment interacts with the issue of how many tasks to assign. While most writing specialists insist, with very good reason, that a single text cannot possibly be representative of a test taker's ability to write in a variety of contexts, there is a trade-off between obtaining more than one writing sample and allowing sufficient time for examinees to complete each task well.

The basic dilemma can be stated as follows: given, say, an hour of total testing time, which will provide more useful information: two 30-minute tasks, or one more complex 60-minute task? There are valid arguments on either side of the issue. With more tasks, test takers have more opportunities to present their best work: if they are not particularly interested in the first task, they may find the second more engaging. One can sample a wider variety of functions and thus of syntax and vocabulary with more than one writing prompt. On the other hand, tasks that can be easily written about in 30 minutes or less may not be sufficiently challenging enough to stretch writers to their limits, and may be less representative of the type of writing students will need to do in their coursework than a more complex task. If a writing task is to be based on reading or the description of a graph, for example, more time will be required.

Ruth and Murphy (1984) found correlations between holistic scores on essays and responses to questionnaire items regarding planning and rereading essays: high-proficiency writers tended to agree with statements such as: 'Because I spent so much time planning, I felt rushed when I actually started writing,' whereas lower-proficiency students did not. Ruth and Murphy suggest that for higher-proficiency students, who have a more complex view of the writing process, shorter writing tasks may not allow them to demonstrate their proficiency as well as longer tasks. To discriminate between higher levels of writing proficiency, therefore, it may make sense to provide fewer long tasks rather than more shorter tasks.

## Instructions

Providing clear instructions for test takers is obviously an important aspect of designing a valid test. As noted in Chapter 4, some research has shown that the amount of detail provided in instructions for writing tests can have an effect on test scores. Bachman and Palmer (1996) provide three guidelines for instructions: (1) they should be simple enough for test takers to understand; (2) they should be short enough not to take up too much of the test administration time; and (3) they should be sufficiently detailed for test takers to know exactly what is expected of them. For a writing task, instructions should include, at a minimum, a specification of the audience and purpose of the writing, some indication of how long the response should be – Carson (2000) suggests that length should be specified in terms of pages (i.e. half a page, one to two pages) rather than structural units such as sentences or paragraphs, as the structural units will emerge from how examinees approach the task – and some indication of how the writing samples will be scored. Figure 5.7 (p. 104), from the Michigan English Language Assessment Battery (MELAB), a test of English for academic purposes, provides an illustration of instructions that meet these criteria.

## Choice of tasks

Whether or not to allow writers to choose among several tasks is an issue that has been discussed at length by scholars. There are several arguments on both sides of the issue. On the one hand, giving writers a choice of task helps to ameliorate the effects of background knowledge and interest: writers may choose to write on the task that they feel they know most about or have the most interest in. This may reduce anxiety and allow writers to perform their best. On the other hand, some studies have shown that writers do not always make the best choice and that choosing among tasks takes up time that could be spent writing. The most persuasive argument against allowing a choice of task has to do with the difficulty of determining whether

---

**MICHIGAN ENGLISH LANGUAGE ASSESSMENT BATTERY**

**PART 1: COMPOSITION**

NAME (PRINT) _____ Date _____
                    (family/surname)        (given/first name)

SIGNATURE _____

**INSTRUCTIONS:**

1.   You will have 30 minutes to write on <u>one</u> of the two topics printed below. If you do not write on one of these topics, your paper will not be scored. If you do not understand the topics, ask the examiner to explain or to translate them.

2.   You may make an outline if you wish, but your outline will not count toward your score.

3.   Write about 1 to 2 pages. Your composition will be marked down if it is extremely short. Write on both sides of the paper. Ask the examiner for more paper if you need it.

4.   You will not be graded on the appearance of your paper, but your handwriting must be readable. You may change or correct your writing, but you should not copy the whole composition over.

5.   Your essay will be judged on clarity and overall effectiveness, as well as on
     -topic development
     -organization
     -range, accuracy, and appropriateness of grammar and vocabulary

---

Figure 5.7  MELAB instructions

tasks are equal in difficulty and how difficulty is measured. This issue was discussed in Chapter 4; as was noted there, task difficulty can consist of factors related to the task (i.e. the discourse mode or cognitive demands of the task), related to the writer (familiarity of the topic) or related to the test raters (expectations of performance on different tasks). If a choice is to be given, therefore, all efforts must be made to ensure that the various tasks are as alike as possible in terms of cognitive demands, complexity of instructions, and so on, and that raters are trained to apply similar criteria on all tasks.

### Transcription mode (handwriting versus word processing)

With the increasing use of computers in education and testing, one important question is whether to ask examinees to write by hand or to enter their essays on a computer. To answer this question, it is important to be aware of the impact of computers on writing, and the advantages and disadvantages of using computers for writing assessment. In many, if not most situations, particularly when one is designing a test for local in-house use, the question is moot as the resources are not available to do computer testing. On the other hand, large-scale institutional tests such as the TOEFL are now being offered on the computer, and it is important to consider the effects of computers on writing. There are three key issues that need to be considered here. First, to what extent are examinees already familiar with computers, and what is the effect of computer familiarity on the ability to take a writing test on the computer? When the TOEFL was moving towards computer delivery of tests, a large-scale study of TOEFL test takers was undertaken to address this issue. The results of the study, reported in Taylor *et al.* (1998), showed that there was little relationship between computer familiarity and TOEFL scores when test takers were given a tutorial on how to use the computer. However, because writing an essay involves more interaction with the keyboard than simply choosing options in a multiple-choice test, the TOEFL currently allows test takers to either handwrite or key in their essays.

The second issue is whether there are consistent observable differences in either the writing process or the end product when hand-written and keyed essays are compared. Research on both of these questions has produced contradictory results, with some studies finding positive effects for word processing and some studies finding negative effects (see Ferris and Hedgcock, 1998, and Pennington, 1996, for in-depth discussions of these issues).

Finally, an important consideration in deciding between hand-written and keyed essays is the implication for scoring. As noted in Chapter 4, some research has suggested that handwritten essays tend to be scored higher than keyed essays, no matter whether the essay was originally composed at the keyboard or on paper (Powers *et al.*, 1994; Arnold *et al.*, 1990, cited in Powers *et al.*, 1994). Powers *et al.* give a number of possible reasons for this finding: first, keyed essays tend to look shorter than handwritten essays, and the relationship between essay length and scores of writing quality is well-documented (Markham, 1976; Hughes *et al.*, 1983; Chase, 1968). In addition, errors in word-processed essays are frequently easier to spot, and judged more negatively, than similar errors in handwritten essays, in part because imprecise handwriting can obscure certain kinds of error, and in part because of a natural tendency to view a computer-generated document as a more polished product than a handwritten one. The third reason why raters may be more sympathetic towards handwritten essays is the fact that such essays frequently show evidence of editing and revision: a word inserted here, a phrase erased and rewritten there. As essay graders are frequently also writing teachers, it may be that this evidence of the writing process is rewarded by higher scores. Powers *et al.* conclude that rater training for word-processed essays must include a discussion of this issue so that raters are conscious of their biases and can compensate for them.

### Use of dictionaries and other reference materials

Traditional language tests generally do not allow the use of dictionaries, as vocabulary knowledge is considered to be part of the skill being tested. However, a broader definition of writing ability, in which one uses all available resources, does not necessarily preclude the use of dictionaries. In fact, one could argue that a good writer *does* know how to use resources such as dictionaries and the appropriate, efficient, occasional use of a dictionary allows a good writer to choose the precise word for his or her meaning.

On the other hand, students do not always know how to use dictionaries effectively, and it may be that using dictionaries will detract from the time available to write which may make students less effective. There is little evidence of the efficacy of dictionary use during a language test. Studies of dictionary use in L2 reading tests (Nesi and Meara, 1991; Bensoussan *et al.*, 1981) suggest that using a dictionary does not significantly affect test scores, but does affect test completion time. This is an area where further research is needed.

### Summary

In this chapter we have looked at the process of test development in terms of three stages: design, operationalization, and administration. An important component of test design is the development of task specifications, which serve both as a blueprint for designing test tasks and as a vehicle for articulating and communicating to various test users the specific ability being tested and the way in which the test tasks are intended to measure that ability. Designing writing tasks involves considering numerous issues from determining the subject matter to deciding on time limits. As we have seen, an overarching concern in designing writing tasks is ensuring that the task allows us to make appropriate inferences about the specific ability that we are interested in, whether this is the development of linguistic competence as displayed through writing, or the development of writing processes and strategies, with linguistic knowledge as a complementary factor. Designing appropriate tasks that tap a specific ability is only half the equation, however. In order to ensure that the inferences that we make about specific abilities are appropriate, we also need to consider how the responses to our tasks are scored. It is to this issue that we turn in Chapter 6.

# CHAPTER SIX

..................................................................................................

# Scoring procedures for writing assessment

In the previous chapter, issues regarding the development and trialing of tasks for writing assessment were discussed. We now turn to the second key component of a writing assessment: procedures for scoring the written product. The scoring procedures are critical because the score is ultimately what will be used in making decisions and inferences about writers. As discussed in Chapter 4, a score in a writing assessment is the outcome of an interaction that involves not merely the test taker and the test, but the test taker, the prompt or task, the written text itself, the rater(s) and the rating scale (Hamp-Lyons, 1990; Kenyon, 1992; McNamara, 1996). Of these elements, two represent central considerations in scoring: defining the rating scale, and ensuring that raters use the scale appropriately and consistently. This chapter discusses these considerations and provides guidelines for designing rating scales, training raters, and ensuring the reliability and validity of scoring. For the purposes of this chapter, I will follow British and Australian usage and refer to the written text that is evaluated by raters as the 'script.' While this term is not widely used in the United States, I find it to be the easiest and most inclusive way to refer to the written response to a task on a writing test, whether it be an essay, a letter, or some other genre.

Table 6.1. *Types of rating scales used for the assessment of writing*

|  | Specific to a particular writing task | Generalizable to a class of writing tasks |
|---|---|---|
| Single score | Primary Trait | Holistic |
| Multiple scores |  | Analytic |

## Rating scales

As McNamara (1996) notes, the scale that is used in assessing performance tasks such as writing tests represents, implicitly or explicitly, the theoretical basis upon which the test is founded; that is, it embodies the test (or scale) developer's notion of what skills or abilities are being measured by the test. For this reason the development of a scale (or set of scales) and the descriptors for each scale level are of critical importance for the validity of the assessment.

### Types of rating scales

One of the first decisions to be made in determining a system for scoring is what type of rating scale will be used: that is, should a single score be given to each script, or will each script be scored on several different features? This issue has been the subject of a great deal of research and discussion over the past three decades. In the composition literature, three main types of rating scales are discussed: **primary trait scales**, **holistic scales**, and **analytic scales**. In recent second-language literature, a fourth type of scale, called a multiple-trait scale, is also frequently referred to (Hamp-Lyons, 1990; Cohen, 1994). However, many of the characteristics ascribed to multiple-trait scales have to do more with procedures for developing and using the scales, rather than with the description of the scales themselves. Thus for the purposes of this book, multiple-trait scales are not distinguished from analytic scales. The three types of scales can be characterized by two distinctive features: (1) whether the scale is intended to be specific to a single writing task or generalized to a class of tasks (broadly or narrowly defined), and (2) whether a single score or multiple scores are given to each script. Table 6.1 summarizes the three types of scales according to this scheme. As the table shows, primary trait scales are specific to a particular writing task, while holistic and analytic scales can be used for grading multiple tasks. These three types of rating scales are discussed in more detail below.

## Primary trait scoring

Primary trait scoring is most closely associated with the work of Lloyd-Jones (1977) for the National Assessment of Educational Progress (NAEP), a large-scale testing program for schools in the US. The philosophy behind primary trait scoring is that it is important to understand how well students can write within a narrowly defined range of discourse (e.g. persuasion or explanation). In primary trait scoring, the rating scale is defined with respect to the specific writing assignment and essays are judged according to the degree of success with which the writer has carried out the assignment. For each writing task in a primary trait assessment, a scoring rubric is created which includes: (a) the writing task; (b) a statement of the primary rhetorical trait (for example, persuasive essay, congratulatory letter) elicited by the task; (c) a hypothesis about the expected performance on the task; (d) a statement of the relationship between the task and the primary trait; (e) a rating scale which articulates levels of performance; (f) sample scripts at each level; and (g) explanations of why each script was scored as it was. A primary trait scoring guide can include several categories on which each script is to be judged. Part of a scoring guide for a primary trait assessment is found in Figure 6.1, taken from Lloyd-Jones (1977). As the figure shows, the scoring rubric is fairly detailed and very specific in terms of how different test takers approach the writing task. It is clear that primary trait scoring is very time- and labor-intensive, as a scoring guide must be developed for every writing task: Lloyd-Jones (1977) estimates that creating a scoring guide takes an average of 60 to 80 hours per task. For this reason alone, primary trait scoring has not been generally adopted in many assessment programs, even though it has the potential of providing rich information about students' abilities, provided that enough samples of writing are collected from each student.

In second-language writing assessment, primary trait assessment has not been widely used, and little information exists on how primary trait scoring might be applied in second-language testing.

Directions: Look carefully at the picture. These kids are having fun jumping on the overturned boat. Imagine you are one of the children in the picture. Or if you wish, imagine that you are someone standing nearby watching the children. Tell what is going on as he or she would tell it. Write as if you were telling this to a good friend, in a way that expresses strong feelings. Help your friend FEEL the experience too. Space is provided on the next three pages.

## NAEP Scoring Guide: Children on Boat

**Background**
*Primary Trait.* Imaginative Expression of Feeling through Inventive Elaboration of a *Point of View.*

**Final Scoring Guide**

ENTIRE EXERCISE

0 No response, sentence fragment
1 Scorable
2 Illegible or illiterate
3 Does not refer to the picture at all
9 I don't know

USE OF DIALOGUE

0 Does not use dialogue in the story.
1 Direct quote from one person in the story. The one person may talk more than once. When in doubt whether two statements are made by the same person or different people, code 1. A direct quote of a thought also counts. Can be in hypothetical tense.
2 Direct quote from two or more persons in the story.

POINT OF VIEW

0 Point of view cannot be determined, or does not control point of view.
1 Point of view is consistently one of the five children. Include "If I were one of the children . . ." and recalling participation as one of the children
2 Point of view is consistently one of an observer. When an observer joins the children in the play, the point of view is still "2" because the observer makes a sixth person playing. Include papers with minimal evidence even when difficult to tell which point of view is being taken.

TENSE

0 Cannot determine time, or does not control tense. (One wrong tense places the paper in this category, except drowned in the present.)
1 Present tense—past tense may also be present if not part of the "main line" of the story.
2 Past tense—If a past tense description is acceptable brought up to present, code as "past." Sometimes the present is used to create a frame for past events. Code this as past, since the actual description is. in the past.
3 Hypothetical time—Papers written entirely in the "If I were on the boat" or "If I were there, I would." These papers often include future references such as "when I get on the boat I will." If part is hypothetical and rest past or present and tense is controlled, code present or past. If the introduction, up to two sentences, is only part in past or present then code hypothetical.

Figure 6.1 Primary trait scoring guide (Lloyd-Jones, 1977)

However, as Hamp-Lyons (1991a) points out, primary trait scoring might be particularly valuable for second-language learners in a school context, where parents, who are themselves not proficient in the language of the school, can benefit from a description of what their child is capable of doing with the language.

## Holistic scoring

Many assessment programs rely on **holistic scoring**, or the assigning of a single score to a script based on the overall impression of the script. In a typical holistic scoring session, each script is read quickly and then judged against a rating scale, or scoring rubric, that outlines the scoring criteria. The existence of a scoring rubric distinguishes holistic scoring from its earlier, less reliable predecessor, **general impression marking**, in which criteria are never explicitly stated. The rubric is complemented by a set of anchor or benchmark scripts at each level that are intended to exemplify the criteria for that level, and raters are carefully trained to adhere to the rubric when scoring scripts. Note, however, that the existence of a rubric, benchmark scripts, and rater training is not limited to holistic scoring; on the contrary, these features are recognized as good practice in writing assessment, regardless of the type of scale used.

A well-known example of a holistic scoring rubric in ESL is the scale used for the TOEFL Writing Test, formerly known as the Test of Written English (TWE) (see Figure 6.2). As can be seen from the figure, the scale contains descriptors of the syntactic and rhetorical qualities of six levels of writing proficiency. Holistic scoring has become widely used in writing assessment over the past 25 years and has a number of positive features. From a practical standpoint, it is faster (and therefore less expensive) to read a script once and assign a single score than to read it several times, each time focusing on a different aspect of the writing. However, as White (1984, 1985), one of the leading proponents of holistic scoring, notes, there are also other advantages to holistic scoring. White maintains that holistic scoring is intended to focus the reader's attention on the strengths of the writing, not on its deficiencies, so that writers are rewarded for what they do well. Holistic scoring rubrics can be designed to focus readers' attention on certain aspects of writing, depending on what is deemed most essential in the context, and thus can provide important

6   An essay at this level
- effectively addresses the writing task
- is well organized and well developed
- uses clearly appropriate details to support a thesis or illustrate ideas
- displays consistent facility in use of language
- demonstrates syntactic variety and appropriate word choice though it may have occasional errors

5   An essay at this level
- may address some parts of the task more effectively than others
- is generally well organized and developed
- uses details to support a thesis or illustrate an idea
- displays facility in the use of language
- demonstrates some syntactic variety and range of vocabulary, though it will probably have occasional errors

4   An essay at this level
- addresses the writing topic adequately but may slight parts of the task
- is adequately organized and developed
- uses some details to support a thesis or illustrate an idea
- demonstrates adequate but possibly inconsistent facility with syntax and usage
- may contain some errors that occasionally obscure meaning

3   An essay at this level may reveal one or more of the following weaknesses:
- Inadequate organization or development
- inappropriate or insufficient details to support or illustrate generalizations
- a noticeably inappropriate choice of words or word forms
- an accumulation of errors in sentence structure and/or usage

2   An essay at this level is seriously flawed by **one** or more of the following weaknesses:
- serious disorganization or underdevelopment
- little or no detail, or irrelevant specifics
- serious and frequent errors in sentence structure or usage
- serious problems with focus

1   An essay at this level
- may be incoherent
- may be undeveloped
- may contain severe and persistent writing errors

0   A paper is rated 0 if it contains no response, merely copies the topic, is off-topic, is written in a foreign language, or consists of only keystroke characters.

Figure 6.2  TOEFL writing scoring guide

information about those aspects in an efficient manner. White also argues that holistic scoring is more valid than analytic scoring methods because it reflects most closely the authentic, personal reaction of a reader to a text, and that, in analytic scoring methods, 'too much attention to the parts is likely to obscure the meaning of the whole' (White, 1984: 409).

On the other hand, holistic scoring has several disadvantages, particularly in second-language contexts. One drawback to holistic scoring is that a single score does not provide useful diagnostic information about a person's writing ability, as a single score does not allow raters to distinguish between various aspects of writing such as control of syntax, depth of vocabulary, organization, and so on. This is especially problematic for second-language writers, since different aspects of writing ability develop at different rates for different writers: some writers have excellent writing skills in terms of content and organization but may have much lower grammatical control, while others may have an excellent grasp of sentence structure but may not know how to organize their writing in a logical way.

Another disadvantage of holistic scoring is that holistic scores are not always easy to interpret, as raters do not necessarily use the same criteria to arrive at the same scores: for example, a certain script might be given a 4 on a holistic scale by one rater because of its rhetorical features (content, organization, development), while another rater might give the same script a 4 because of its linguistic features (control of grammar and vocabulary). Holistic scores have also been shown to correlate with relatively superficial characteristics such as length and handwriting (Markham, 1976; Sloan and McGinnis, 1982). Holistic scoring has also come under criticism in recent years for its focus on achieving high inter-rater reliability at the expense of validity, as discussed in Chapter 3.

## Analytic scoring

In analytic scoring, scripts are rated on several aspects of writing or criteria rather than given a single score. Depending on the purpose of the assessment, scripts might be rated on such features as content, organization, cohesion, register, vocabulary, grammar, or mechanics. Analytic scoring schemes thus provide more detailed information about a test taker's performance in different aspects of writing and are for this reason preferred over holistic schemes by many writing specialists.

One of the best known and most widely used analytic scales in ESL was created by Jacobs *et al.* (1981) (see Figure 6.3). In the Jacobs *et al.* scale, scripts are rated on five aspects of writing: content, organization, vocabulary, language use, and mechanics. The five aspects are differentially weighted to emphasize first content (30 points) and next language use (25 points), with organization and vocabulary weighted equally (20 points) and mechanics receiving very little emphasis (5 points). This scale has been adopted by numerous college-level writing programs, and is accompanied by training materials and sample compositions so that users can fairly quickly learn to apply the scale. A slightly different approach to analytic scoring for second-language writing assessment is a set of scales developed for the Test in English for Educational Purposes (TEEP) by Cyril Weir (1988), reproduced as Figure 6.4. Instead of a single scale composed of a number of subscales, Weir's scheme consists of seven scales, each divided into four levels with score points ranging from 0 to 3. The first four scales are related to communicative effectiveness, while the others relate to accuracy. Like the Jacobs *et al.* scale, the TEEP scale was extensively piloted and revised to make sure that it could be applied reliably by trained raters. A third example of an analytic scoring system is the Michigan Writing Assessment Scoring Guide (Hamp-Lyons, 1990; 1991b) for grading an entry-level university writing examination (see Figure 6.5). The Michigan Writing Assessment is scored on three rating scales: Ideas and Arguments, Rhetorical Features, and Language Control. Like the TEEP scales, the three scales are not combined in a single score, but are reported separately and thus provide valuable diagnostic information to teachers and test takers. A distinguishing feature of this .assessment is that the scales were locally developed in consultation with the university faculty, both within and outside of composition, and incorporate considerations of good writing as defined by a variety of constituents. As a result, Hamp-Lyons (1991b) states that the assessment has had a positive reception among students, faculty, advisors, and other community members because it reflects the concerns of and is easily interpreted by these varied constituencies. The examples of analytic scales presented here reflect an understanding that has become well established in writing assessment: that is, the importance of using an explicit and detailed scoring rubric. Criticisms of analytic scoring that

---

### ESL COMPOSITION PROFILE

STUDENT               DATE           TOPIC

| SCORE | LEVEL | CRITERIA | COMMENTS |
|---|---|---|---|
| **CONTENT** | 30-27 | EXCELLENT TO VERY GOOD: knowledgeable • substantive • thorough development of thesis • relevant to assigned topic | |
| | 26-22 | GOOD TO AVERAGE: some knowledge of subject • adequate range • limited development of thesis • mostly relevant to topic, but lacks detail | |
| | 21-17 | FAIR TO POOR: limited knowledge of subject • little substance • inadequate development of topic | |
| | 16-13 | VERY POOR: does not show knowledge of subject • non-substantive • not pertinent • OR not enough to evaluate | |
| **ORGANIZATION** | 20-18 | EXCELLENT TO VERY GOOD: fluent expression • ideas clearly stated/supported • succinct • well-organized • logical sequencing • cohesive | |
| | 17-14 | GOOD TO AVERAGE: somewhat choppy • loosely organized but main ideas stand out • limited support • logical but incomplete sequencing | |
| | 13-10 | FAIR TO POOR: non-fluent • ideas confused or disconnected • lacks logical sequencing and development | |
| | 9-7 | VERY POOR: does not communicate • no organization • OR not enough to evaluate | |
| **VOCABULARY** | 20-18 | EXCELLENT TO VERY GOOD: sophisticated range • effective word/idiom choice and usage • word form mastery • appropriate register | |
| | 17-14 | GOOD TO AVERAGE: adequate range • occasional errors of word/idiom form, choice, usage *but meaning not obscured* | |
| | 13-10 | FAIR TO POOR: limited range • frequent errors of word/idiom form, choice, usage • *meaning confused or obscured* | |
| | 9-7 | VERY POOR: essentially translation • little knowledge of English vocabulary, idioms, word form • OR not enough to evaluate | |
| **LANGUAGE USE** | 25-22 | EXCELLENT TO VERY GOOD: effective complex constructions • few errors of agreement, tense, number, word order/function, articles, pronouns, prepositions | |
| | 21-18 | GOOD TO AVERAGE: effective but simple constructions • minor problems in complex constructions • several errors of agreement, tense, number, word order/function, articles, pronouns, prepositions *but meaning seldom obscured* | |
| | 17-11 | FAIR TO POOR: major problems in simple/complex constructions • frequent errors of negation, agreement, tense, number, word order/function, articles, pronouns, prepositions and/or fragments, run-ons, deletions • *meaning confused or obscured* | |
| | 10-5 | VERY POOR: virtually no mastery of sentence construction rules • dominated by errors • does not communicate • OR not enough to evaluate | |
| **MECHANICS** | 5 | EXCELLENT TO VERY GOOD: demonstrates mastery of conventions • few errors of spelling, punctuation, capitalization, paragraphing | |
| | 4 | GOOD TO AVERAGE: occasional errors of spelling, punctuation, capitalization, paragraphing *but meaning not obscured* | |
| | 3 | FAIR TO POOR: frequent errors of spelling. punctuation, capitalization, paragraphing • poor handwriting • *meaning confused or obscured* | |
| | 2 | VERY POOR: no mastery of conventions • dominated by errors of spelling, punctuation, capitalization, paragraphing • handwriting illegible • OR not enough to evaluate | |

TOTAL SCORE     READER     COMMENTS

---

Figure 6.3 Jacobs *et al.*'s (1981) scoring profile

A. *Relevance and adequacy of content*
  0. The answer bears almost no relation to the task set. Totally inadequate answer.
  1. Answer of limited relevance to the task set. Possibly major gaps in treatment of topic and/or pointless repetition.
  2. For the most part answers the tasks set, though there may be some gaps or redundant information.
  3. Relevant and adequate answer to the task set.

B. *Compositional organisation*
  0. No apparent organisation of content.
  1. Very little organisation of content. Underlying structure not sufficiently controlled.
  2. Some organisational skills in evidence, but not adequately controlled.
  3. Overall shape and internal pattern clear. Organisational skills adequately controlled.

C. *Cohesion*
  0. Cohesion almost totally absent. Writing so fragmentary that comprehension of the intended communication is virtually impossible.
  1. Unsatisfactory cohesion may cause difficulty in comprehension of most of the intended communication.
  2. For the most part satisfactory cohesion although occasional deficiencies may mean that certain parts of the communication are not always effective.
  3. Satisfactory use of cohesion resulting in effective communication.

D. *Adequacy of vocabulary for purpose*
  0. Vocabulary inadequate even for the most basic parts of the intended communication.
  1. Frequent inadequacies in vocabulary for the task. Perhaps frequent lexical inappropriacies and/or repetition.
  2. Some inadequacies in vocabulary for the task. Perhaps some lexical inappropriacies and/or circumlocution.
  3. Almost no inadequacies in vocabulary for the task. Only rare inappropriacies and/or circumlocution.

E. *Grammar*
  0. Almost all grammatical patterns inaccurate.
  1. Frequent grammatical inaccuracies.
  2. Some grammatical inaccuracies.
  3. Almost no grammatical inaccuracies.

F. *Mechanical accuracy I (punctuation)*
  0. Ignorance of conventions of punctuation.
  1. Low standard of accuracy in punctuation.
  2. Some inaccuracies in punctuation.
  3. Almost no inaccuracies in punctuation.

G. *Mechanical accuracy II (spelling)*
  0. Almost all spelling inaccurate.
  1. Low standard of accuracy in spelling.
  2. Some inaccuracies in spelling.
  3. Almost no inaccuracies in spelling.

Figure 6.4 TEEP attribute writing scales (Weir, 1990)

## MICHIGAN WRITING ASSESSMENT SCORING GUIDE

### English Composition Board: Criteria for Reading the Assessment

| | Ideas and Arguments | Rhetorical Features | Language Control |
|---|---|---|---|
| 6 | The essay deals with the issues centrally and fully. The position is clear, and strongly and substantially argued. The complexity of the issues is treated seriously and the viewpoints of other people are taken into account very well. | The essay has rhetorical control at the highest level, showing unity and subtle management. Ideas are balanced with support and the whole essay shows strong control of organization appropriate to the content. Textual elements are well connected through logical or linguistic transitions and there is no repetition or redundancy. | The essay has excellent language control with elegance of diction and style. Grammatical structures and vocabulary are well-chosen to express the ideas and to carry out the intentions. |
| 5 | The essay deals with the issues well. The position is clear and substantial arguments are presented. The complexity of the issues or other viewpoints on them have been taken into account. | The essay shows strong rhetorical control and is well managed. Ideas are generally balanced with support and the whole essay shows good control of organization appropriate to the content. Textual elements are generally well connected although there may be occasional lack of rhetorical fluency: redundancy, repetition, or a missing transition. | The essay has strong language control and reads smoothly. Grammatical structures and vocabulary are generally well-chosen to express the ideas and to carry out the intentions. |
| 4 | The essay talks about the issues but could be better focused or developed. The position is thoughtful but could be clearer or the arguments could have more substance. Repetition or inconsistency may occur occasionally. The writer has clearly tried to take the complexity of the issues or viewpoints on them into account. | The essay shows acceptable rhetorical control and is generally managed fairly well. Much of the time ideas are balanced with support, and the organization is appropriate to the content. There is evidence of planning and the parts of the essay are usually adequately connected, although there are some instances of lack of rhetorical fluency. | The essay has good language control although it lacks fluidity. The grammatical structures used and the vocabulary chosen are able to express the ideas and carry the meaning quite well; although readers notice occasional language errors. |

| | Ideas and Arguments | Rhetorical Features | Language Control |
|---|---|---|---|
| 3 | The essay considers the issues but tends to rely on opinions or claims without the substance of evidence. The essay may be repetitive or inconsistent; the position needs to be clearer or the arguments need to be more convincing. If there is an attempt to account for the complexity of the issues or other viewpoints this is not fully controlled and only partly successful. | The essay has uncertain rhetorical control and is generally not very well managed. The organization may be adequate to the content, but ideas are not always balanced with support. Failures of rhetorical fluency are noticeable although there seems to have been an attempt at planning and some transitions are successful. | The essay has language control which is acceptable but limited. Although the grammatical structures used and the vocabulary chosen express the ideas and carry the meaning adequately, readers are aware of language errors or limited choice of language forms. |
| 2 | The essay talks generally about the topic but does not come to grips with ideas about it, raising superficial arguments or moving from one point to another without developing any fully. Other viewpoints are not given any serious attention. | The essay lacks rhetorical control most of the time, and the overall shape of the essay is hard to recognize. Ideas are generally not balanced with evidence, and the lack of an organizing principle is a problem. Transitions across and within sentences are attempted with only occasional success. | The essay has rather weak language control. Although the grammatical structures used and vocabulary chosen express the ideas and carry the meaning most of the time, readers are troubled by language errors or limited choice of language forms. |
| 1 | The essay does not develop or support an argument about the topic, although it may 'talk about' the topic. | The essay demonstrates little rhetorical control. There is little evidence of planning or organization, and the parts of the essay are poorly connected. | The essay demonstrates little language control. Language errors and restricted choice of language forms are so noticeable that readers are seriously distracted by them. |

Figure 6.5 Michigan writing assessment scoring guide

appeared twenty or thirty years ago pointed out quite rightly that scoring scripts on such features as 'diction' or 'flavor' was highly subjective because of the use of vague, indefinable criteria. Current scholarship (e.g. Weir, 1990; Hamp-Lyons, 1990; Alderson, 1991; Bachman and Palmer, 1996) emphasizes the need for clearly defined criteria and well-articulated levels for each scale or subscale within an analytic scoring scheme.

As mentioned above, the primary advantage of an analytic scoring scheme over a holistic scheme is that it provides more useful diagnostic information about students' writing abilities. However, analytic scoring has a number of other advantages over holistic scoring as well. First, some research suggests that analytic scoring is more useful in rater training, as inexperienced raters can more easily understand and apply the criteria in separate scales than in holistic scales (Francis, 1977, and Adams, 1981, both cited in Weir, 1990). Analytic scoring is particularly useful for second-language learners, who are more likely to show a marked or uneven profile across different aspects of writing: for example, a script may be quite well developed but have numerous grammatical errors, or a script may demonstrate an admirable control of syntax but have little or no content (see Hamp-Lyons, 1991b, for a fuller discussion of this issue). Finally, analytic scoring can be more reliable than holistic scoring: just as reliability tends to increase when additional items are added to a discrete-point test, so a scoring scheme in which multiple scores are given to each script tends to improve reliability (Hamp-Lyons, 1991b; Huot, 1996).

The major disadvantage of analytic scoring is that it takes longer than holistic scoring, since readers are required to make more than one decision for every script. An additional problem with some analytic scoring schemes is that, if scores on the different scales are combined to make a composite score, a good deal of the information provided by the analytic scale is lost. It may also be the case that raters who are experienced at using a particular analytic scoring system may actually rate more holistically than analytically if scores are combined into a single score: experienced raters may target their ratings towards what they expect the total score to come out to be, and revise their analytic scores accordingly (Charlene Polio, personal communication, 1998).

To summarize, the choice about the kind of rating scale to use is not always clear-cut. A useful approach to making a decision is to appeal to the Bachman and Palmer (1996) framework of test usefulness discussed in Chapter 3. Table 6.2 presents a comparison of holistic and analytic scales based on the six qualities of test usefulness: reliability, construct validity, practicality, impact, authenticity, and interactiveness. As Bachman and Palmer note, the choice of testing procedures involves finding the best possible combination of these qualities and deciding which qualities are most relevant in a given situation. For example, if large numbers of students need to be

Table 6.2. *A comparison of holistic and analytic scales on six qualities of test usefulness*

| Quality | Holistic Scale | Analytic Scale |
|---|---|---|
| Reliability | lower than analytic but still acceptable | higher than holistic |
| Construct Validity | holistic scale assumes that all relevant aspects of writing ability develop at the same rate and can thus be captured in a single score; holistic scores correlate with superficial aspects such as length and handwriting | analytic scales more appropriate for L2 writers as different aspects of writing ability develop at different rates |
| Practicality | relatively fast and easy | time-consuming, expensive |
| Impact | single score may mask an uneven writing profile and may be misleading for placement | more scales provide useful diagnostic information for placement and/or instruction; more useful for rater training |
| Authenticity | White (1995) argues that reading holistically is a more natural process than reading analytically | raters may read holistically and adjust analytic scores to match holistic impression |
| Interactiveness* | n/a | n/a |

*Interactiveness, as defined by Bachman and Palmer, relates to the interaction between the test taker and the test. It may be that this interaction is influenced by the rating scale if the test taker knows how his/her writing will be evaluated; this is an empirical question.

placed into writing courses in a limited time with limited resources, a holistic scale may be the most appropriate based on considerations of practicality. In this case, issues of reliability, validity, and impact can be ameliorated by the possibility of adjusting placements within the first week of class. On the other hand, a test of writing used for research purposes may have reliability and construct validity as central concerns, and practicality and impact may be of lesser significance. These issues must be resolved by the test users in considering all aspects of the situation.

## Designing the scoring rubric

### Factors to consider in designing a scoring rubric

Once it is determined what kind of rating scale is to be used, the next step is to design the scale, or scoring rubric, itself. The scoring rubric is critical, as it represents as explicitly as possible the definition of the skill(s) that the test is intended to measure, as mentioned above. However, it is not enough for a rubric to be clear and explicit: it must also be useable and interpretable, certainly by raters, and preferably by any and all stakeholders in the testing process, particularly test takers and decision makers. Factors to consider when designing a scoring rubric are as follows:

**(a) Who is going to use the scoring rubric?** Alderson (1991) notes that rating scales can have three distinct functions, depending on who is using them. **Constructor-oriented scales** are intended to guide the construction of tests at appropriate levels and thus include reference to the kinds of writing tasks that examinees would be expected to encounter, as in the following example from the American Council for the Teaching of Foreign Languages (ACTFL) writing scale: 'Can write a personal letter on simple everyday topics or a simple report on an everyday event' (ACTFL, 1985, cited in Alderson, 1991). **Assessor-oriented scales** are intended to guide the rating process, and focus on comparing the written text with descriptors on the scale. Finally, **user-oriented scales** are written with a focus on providing useful information to help test users interpret test scores. Alderson argues that it is important to be clear about the main function of a scale, and that problems are likely to arise when a scale intended for one purpose is used for another.

**(b) What aspect(s) of writing are most important, and how will they be divided up?** The Michigan Writing Assessment scale discussed above has a single category for language use. In some situations, however, in other situations it may be more appropriate to have separate scales for vocabulary use and grammatical accuracy. More detailed information about various aspects of language use would be particularly appropriate when the focus of the assessment is on the acquisition of specific language subskills, such as in low-proficiency non-academic classes or general foreign-language instruction. In post-secondary academic settings, and specifically when a test is being used to certify proficiency for academic study or to exempt students from composition courses, more emphasis will be placed on communicative effectiveness and less on specific language features, making a general category for language use more appropriate.

**(c) How many points, or scoring levels, will be used?** It is important to be able to distinguish between writers of different abilities; however, there are limits to the number of distinctions that raters can reliably make. Many large-scale assessment programs such as the TOEFL use a six-point scale; however, others have used nine-point scales with success. Part of this decision is determined by the range of performances that can be reasonably expected of the population of test takers; another consideration is the use to which the test will be put. If the test is being used primarily to make pass/fail decisions (as in a university writing competence examination, for example) fewer score points may be needed. If the test will be used to place students into different courses, on the other hand, more score points will be needed. Bachman and Palmer (1996) recommend using more score points than there are decisions to be made, since ratings are never completely reliable; that is, since independent raters will not necessarily agree on exact scores. The background and experience of raters may also influence the number of score points to be used: more experienced raters may be able to make finer distinctions between scripts than less experienced raters, and thus may be able to make use of more score points on a scale reliably.

Some questions about scale points can only be determined through empirical means in pre-testing, by trying out the scale with a wide variety of scripts and raters to determine whether raters are able to use the entire range of scores and distinguish between scale steps reliably. For example, if pre-testing showed that raters were only using four out of six scale points on a scale, scale developers might consider eliminating the other two scale points altogether or rewording the descriptors so that distinctions between the levels would be easier for raters to make. Pollitt (1990) points out that the number of points on a rating scale that can be distinguished reliably is a function of the overall reliability of the test, claiming that it is overly optimistic to expect a test of writing to be able to distinguish reliably between five scale points or more.

**(d) How will scores be reported?** If an analytic score is used, scale scores can either be combined for a total score, as is done in the Jacobs *et al.* (1981) scale, or scale scores can be reported separately for diagnostic purposes. Combining scores has the obvious advantage of providing a single score to be used in decision-making (for example, for cut-off scores for placement, exit, or exemption purposes), and combined scores tend to be more reliable than the separate part scores. However, combining scores also has the effect of negating the principal advantage of an analytic scale, which is to provide richer information about students' abilities. Since the same score can be achieved by people with varying profiles (for example, strong in syntax, weak in rhetoric, or vice versa) a composite score is difficult to interpret, except for those test takers who earn very high or very low scores.

Reporting separate scores provides more useful diagnostic information and generally provides a more accurate picture of test takers' abilities in writing. However, separate scores can be harder for test users to interpret quickly and cannot be combined easily with other parts of a test battery for decision-making purposes. For this issue the audience for test results must be kept in mind: program administrators who have to make quick decisions about many students may prefer a single score, while advisors helping students decide which of several courses to take would probably prefer the richer information provided by separate scores.

A related issue is whether, and how much, to weight different components of writing ability in an analytic scale. Jacobs *et al.* (1981) have differential weightings of the various components already built into their scale, with content receiving the most weight and mechanics the least. Hamp-Lyons (1991b), on the other hand, recommends weighting all components equally, suggesting that if one component is to be weighted more heavily than others in a given context, a focused holistic scale might be more appropriate. Weighting of scores has two complementary but distinct aspects that must be taken into consideration: it represents an explicit statement of a theory of writing ability (i.e. that certain aspects are more or less important/relevant/involved than others), and it also has consequences for the final scores that are the basis for decisions. The effects of weighting on final scores depend not just on the weights given to each component, but also on other statistical factors, such as the amount of variation within each component, and the correlations, or relationships between components. For this reason, if weighting is to be considered, the advice of a statistician familiar with these issues should be sought.

## Writing scale descriptors

Once these issues have been resolved, at least preliminarily, the descriptors for the various levels of the scale itself can be written. This can be done *a priori*, by defining in advance the ability being measured and then describing a number of levels of attainment, from none to complete mastery. This is the approach advocated by Bachman and Palmer (1996) and shown in Figure 6.6, from a set of scales used for placement into a university writing program. The advantage of this approach, according to Bachman and Palmer, is that it allows one to make inferences about a test taker's language ability on an absolute scale rather than relative to other test takers or to native speakers. However, a potential problem with this approach is that the scale descriptors tend to make imprecise distinctions between the levels (e.g. 'excellent,' 'very good,' 'good,' and so on). It is likely that inexperienced raters may have difficulties making these distinctions reliably without extensive training and repeated exposure to texts that instantiate the various scale levels. Another approach is to generate scale descriptions empirically, through the examination of actual scripts and/or operational ratings of writing performances. North and Schneider (1998) describe five data-based methods of scale construction that involve expert judgements of the key features at different levels of performance, statistical analysis of ratings vis-à-vis scale descriptors, or textual features of performances at different levels. The most common of these methods involves gathering sample scripts on a prototype writing task from students at all relevant levels of proficiency and, with a group of instructors familiar with the proficiency levels, defining the characteristics that differentiate the samples. In this case the definitions ordinarily take the form of verbal description rather than levels of mastery, although there is certainly an explicit rank ordering of these descriptions in terms of quality. These descriptions frequently refer to such notions as audience awareness, overall communicative effectiveness, and effect on the reader – notions which do not lend themselves easily to the levels-of-mastery approach. The rating scales in Figures 6.2 and 6.4 above were developed in this manner. North and Schneider (1998) caution that this method of scale

| Levels of ability/mastery | Description |
|---|---|
| 0    None | *No evidence of knowledge* of syntax<br><br>Range: zero<br>Accuracy: not relevant |
| 1    Limited | *Limited knowledge* of syntax<br><br>Range: small<br>Accuracy: poor, moderate, or good accuracy. If test taker only attempts a very few structures, accuracy may be good. |
| 2    Moderate | *Moderate knowledge* of syntax<br><br>Range: medium<br>Accuracy: moderate to good accuracy within range. If test taker attempts structures outside of the range that is controlled, accuracy may be poor. |
| 3    Extensive | *Extensive knowledge* of syntax.<br><br>Range: large, few limitations<br>Accuracy: good accuracy, few errors |
| 4    Complete | *Evidence of complete knowledge* of syntax<br><br>Range: evidence of unlimited range<br>Accuracy: evidence of complete control |

Figure 6.6  Scale: knowledge of syntax (Bachman and Palmer, 1996)

construction, which relies on expert judgement rather than statistical analyses, may be most useful for limited, specific contexts rather than for very large-scale (i.e. statewide or international) assessments.

The choice between *a priori* and empirical development of rating scales may depend in part on philosophical orientation – in particular, the degree to which one believes that the most important aspects of the ability being tested can be measured on a scale of none to complete mastery – and also on factors related to the purpose of the assessment. The mastery approach advocated by Bachman and Palmer (1996) is particularly appropriate if the construct is conceived of as an inherent ability (i.e. a student 'has' ability X) rather than in terms of a pragmatic ascription (i.e. a student 'can do' X, without reference to the exact nature of the underlying ability). The mastery approach is useful when we want to make inferences about underlying abilities, as in diagnostic tests, while the pragmatic approach is useful when we want to predict how someone will perform on future similar tasks. One disadvantage of the pragmatic approach, according to Bachman and Palmer, is its inadequacy for making generalizations: if we are simply predicting how one will perform in the future on the basis of specific performance without referring to an underlying ability, we may not be able to generalize that performance to other task types.

However the different scale levels are described, these characteristics form the basis for a preliminary scoring rubric against which further scripts can be judged. At this point, descriptors can be added, deleted, or modified until raters can agree on scores in the majority of cases. If the scoring rubric is to be used with a number of different writing tasks, the next step would be to apply the rubric to a variety of tasks to make sure that the descriptors are relevant and applicable to these new tasks. It is also helpful to devise a training procedure at this point to make sure that new raters are able to learn to apply the scoring rubric appropriately. Training procedures are discussed at length in the next section of this chapter.

It should be noted that the process of developing a scoring rubric, as in all aspects of test development, is iterative: it may well be that decisions about the aspects of writing to be scored and the number of score points for each aspect will need to be revisited one or more times as a result of trying out the rubric on actual scripts. For example, it may be that raters can reliably distinguish between five levels for one aspect of writing, but only four levels for another, or it may be that raters cannot reliably distinguish between two aspects, which may need to be collapsed into a single category.

## Calculating total scores

Before the scoring rubric can be finalized, decisions need to be made about calculating reported scores, in particular, if and how a total score will be derived from individual raters' scores, how much tolerance for discrepancies in ratings will be allowed, and what procedures will be followed in adjudicating discrepancies. For the purposes of this discussion, it is assumed that two raters will read and score each script independently of each other, with a third, senior rater, reading the sample in case of discrepancies.

In the simplest case, when the two raters are in agreement, the reported score can be the sum or the average of the two raters' scores. The practice of combining scores in these ways has the effect of doubling the possible range of scores (for example, if a six-point scale is used, the reported scores will range from 2 to 12 if scores are added together, or from 1 to 6, maintaining the original scale, with half-point intervals, if the scores are averaged).

Another factor that must be decided is the amount of variability among ratings that will be considered acceptable. Common practice on a six-point scale is that ratings more than one score point apart (e.g. one score of 3 and one of 5) are considered discrepant and must be resolved. In some testing programs where there is a specific pass/fail boundary (e.g. a score of 4 on a 6-point scale is passing, while a score of 3 is failing), if the two scores fall on either side of the boundary a third rater must resolve the discrepancy, even if the scores are only a point apart. Procedures for incorporating a third rating in the reported score vary from institution to institution: in some cases, the reported score is the average of the two closest scores, while in others all three scores are averaged. In the case of a third rater adjudicating at a pass/fail boundary, the third rater's judgement will normally prevail and the two scores on the same side of the boundary will be used in calculating the final score.

## The scoring process

Once the scoring rubric has been finalized, the next step is to select raters and design a process for the operational scoring of scripts. Much of the literature on large-scale testing has been concerned with procedures for obtaining satisfactory levels of reliability in an efficient manner; these procedures are introduced in this section.

### Procedures for assuring reliability

In Chapter 3, several possible sources of unreliability were discussed, and in Chapter 5 I discussed procedures for assuring consistency or reliability of tasks or prompts. In this section I will discuss another potential source of unreliability in writing assessment: inconsistencies in scoring. Of these, there are two main types: (1) inconsistencies in the ratings of a single scorer across different scripts of similar quality or the same script on different occasions, and (2) inconsistencies between different scorers. Both of these potential sources of unreliability can be addressed by the procedures described in this section. Procedures for estimating the effects of these two kinds of scorer inconsistency on test scores are discussed later in this chapter.

White (1984) outlined six practices and procedures that are important for maintaining high reliability in large-scale assessments. Two of these have already been discussed: the use of a scoring rubric that details explicitly the criteria to be used in scoring, and the use of sample scripts in training that exemplify points on the scale. It is only when all raters are in close agreement on the scores for these sample scripts that reliable scoring can take place. White's other recommendations are as follows:

- Each script must be scored independently by at least two raters, with a third rater adjudicating in cases of discrepancy.

- Scoring should be done in a controlled reading, by which is meant that a group of readers meets together to grade scripts at the same place and time. Two advantages of controlled reading are that the circumstances under which scripts are read are controlled, thus eliminating unnecessary sources of error variance, and that a positive social environment is formed which helps to enforce and maintain the rating standards. Unfortunately, group scoring is not always feasible; Alderson *et al.* (1995: 133–5) present alternatives for scoring when this is the case.

- Checks on the reading in progress by reading leaders (sometimes called Table Leaders) help to ensure that individual readers are maintaining the agreed-upon standards for grading.

- Evaluation and record keeping are essential for an ongoing assessment program so that reliable readers are kept on and unreliable readers are retrained or dropped if necessary.

White also makes the important point that the tone set by the reading leaders has a tremendous influence on the success of the reading. If a reading is led with sensitivity and respect, it can be an enjoyable and professionally valuable experience for readers; on the other hand, poorly run readings, in which readers feel exploited or coerced, can turn readers against the grading process, which in turn can have negative effects on the scoring itself.

## Rater training

Building on White's recommendations and procedures followed in large-scale writing assessment sessions such as those conducted by Educational Testing Service, the following process is recommended for instituting rater training for writing assessment. Specific circumstances will dictate to what extent this exact process can be followed, but the major elements should be part of any rater training. For example, if a small number of scripts are to be read and only two or three raters are involved, a less complex procedure might be appropriate. Similarly, if the same raters are used for frequent rating sessions, a full-scale rater training session might not be needed for every test administration.

The leader (or preferably a team) should read through the scripts to find anchor/benchmark scripts that exemplify the different points on the scale. Depending on the size of the reading, the complexity of the scale, the number of readers, and their experience, anything from three to ten sets of anchor scripts may be required. It is also helpful to include in the training sets scripts that exemplify certain problematic situations, for example, scripts that do not respond to the task or simply copy the prompt, or scripts that represent the borderline between two critical levels (e.g. passing and failing).

The first set of scripts is generally given to raters in order (from highest to lowest or vice versa) with the appropriate scores indicated, and should be as unambiguous a set as possible. This set is used to familiarize readers with the scale and to instantiate certain features of the rubric. The leader can use these scripts to describe for the readers what is meant by phrases in the rubric (e.g. 'appropriate introduction,' 'minor errors'). At this and every point questions are raised by readers and discussed with the whole group.

Once the readers feel comfortable with the scale as defined by the leader and instantiated in the first set or sets of anchor scripts, a set can be given that includes one script at each level in random order. Readers can be told that there should be one script at each level and given a chance to rate the scripts themselves. Once readers are able to handle this task, more problematic sets can be given out, which may have more than one script at a given level or may be less clearly representative of certain points of the scale.

It should be noted that it is virtually impossible to get a large group of raters to agree on exact scores and that some disagreement among raters is inevitable. In training raters, it is important to communicate to raters the amount of variability that is acceptable and to let them know that they are not required to be perfectly accurate at all times. Raters who consistently rate higher or lower than the rest of the group should be given feedback and perhaps additional training to bring their scores into alignment with the rest of the group.

In a large reading, additional retraining may be required at certain points. For example, if the reading takes place over more than one day, one or two sets of anchor scripts can be used to recalibrate readers each day. Similarly, if raters will be reading more than one topic, anchor scripts for each topic should be used if possible.

Once live rating is under way, it is important to ensure that scoring is independent – that is, that raters do not see and therefore cannot be influenced by scores given by other raters – and, of course, procedures for maintaining independence of scores must be devised well in advance. These procedures can be as complex as assigning different codes for scores to each rater or using invisible ink, or as simple as designing a rating sheet that can be folded in half once the first score is given so that it is hidden from the second rater. Whatever procedure is used, it is essential for the integrity of the scoring process that raters arrive at their scores independently, without reference to scores given by other raters. For this reason it is also important that raters do not write comments or underline errors when scoring scripts, to avoid influencing the scores given by other raters.

## Special problems in scoring

In this section, some common problems in scoring writing are discussed. In an ideal world, writing prompts would be written so that every test taker could understand exactly what was required and would respond appropriately within his or her ability level. In the same ideal world, every test taker would agree to go along with the task set by the test writers in exactly the way the test writers envision. However, in the real world these conditions are virtually impossible to meet. It then becomes incumbent upon the test writers (or readers, if they are different people) to determine to what extent fulfilling the exact task set forth in the writing prompt should be part of the scoring procedure. While it is impossible to foresee every problem that might occur, it is advisable to anticipate as far as possible the kinds of problems that might occur with a given prompt, to reduce the possibility that different raters will approach problematic scripts differently and thus introduce unwanted errors into the scoring procedures. Three types of problematic scripts will be discussed in this section: (1) scripts that are complete but do not address the intended task or fail to address parts of the task, (2) scripts that have clearly been written from memory rather than in response to the prompt, and (3) incomplete scripts – that is, scripts in which the writer has demonstrated an understanding of the important features of the task but was unable to complete the task in the allotted time (for example, the conclusion may be missing).

### *Off-task scripts*

A writing prompt ordinarily contains specific instructions to the test taker about what topic to address and how to approach the topic – for example, compare and contrast two things, outline the causes of a particular problem, or give advantages and disadvantages of some course of action. One problematic area in scoring is a script that misconstrues these instructions – listing solutions to a problem rather than the causes, for instance, or providing only advantages and not disadvantages. In such cases the raters need to decide the extent to which task fulfillment is essential to the scoring. Decisions about task fulfillment are based on the purpose of the assessment and the type of scoring that is used. For the TOEFL, for example, the test writers and users are interested primarily in a general sense of a person's ability to create a coherent written text, not the quality of the ideas or the persuasiveness of the essay. In addition, the TOEFL Writing Test is intended to test writing and not reading ability. For these reasons, raters are told that an essay can be considered on-topic and ratable if it can at all be reasonably construed to have something to do with the prompt. For example, if the prompt required test takers to discuss the advantages of books over movies, an essay that simply discussed a recent book that the writer had read would not be considered off-topic. On the other hand, in primary trait scoring, task fulfillment is central to the scoring guide, and a script that did not address the demands of the task would receive a low score no matter how beautifully written it was. This issue harks back to the distinction between the strong and weak senses of performance testing discussed in Chapter 3.

From these examples, it is clear that what constitutes task fulfillment lies in the purpose of the assessment and the type of scoring that is used. For example, with assessments whose main purpose is obtaining a ratable sample of writing that will demonstrate control of syntax and vocabulary, the degree to which writers follow the instructions exactly will be less important than for assessments whose purpose is to assess writers' ability to successfully communicate in writing, such as is typically of interest in academic settings.

### Memorized scripts

Determining task fulfillment is particularly problematic in the case of memorized scripts: if it becomes generally known that readers are merely looking for a scorable sample of writing rather than the ability to accomplish a specific task through writing, some test takers may prepare for the test by memorizing a well-written script and writing it out from memory during the test. Obviously a memorized script does not provide an accurate sample of a test taker's ability, since there is no way of knowing the author or source of the script. Thus, steps must be taken to avoid the possibility of memorized scripts being proffered or accepted for scoring. This argues for requiring at least some adherence to the task in order for a script to be acceptable, although again it is a matter of degree, depending on the circumstances. Generally, the more specifically a writing test is geared to a particular situation, the more important the notion of task fulfillment becomes. For example, task fulfillment may be less important in a general proficiency test for placement into university-level foreign-language classes, where students may have no genuine need for using the language outside of the classroom, while it becomes much more critical in a vocational or professional LSP course that is preparing students to use English in their professions.

### Incomplete responses

Another issue that must be resolved is that of incomplete responses. This issue becomes particularly pertinent in cases where task fulfillment is an integral part of the scoring rubric. If a test taker makes a promising beginning to a script but does not complete it, the reader's dilemma is whether to score the script based on the strength of what has been written, assuming that the writer could have made an appropriate conclusion given enough time, or whether to adhere strictly to the wording of the rubric and score the script on the basis of what is present in the script. Again, to resolve this dilemma one must consider the purpose of the assessment and the impact that decisions will have on test takers. In a fairly low-stakes test such as a placement test, where additional information can be gathered after the fact to support or revise a decision, one might decide in favor of the former approach. On a higher-stakes test, on the other hand, especially in an academic context where a writing test is supposed to be indicative of other types of academic writing, one can be stricter about the rating criteria and judge incomplete scripts more severely.

The fact that it is impossible to know ahead of time which of these or other unanticipated problems will occur during a live reading makes the pre-testing of prompts, as discussed in Chapter 5, critical. Sample scripts on a topic are essential for providing information about the variations in responses that can inform rater training, and it is important for scoring leaders to be aware of and anticipate the kinds of problems that may arise during the reading. For example, scoring leaders should be prepared with advice on how to deal with poor handwriting, extremely brief responses, or uncreative or simplistic responses. When unanticipated problems arise during operational rating, it may be worthwhile keeping a written record of the problem and its resolution so that raters are consistent in dealing with the problem should it recur later on. Careful consideration of the implications of decisions regarding problem scripts is critical to ensuring a successful scoring session.

## Evaluating scoring procedures

As with other aspects of testing, scoring procedures can be evaluated according to the criteria of test usefulness outlined in Bachman and Palmer (1996). In particular the aspects of reliability, validity, and practicality need to be evaluated with reference to scoring procedures. Of these qualities of usefulness, procedures for evaluating reliability are the best known.

### Assessing reliability of scores

There are a number of ways to investigate the reliability or consistency of raters. Two important aspects of reliability are intra-rater reliability (self-consistency) and inter-rater reliability (agreement between raters). Intra-rater reliability refers to the tendency of a rater to give the same score to the same script on different occasions, while inter-rater reliability refers to the tendency of different raters to give the same scores to the same scripts. In the simplest cases, the reliability of ratings on a holistic scale between two raters, or between the scores given to the same samples by one rater on two different occasions, can be calculated by means of a correlation coefficient. This statistic is a number between 0 and 1 indicating the strength of the relationship between two sets of scores. A correlation coefficient close to 0 indicates that there is little or no relationship between the scores given by the first rater and those given by the second (or on the second occasion), while a coefficient close to 1 indicates a strong relationship between the sets of scores. The formulas for calculating the appropriate statistic, either the Spearman rank-order correlation coefficient or the Pearson product-moment correlation coefficient, can be found in any standard textbook on statistics, and reliability coefficients are easily calculated on readily available spreadsheet software such as Microsoft Excel.

A complementary approach to investigating inter-rater reliability, particularly when more than two raters are involved, is through the analysis of variance (ANOVA). ANOVA can be used to compare the distribution of scores given by a set of raters (assuming they have all scored the same scripts). The two main statistics used to describe the distribution of scores are the **mean**, or average score, and the **standard deviation**, or the average amount that scores differ from the mean. ANOVA can be used to determine whether there is any statistical difference between the mean scores of raters; that is, if some raters tend to give higher or lower scores than other raters, irrespective of the correlation among raters' scores. Further information about analysis of variance can be found in a textbook on statistics; useful discussions of both intra- and inter-rater reliability can be found in Alderson *et al.*, (1995), Hatch and Lazaraton (1991), and Bachman (forthcoming).

Beyond inter-rater reliability, there are several ways of looking at rater agreement. To judge the overall success of a rating session, the scores given by the first and second readers can be cross-tabulated, as in Table 6.3. White (1984) states that an average reading using a six-point scale will have 7–10% of the ratings more than one point apart, while in an excellent reading only 5% of ratings will be discrepant. In the table, numbers outside the shaded area represent discrepant

Table 6.3. *Example rating summary*

| SCORE | Rater 1 | | | | | | |
|---|---|---|---|---|---|---|---|
| Rater 2 | 1 | 2 | 3 | 4 | 5 | 6 | Total |
| 1 | 4 | 2 | | | | | 6 |
| 2 | 2 | 8 | 5 | 2 | | | 17 |
| 3 | 1 | 6 | 12 | 7 | 2 | | 28 |
| 4 | | 2 | 9 | 15 | 7 | 1 | 34 |
| 5 | | | 2 | 8 | 12 | 4 | 26 |
| 6 | | | | 1 | 3 | 5 | 9 |
| Total | 7 | 18 | 28 | 33 | 24 | 10 | 120 |

scores, or cases where the two readers were more than one point apart. A total of 11 scores, or slightly over 9% of the total number of scores, are discrepant in this example, indicating an acceptable degree of rater disagreement, according to this, admittedly rule-of-thumb, standard. For an overall indication of rater agreement using a table such as Table 6.3, a coefficient of relationship (called kappa) can be derived, and this can be interpreted much the same way as a correlation coefficient, described above. The reader is referred to the references listed above for further details about this statistic. For individual readers, statistics can be compiled to include the number of scripts read, the number of scripts read that needed to be adjudicated by a third reader, and the number of times discrepancies were resolved in the reader's favor. This information can be useful for providing feedback to readers regarding their accuracy and efficiency or for determining whether to reuse raters in future readings.

## Assessing validity of scoring procedures

In addition to considering the reliability of scores, it is important to investigate how scoring procedures affect the construct validity of a writing test – that is, the validity of inferences made on the basis of test results. Looking at construct validity in terms of scoring procedures is somewhat less straightforward than investigating reliability, however, as it involves investigation of a multitude of factors from a variety of perspectives. One can start by asking a few basic questions.

First, do the scoring procedures – in particular, the scoring guide – accurately reflect the construct being measured? As discussed previously, the scoring guide represents an explicit statement of what aspects of writing are being considered as part of the construct, and thus the first question is whether that is in fact the case. For example, if we are interested primarily in accuracy of content and logical organization in writing, the scoring guide should not focus heavily on grammar.

Another important question is whether the scoring procedures are being implemented in an appropriate way. This question relates to rater behavior: if raters are not basing their judgements on the scale as defined in the scoring guide, questions must be asked about what is actually being measured, since the scoring guide, as mentioned above, represents the construct. The studies of rater behavior cited in Chapter 4, particularly those using think aloud protocols to investigate raters' decision-making processes, relate to this question and can serve as models for similar studies on a local level. Alternatively, a debriefing session following rating can be held to discuss how raters are interpreting the scale or any problems or concerns that may have arisen during the scoring session. Information from these sessions can then feed into further refinements of the scoring guide.

A third question is whether the scores obtained from the test allow us to make appropriate inferences about writing ability and thus appropriate decisions about test takers. To answer this question, we thus need to evaluate our scoring procedures in terms of their effect on outcomes. Outcomes can be assessed both in terms of consequences for individual test takers and in terms of consequences for the educational system or teaching program (cf. the discussion of washback in Chapter 3). For individuals, one way to assess the consequences of scoring procedures is to investigate the appropriateness of decisions made on the basis of the test scores. For example, if a writing test is being used for placement, the percentage of placements that were later changed based on additional information can be calculated, thus giving an indication of how well the test is functioning for this purpose.

On a systemic level, scoring procedures can have an effect (positive or negative) on instruction in a number of ways. First, disseminating the rating criteria among teachers, students, and other stakeholders allows for frank discussion of, and ideally consensus about, the goals of writing instruction and the expected outcomes for students. Dissemination of rating criteria can lead to instructional changes, if teachers gear their instruction towards the aspects of writing that are seen as valued because they are emphasized in the criteria. By the same token, students may be motivated to work on those aspects of writing if they are aware of how their writing will be scored.

The type of rating scale used – holistic, analytic, or primary trait – is also relevant in this regard. Using an analytic scoring guide rather than a holistic one can have beneficial effects as it provides more information about the strengths and weaknesses of students and may allow instructors and curriculum developers to tailor instruction more closely to the needs of their students.

### Evaluating the practicality of scoring procedures

As discussed in Chapter 3, the practicality of a test is a matter of the availability of resources vis-à-vis the resources required to develop, administer, and score the test. Given a finite amount of resources for testing, it may be necessary to optimize the allocation of resources to reach the desired levels of the various aspects of test usefulness. This may take the form of a cost–benefit analysis. For instance, one may believe that an analytic scale may provide more useful information about test takers' abilities than a holistic scale, but the time required to provide analytic scores may not be worth the added benefits. As another example, if inter-rater reliability is not sufficiently high, several options might be explored: increase the number of writing tasks, increase the number of raters, or devote more time to refining the rating scale and training raters. The costs and benefits for each option will have to be weighed against the availability of resources.

On a more mundane level, following an operational scoring session, it is generally a good idea for scoring leaders to meet with raters to discuss ways in which the scoring process could be streamlined without sacrificing reliability or validity: could training have been more efficient, for example, or was the system for tracking scripts and reporting scores too cumbersome? Even when a scoring system has been in place for a long period of time, it is useful to hold such debriefing sessions regularly, as new ideas and new technologies (see Chapter 10) may arise that can be useful for increasing the efficiency of scoring.

## Summary

This chapter has provided a discussion of scoring procedures for writing assessment, focusing on the use and development of rating scales and procedures for training, monitoring, and evaluating raters. The next chapter brings together many of the issues raised in this chapter and the previous one by presenting both the writing tasks and scoring procedures for several illustrative writing tests for different purposes.

Many of the procedures described in this chapter were developed originally to counter the criticism that subjective scoring of writing could never be reliable and that it thus was, if not impossible, at least highly impractical, to test writing by having test takers actually write, particularly in large-scale assessment. A great deal of attention has therefore, and with good reason, been focused on increasing reliability of scoring. Recently, however, the focus has shifted towards ensuring the validity of scoring, an issue that will be revisited in Chapter 10.

It is also becoming increasingly clear that, while timed impromptu writing has its place in writing assessment, for many purposes a single script written under time restrictions is insufficient, as it provides a very restricted picture of what test takers are able to accomplish with writing in the real world. Furthermore, timed writing tests, while useful for large-scale assessment, are of less value in classroom-based assessment of writing, for reasons that are discussed in Chapter 8. In Chapters 9 and 10, therefore, we will turn from timed writing tests to alternative forms of writing assessment: classroom-based writing evaluation, and portfolio assessment.

.....................................................................................................................

# CHAPTER SEVEN

# Illustrative tests of writing

## Introduction

In Chapters 5 and 6, issues in developing writing tasks and scoring procedures for large-scale assessment were discussed. This chapter presents examples from several tests of second-language writing as a way of illustrating how test developers have dealt with some of the issues raised in the previous two chapters for specific groups of test takers. These issues include:

- defining the writing construct for the purpose of the test;
- designing writing tasks from specific TLU domains so that they are likely to be authentic for prospective examinees;
- developing scoring criteria that reflect the most important aspects of writing for those test takers; and
- balancing the various aspects of test usefulness for a particular situation.

Five tests will be discussed in this chapter. Three of them are well-known language tests that include writing as a distinct component of the test: these are the TOEFL, the International English Language Testing System (IELTS), and the UCLES First Certificate in English (FCE). Scores on these tests are internationally recognized for such purposes as university admissions or certification of language proficiency for employment. The other two tests that will be discussed are tests of quite a different nature. The Basic English Skills Test (BEST), developed by the Center for Applied Linguistics in Washington, D.C., is a test intended for adult immigrant learners of English who are not necessarily literate in their first language and who need basic functional English skills for everyday life. The Contextualized Writing Assessment (CoWA), produced by the Minnesota Language Assessment Project, is part of a battery of foreign-language tests for secondary and post-secondary students of French, German, and Spanish. These two tests have been included as examples of writing tests for lower-proficiency students who do not need to use their second language for professional or academic purposes. As the following discussion will illustrate, the goals of the test and the characteristics of the examinees have implications for the nature of the writing tasks, the scoring procedures, and the consideration of the aspects of test usefulness.

For each test, the following information is provided:

1.  The purpose of the test, as defined by the test author or publisher, and the specific population for whom the test is intended. This section also includes information about additional uses of the test other than those intended by the author or publisher.

2.  A description of the test content; specifically the number and type of writing tasks.

3.  A description of the rating scale used and the scoring procedures.

4.  A discussion of the distinctive features of the test, including (a) how the writing construct is defined, either explicitly by the test publisher, or implicitly, as can be inferred from the writing tasks and scoring rubrics; (b) how the test developers have approached task authenticity for the population of test takers; and (c) how the test developers have balanced among the various qualities of test usefulness in light of the test purpose and the intended test-taker population.

## Test of English as a Foreign Language (TOEFL)

### Purpose

The purpose of the TOEFL test is to evaluate the English proficiency of people whose native language is not English. TOEFL scores are used primarily in decisions about admission to colleges and universities in the United States and Canada, but TOEFL scores are also used by other entities such as government agencies and scholarship programs, and for admission to higher education institutions in other countries. Until 1998, the TOEFL itself did not contain a writing section. In that year the Test of Written English (TWE), a 30-minute writing test, was given along with the TOEFL at certain test administrations, but the TWE score was not incorporated into the total TOEFL score. Along with other changes to the test, writing became a part of every test when the computer-based TOEFL was introduced in July 1998.

The computer-based TOEFL is administered at individual computer stations in four sections: listening, structure, reading, and writing. Total testing time, which includes a mandatory computer tutorial, is approximately four hours. The writing section itself is strictly timed at 30 minutes.

## Test content

The TOEFL writing test consists of a single essay. According to the TOEFL Bulletin (ETS 2000), the purpose of the writing test is 'to demonstrate [test takers'] ability to write in English. This includes the ability to generate and organize ideas, to support those ideas with examples or evidence, and to compose in standard written English in response to an assigned topic' (p. 41).

Several sample TOEFL prompts are found in Figure 7.1 on page 143. All TOEFL writing prompts are disclosed; that is, the most current TOEFL bulletin contains a list of all possible prompts that could be administered. The 2000–2001 bulletins list 155 potential topics. Examinees are not given a choice of prompt, and must write on the assigned prompt, which is selected randomly by computer from the several dozen prompts in use at any given time. TOEFL writing prompts are of two types: those that require test takers to express and support an opinion, and those that require test takers to choose and defend a position on an issue. These tasks are based on the types of writing identified in a survey by Bridgeman and Carlson (1983) as important for academic work (ETS, 1989).

The instructions that appear on the computer screen for examinees are shown in Figure 7.2. Examinees may write their essays by hand or on the computer. Handwritten essays are scanned into a computer before being scored.

Some people think that children should begin their formal education at a very early age and should spend most of their time on school studies. Others believe that young children should spend most of their time playing. Compare these two views. Which view do you agree with? Why?

Should government spend more money on improving roads and highways, or should government spend more money on improving public transportation (buses, trains, subways)? Why? Use specific reasons and details to support your essay.

Do you agree or disagree with the following statement? People are never satisfied with what they have; they always want something more or something different. Use specific reasons to support your answer.

You have the opportunity to visit a foreign country for two weeks. Which country would you like to visit? Use specific reasons and details to explain your choice.

Figure 7.1 Sample TOEFL writing prompts (ETS, 2000)

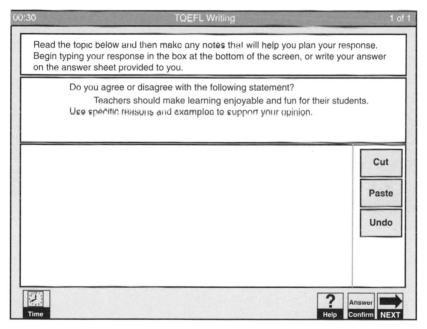

Figure 7.2 Instructions for computer-based TOEFL writing test (ETS, 1998)

## Scoring

The TOEFL writing is scored on a six-point holistic scale. This scale was presented as Figure 6.2; it is reproduced here again as Figure 7.3. The rating scale addresses the following aspects of writing: overall

6   An essay at this level
    • effectively addresses the writing task
    • is well organized and well developed
    • uses clearly appropriate details to support a thesis or illustrate ideas
    • displays consistent facility in use of language
    • demonstrates syntactic variety and appropriate word choice though it may have occasional errors

5   An essay at this level
    • may address some parts of the task more effectively than others
    • is generally well organized and developed
    • uses details to support a thesis or illustrate an idea
    • displays facility in the use of language
    • demonstrates some syntactic variety and range of vocabulary, though it will probably have occasional errors

4   An essay at this level
    • addresses the writing topic adequately but may slight parts of the task
    • is adequately organized and developed
    • uses some details to support a thesis or illustrate an idea
    • demonstrates adequate but possibly inconsistent facility with syntax and usage
    • may contain some errors that occasionally obscure meaning

3   An essay at this level may reveal **one** or more of the following weaknesses:
    • inadequate organization or development
    • inappropriate or insufficient details to support or illustrate generalizations
    • a noticeably inappropriate choice of words or word forms
    • an accumulation of errors in sentence structure and/or usage

2   An essay at this level is seriously flawed by one or more of the following weaknesses:
    • serious disorganization or underdevelopment
    • little or no detail, or irrelevant specifics
    • serious and frequent errors in sentence structure or usage
    • serious problems with focus

1   An essay at this level
    • may be incoherent
    • may be undeveloped
    • may contain severe and persistent writing errors

0   A paper is rated 0 if it contains no response, merely copies the topic, is off-topic, is written in a foreign language, or consists of only keystroke characters.

Figure 7.3  TOEFL writing scoring guide (ETS, 2000)

effectiveness of the response to the writing task, organization and development, use of details, facility with use of language, syntactic variety and word choice. The TOEFL writing test is factored into the structure/writing score, contributing approximately half of the scaled total score for this section. In addition, the essay rating appears separately on the score report. When the TWE was administered as a separate test, scoring was centralized; that is, raters met together following each administration of the test to rate the essays, following procedures similar to those outlined in Chapter 6. Right before this centralized rating session, a chief reader, assistant chief readers, and table leaders selected sample essays to calibrate the raters to the scoring rubric and essay topic, and then monitored the performance of a large number of raters throughout the two- to three-day reading.

Now, however, since testing is done every day, scoring is also done nearly every weekday and also on some Saturdays. A smaller number of raters on any given day score TOEFL writing responses via the Online Scoring Network of Educational Testing Service. These qualified raters, working from an ETS-established scoring center or from their homes using a Web interface, are presented on their computer monitors with virtual 'folders' of keyed essays and images of handwritten essays on a given topic. Raters have access to sample essays, both keyed and handwritten, on all topics at all score points and work under the supervision of Scoring Leaders who monitor the performance of these raters in real time and can contact them and be contacted while scoring is taking place. In addition, all raters must pass a calibration test at the beginning of each scoring day before they begin scoring. Scoring Leaders can also observe rater performance on 'monitor papers,' pre-scored papers that are co-mingled with the responses that are being scored (Robert Kantor, personal communication, March 2000).

Just as with the paper TWE, the reported score is the average of the two raters' scores. In case of a discrepancy of two points or more, an experienced rater reads the essay and the final score is the average of the two closest scores.

## Discussion

The TOEFL is a high-stakes test, as test results are used in admissions decisions for colleges and universities and thus have important consequences for test takers. It is also administered on a very large scale, and the logistics for scoring the essays and calculating and reporting test scores in a timely fashion are therefore extremely complex. Furthermore, the addition of a compulsory writing test is a relatively new development in the TOEFL, which has its roots in the American psychometric tradition of discrete-point testing. These factors have all been important in determining the structure and content of the TOEFL writing test. Some of the distinctive features of the TOEFL writing test include the use of a single task written along a set of fairly narrow parameters, no choice between tasks, a holistic scale that is used for scoring all tasks, highly structured procedures for achieving inter-rater reliability, and the optional use of hand-writing or keying in essays. An additional feature, the practice of combining the writing score with the structure score, has implications for the definition of the construct, and is discussed below.

### *Construct*

As noted above, the stated definition of 'writing ability' as measured by the TOEFL writing test involves the ability to 'generate and orga-nize ideas, to support those ideas with examples or evidence, and to compose in standard written English in response to an assigned topic.' The descriptors on the rating scale focus on these compo-nents of writing, addressing task fulfillment, organization and devel-opment, use of details to support an argument, and facility with language, including syntactic variety, appropriateness of word choice, and linguistic accuracy. The TOEFL writing test does not attempt to measure students' abilities to write in different genres or for different audiences or purposes; in this respect the construct being measured is limited to a narrow focus: the ability to write argumentative discourse on an impromptu topic. Furthermore, there seems to be an implicit bias towards privileging linguistic accuracy over other aspects of writing such as task fulfillment and develop-ment in the TOEFL writing test, as evidenced by the fact that the writing score is reported as part of the structure score of the test.

### *Authenticity*

The TOEFL is primarily intended for academically oriented test takers, and thus the tasks on the writing test focus on an important aspect of academic English: the ability to present and support an argument. The TOEFL writing tasks are thus authentic to the extent that argumentative prose is an important genre of academic writing. However, the authenticity of the TOEFL writing tasks is limited by the fact that there is no opportunity to read about or discuss the assigned topic before writing about it, in contrast to the vast majority of academic writing assignments. This point is discussed in more detail in Chapter 8. Authenticity is also limited by the fact that test takers are not allowed a choice of prompts, thus reducing the likelihood that test takers will find a specific prompt relevant to their background, interests, and writing goals. On the other hand, as more and more students come to rely on computers in their academic programs, the fact that students are allowed to key in their essays may increase the authenticity of the task for some test takers.

### *Other aspects of test usefulness*
As noted above, the TOEFL is a high-stakes test that is administered on a very large scale. For these reasons, reliability and practicality are important aspects of test usefulness for the TOEFL. Some of the distinctive features of the TOEFL writing test can be seen as arising from the desire to provide scores reliably and efficiently; for example, the use of a single writing prompt written along very narrow parameters and the lack of choice between prompts. Reliability of scoring is achieved through careful pre-testing of prompts and rigorous training and monitoring of raters. While construct validity could be enhanced through the administration of multiple writing tasks, the constraints of practicality mitigate against this: multiple tasks would greatly increase the administration and scoring time, requiring substantially more human resources and ultimately increasing the cost of the test to the examinee. Similarly, interactiveness could be increased by offering a choice of prompts to examinees, who may have more relevant background knowledge on one topic than another, or may find one more engaging than another. However, offering a choice of prompts may decrease reliability, as discussed in earlier chapters. Finally, it should be noted that potential impact was an important consideration in making writing an obligatory component of the TOEFL, as it was felt that including writing on the test might lead to more writing instruction and practice for potential examinees. It is intriguing to note that the developers of the TOEFL decided to publish all TOEFL prompts, perhaps for the purpose of promoting beneficial washback by providing opportunities for examinees to practice the specific task type that is tested by the TOEFL. The

number of prompts (155) is sufficiently large so that someone attempting to memorize essays on all of them would most probably improve their language competence from the extraordinary effort that such a task would require.

An interesting aspect of the TOEFL is the option that test takers have to key in their essays rather than writing them by hand. As discussed above, this option may make the test more authentic for some students who are accustomed to using computers for composing, and it certainly simplifies the scoring process, as keyed essays can be more easily sent out to raters. However, questions remain about the effects of word processing on essay tests, in terms of both the composing process and the influence of word processing on raters' judgements, as discussed in Chapter 5. More research is necessary in this area to determine whether the benefits of allowing students to key in their essays outweigh the potential disadvantages.

## Cambridge First Certificate in English (FCE)

### Test purpose

The First Certificate in English examination is part of a suite of English language examinations at five levels of proficiency administered by the University of Cambridge Local Examinations Syndicate (UCLES, 2001). These examinations are used to certify English language proficiency for a variety of purposes. Examinees who pass the FCE, which is the third level of proficiency in the UCLES system, are presumed to have sufficient language proficiency for office work or to pursue a training course in English. Approximately 80 per cent of examinees who take the FCE do so following a course of study tailored to the exam, and examinees' reasons for taking the test are roughly equally divided between employment, study, and personal interest (UCLES, 2000).

The FCE consists of five different papers focusing on different language skill areas: reading, writing, listening, speaking, and use of English. The second paper, which is the focus of this discussion, is the writing paper.

## Test content

The FCE Writing Paper consists of two writing tasks: a compulsory task that all examinees complete, and an optional task from a choice of four. The compulsory task in Part 1 is a 'transactional' letter, i.e. a request for action or a response to a request for action, and is based on input materials such as advertisements or short articles. In Part 2 one of the optional tasks is based on the reading of one of five books specified in advance. The other optional tasks are drawn from a variety of genres, including non-transactional letters, discursive compositions, narratives, and descriptions. Examinees are asked to write between 120 and 180 words for each task, and the total time for the test is 1 hour 30 minutes. Figure 7.4 presents a sample paper.

## Scoring

The FCE writing tasks are scored on a six-band scale, reproduced as Figure 7.5 (on p. 152). The FCE literature calls this scale a 'general impression scale,' but it is not to be confused with what has been termed 'general impression marking' – that is, rating without an explicit scale – as discussed in Chapter 6. In addition to the general impression scale, a task-specific scoring rubric (called the 'task-specific mark scheme') is drafted in advance of each test administration and is finalized after consideration of actual written samples or scripts. The task-specific mark scheme summarizes the content, organization and cohesion, range of structures and vocabulary, register and format, and desired effect on the target reader of the task. Organization of the coverage of content points is important in Part 1, while the range of structures and vocabulary used is indicative of performance in Part 2. Band 3 describes a 'satisfactory' level of performance, and within the bands examiners place a script more exactly at the bottom, middle or top of the band range, e.g. 3.1, 3.2, 3.3. These scores are converted to provide a score out of 20 for each piece of writing (Linda Taylor, personal communication, March 2001). Scoring is done by a panel of trained examiners divided into small teams, each with a very experienced examiner as Team Leader. The Principal Examiner guides and monitors the scoring process, beginning with a meeting of the Principal Examiners and the Team Leaders. This is held immediately after the test administration and begins the process

**Part 1**

You **must** answer this question.

1    You recently entered a competition and have just received this letter from the
     organiser. Read the letter, on which you have made some notes. Then, using
     all the information in your notes, write a suitable reply.

> Congratulations! You have won first prize in our competition–
> two weeks at Camp California in the U.S.A. All accommodation
> and travel costs are paid for, including transport to and from the
> airport. We now need some further information from you:
>
> *only July because...*
>
> • When would you like to travel?
>
> • Accommodation at Camp California is in tents or log cabins,
>   which would you prefer?
>
> *say which and why*
>
> • You will have the chance to do two activities while you are at
>   the Camp. Please choose two from the list below and tell
>   us how good you are at each one.
>
> *tell them*
>
> Basketball   Swimming   Golf      Painting      Climbing
> Singing      Sailing    Tennis    Photography   Surfing
>
> Is there anything you would like to ask us?
>
> Yours sincerely
>
> *clothes, money...*
>
> Helen Ryan
> Competition Organiser

Write a **letter** of between **120** and **180** words in an appropriate style on the
opposite page.

Do not write any postal addresses.

**Part 2**

Write an answer to **one** of the questions **2–5** in this part. Write your answer in
**120–180** words in an appropriate style on the opposite page. Put the question
number in the box.

2    Your English class is going to make a short video about daily life at your

school. Your teacher has asked you to write a report, suggesting which lessons and other activities should be filmed, and why.

Write your **report**.

3　You have recently had a class discussion about shopping. Now your English teacher has asked you to write a composition, giving your opinions on the following statement:

*Shopping is not always enjoyable.*

Write your **composition**.

4　Last month, you enjoyed helping at a pop concert and your pen friend Kim wants to hear about your experience. Write a letter to Kim, describing what you did to help **and** explaining what you particularly liked about the experience.

Write your **letter**. Do not write any postal addresses.

5　Answer **one** of the following two questions based on your reading of **one** of these set books. Write **(a)** or **(b)** as well as the number **5** in the question box, and the **title** of the book next to the box.

*Best Detective Stories of Agatha Christie* – Longman Fiction
*The Old Man and the Sea* – Ernest Hemingway
*Cry Freedom* – John Briley
*Wuthering Heights* – Emily Brontë
*A Window on the Universe* – Oxford Bookworms Collection

**Either (a)**　'Sometimes the bad characters in a story are more interesting than the good ones.' Is this true of the book you have read? Write a **composition**, explaining your views with reference to the book or one of the short stories you have read.

**Or**　**(b)**　'This is such a marvellous book you will want to read it again.' Write an **article** for your college magazine, saying whether you think this statement is true of the book or one of the short stories you have read.

Figure 7.4　Sample FCE paper (UCLES, 1997)

of establishing a common standard of assessment by the selection of sample scripts for all the tasks on the Writing Paper. During marking, each examiner is apportioned scripts chosen on a random basis from the entire entry in order to ensure there is no concentration of good or weak scripts or of one large center of one country in the allocation of any one examiner. Writing scripts are not double-rated as a matter of routine, although a rigorous process of co-ordination and checking by Team Leaders is carried out before and during the marking process, and procedures for examiner-scaling are in place in order to minimize subjectivity.

**Band 5**  Full realisation of task set shown by:

- Coverage of points required with evidence of original output.
- Wide range of structure and vocabulary demonstrating control of language.
- Clear organisation with a variety of linking devices.
- Presentation and register wholly appropriate to purpose and audience throughout.

Overall: a very positive effect on the target reader.

**Band 4**  Good realisation of task set shown by:

- Coverage of points required with sufficient detail.
- Good range of structure and vocabulary; generally accurate.
- Effective organisation; suitable linking devices.
- Presentation and register appropriate to purpose and audience.

Overall: a positive effect on the target reader.

**Band 3**  Task set is reasonably achieved by:

- Coverage of main points required.
- Adequate range of structure and vocabulary; some errors.
- Adequate organisation; simple linking devices.
- Presentation and register on the whole appropriate to purpose and audience.

Overall: a satisfactory effect on the target reader.

**Band 2**  Task set attempted but not adequately achieved because of:

- Some omissions and/or irrelevant material.
- Range of structure and vocabulary rather limited; errors may obscure communication.
- Inconsistent organisation; few linking devices.
- Unsuccessful attempts at appropriate presentation and register.

Overall: message not clearly communicated to target reader.

**Band 1**  Task set not achieved because of:

- Notable omissions and/or considerable irrelevance.
- Narrow range of vocabulary and structure; little or no language control.
- Lack of organisation and linking devices.
- Little or no awareness of appropriate presentation and register.

Overall: a very negative effect on the target reader.

**Band 0**  Too little language for assessment.

Figure 7.5  FCE scoring rubric (UCLES, 1997)

The FCE Writing Paper is weighted to 40 points, as are the four other FCE papers. After weighting, the five FCE papers total 200 points. The candidate's FCE grade is based on the total score gained by the candidate in all five papers. Candidates do not 'pass' or 'fail' in a particular paper, but rather in the examination as a whole. Results are reported as three passing grades (A, B, and C) and two failing grades (D and E). Every candidate receives a Statement of Results showing their FCE grade and also a graphical display of their performance in each of the five test papers. These are shown against the scale Exceptional – Good – Borderline – Weak and indicate the candidate's relative performance in each paper.

## Discussion

Like the TOEFL, the FCE is a relatively high-stakes test, as a passing score on the test is a requirement for certain types of employment or areas of study. The FCE is taken by a wider range of candidates than the TOEFL, however, and for more varied purposes, and this consideration has certain consequences for test design. Some of the distinguishing features of the FCE vis-à-vis the TOEFL are: a longer testing time for writing (90 minutes as opposed to 30 minutes); one compulsory and one optional task as opposed to a single compulsory task; a wider variety of task types; task-specific marking schemes; and lack of double rating for all writing samples.

### Construct
Compared to the TOEFL, the construct being measured by the FCE is somewhat more difficult to define, as test takers have several very different writing options to choose from. The published FCE literature does not provide an explicit definition of the writing construct other than stating that 'candidates are assessed as to their ability to write non-specialised task types such as letters, articles, reports and compositions for a given purpose and target reader' (UCLES, 2001). The FCE, with two tasks, samples the domain of interest somewhat more widely than the TOEFL, and the different rating scales reflect the fact that different genres and tasks make use of different dimensions of writing ability and thus may give a truer picture of the test takers' range of abilities in writing than does the TOEFL. On the other hand,

the variety of possible test tasks in the FCE may make it difficult to say exactly what it is that the FCE is testing, as two test takers writing on very different tasks may arrive at similar scores through very different means.

### Authenticity

The issue of what constitutes an authentic writing task for FCE test takers is rather difficult to define, since authenticity is related to the TLU situations of the test takers, which are quite heterogeneous among the FCE candidature. While some test takers may need to write in English for educational or employment purposes, others may only need to use English for occasional correspondence, for example in making travel arrangements. The developers of the FCE have chosen to allow test takers a choice between several different task types, in the hopes that test takers will find one of the tasks relevant to their backgrounds and goals for learning English. The tasks themselves simulate genuine real-world tasks, and the fact that an audience and purpose are specified for each task adds to their authenticity. Furthermore, the rating scale specifically addresses the appropriateness of the writing vis-à-vis the specified audience and purpose in terms of register and presentation, which also adds to the authenticity of the test, as test takers are rewarded for tailoring their response to a specific audience. On the other hand, the variety of test tasks may detract from reliability and make it more difficult to ensure that the test is measuring the same construct for different test takers, as mentioned above.

### Other aspects of test usefulness

Whereas the TOEFL writing test privileges reliability by restricting the task types to a narrow range and by double rating all scripts, the FCE privileges authenticity and interactivity, by allowing examinees to respond to the task that they feel best equipped to handle given their own background characteristics and language use needs. Furthermore, the FCE uses two writing tasks rather than one, which allows generalization to a broader domain of writing. However, the use of multiple writing tasks increases the amount of resources that must be dedicated to test scoring. Instead of double-rating each script, therefore, the developers of the FCE have chosen to address reliability through other, less costly means, as described above.

# International English Language Testing System (IELTS)

## Test purpose

The purpose of IELTS (IELTS, 2002) is to assess the language ability of candidates who need to study at the post-secondary or university level or work in a professional capacity where English is used as the language of communication. Thus the level of English targeted by IELTS is more similar to the TOEFL than to the FCE, which is targeted at a somewhat lower level of English proficiency. IELTS is jointly managed by UCLES, The British Council, and IDP Education Australia. The test consists of four sections. Listening, Speaking, Reading, and Writing. For the Reading and Writing sections, candidates choose either the General Training or Academic Module. Both the General Training and Academic Writing Modules take 60 minutes. Total test time is 2 hours 45 minutes.

## Test content

Both the General Training and Academic Modules consist of two tasks, a shorter task of at least 150 words and a longer task of at least 250 words. Examinees are advised to spend 20 minutes on the first task and 40 minutes on the second task. The main differences between the two modules are the topic areas (general versus academic) and the complexity of the tasks.

### General Training Module
In the General Training Module, the first task is to respond to a given problem with a letter of request or explanation (see Figure 7.6 for a sample task). The second task requires examinees to write an essay or report in which they provide factual information, outline a problem and suggest a solution, present and justify an opinion, or present and evaluate an argument (an example is provided in Figure 7.7). For both tasks, the topics are of general interest.

### Academic Module
In the Academic Module, the first task requires examinees to look at a diagram or table and to present the information in their own words (see Figure 7.8). In this task, examinees might be asked to organize,

**WRITING TASK 1**

You should spend about 20 minutes on this task.

> *You rent a house through an agency. The heating system has stopped working. You phoned the agency a week ago but it has still not been repaired.*
>
> *Write a letter to the agency. Explain the situation and tell them what you want them to do about it.*

You should write at least 150 words.

You do **NOT** need to write your own address.

Begin your letter as follows:

*Dear Sir/Madam:*

Figure 7.6 IELTS general training writing task 1 (sample)

**WRITING TASK 2**

You should spend about 40 minutes on this task.

You have to write about the following topic.

> *Some businessmen now say that no one can smoke cigarettes in any of their offices. Some governments have banned smoking in all public places.*
>
> *This is a good idea but it alo takes away some of our freedom.*
>
> *Do you agree or disagree?*
>
> *Give reasons for your answer.*

You should write at least 250 words.

Figure 7.7 IELTS general training writing task 2 (sample)

present, and compare data, describe an object, a process, or a sequence of events, or explain how something works. For the second task, examinees are presented with a point of view, argument, or problem; they must either present the solution to a problem, present and justify an opinion, compare and contrast evidence, opinions and implications, or evaluate and challenge ideas, evidence or an argument (Figure 7.9). Topics are of general interest and the issues raised are 'interesting, suitable for and easily understood by candidates entering postgraduate or undergraduate studies' (IELTS, January 2002, p 12).

**WRITING TASK 1**

You should spend about 20 minutes on this task.

> *The graph below shows the different modes of transportation used to travel to and from work in one European city, in 1950, 1970 and 1990.*
>
> *Write a report for a University lecturer describing the information shown below.*

You should write at least 150 words.

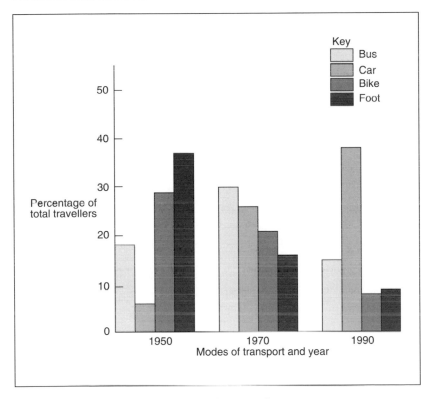

Figure 7.8  IELTS academic writing task 1 (sample)

## Scoring

Scores on the IELTS are reported as band scores between 1 (non user) and 9 (expert user). Separate band scores are reported for each skill section as well as an overall band score. The overall band descriptors are found in Figure 7.10. IELTS also provides guidelines for inter-

---

**WRITING TASK 2**

You should spend about 40 minutes on this task.

Present a written argument or case to an educated reader with no specialist knowledge of the following topic.

> *It is inevitable that as technology develops traditional cultures must be lost. Technology and tradition are incompatible – you cannot have both together.*
>
> *To what extent do you agree or disagree with this opinion?*

You should use your own ideas, knowledge and experience and support your arguments with examples and relevant evidence.

You should write at least 250 words.

---

Figure 7.9  IELTS acadmic writing task 2 (sample)

preting the band scores in terms of acceptability for different types of academic or training courses (see Table 7.1). Writing scripts are assessed by trained and certificated IELTS examiners at the local testing center. Each task is assessed independently and the assessment of Task 2 carries more weight in marking than Task 1, in accordance with the recommended time allocation. Task 1 scripts are assessed on the following criteria: Task Fulfilment; Coherence and Cohesion; Vocabulary and Sentence Structure. Task 2 scripts are assessed on Arguments, Ideas and Evidence; Communicative Quality; Vocabulary and Sentence Structure. Detailed rating scale descriptors have been developed which describe written performance at the 9 IELTS bands. These rating scale descriptors are confidential but the IELTS Specimen Materials provide sample candidate scripts and the band scores awarded together with examiner comments. Second marking is compulsory where inconsistent profile scores are identified across the four skills. In addition, regular sample monitoring is conducted to maintain a check on the system-wide reliability of writing assessment. Centers are requested to send a certain number of scripts to UCLES over a specific period. The scripts are selected in such a way as to ensure that all examiners working during that period are represented. Feedback on each examiner's performance is given to each center monitored (Linda Taylor, personal communication, April 2001).

**9 Expert User**
Has fully operational command of the language: appropriate, accurate and fluent with complete understanding.

**8 Very Good User**
Has fully operational command of the language with only occasional unsystematic inaccuracies and inappropriacies. Misunderstandings may occur in unfamiliar situations. Handles complex detailed argumentation well.

**7 Good User**
Has operational command of the language, though with occasional inaccuracies, inappropriacies and misunderstandings in some situations. Generally handles complex language well and understands detailed reasoning.

**6 Competent User**
Has generally effective command of the language despite some inaccuracies, inappropriacies and misunderstandings. Can use and understand fairly complex language, particularly in familiar situations.

**5 Modest User**
Has partial command of the language, coping with overall meaning in most situations, though is likely to make many mistakes. Should be able to handle basic communication in own field.

**4 Limited User**
Basic competence is limited to familiar situations. Has frequent problems in understanding and expression. Is not able to use complex language.

**3 Extremely Limited User**
Conveys and understands only general meaning in very familiar situations. Frequent breakdowns in communication occur.

**2 Intermittent User**
No real communication is possible except for the most basic information using isolated words or short formulae in familiar situations and to meet immediate needs. Has great difficulty understanding spoken and written English.

**1 Non User**
Essentially has no ability to use the language beyond possibly a few isolated words.

**0 Did not attempt the test**
No assessable information provided.

Figure 7.10.  IELTS bands (IELTS, 2002: 20)

Table 7.1. *IELTS band interpretations (IELTS, 2002: 22)*

| Band | Linguistically demanding **academic** courses | Linguistically less demanding **academic** courses | Linguistically demanding **training courses** | Linguistically less demanding **training courses** |
|---|---|---|---|---|
| | e.g. Medicine, Law, Linguistics, Journalism, Library Studies | e.g. Agriculture, Pure Mathematics, Technology, Computer-based work, Tele-communications | e.g. Air Traffic Control, Engineering, Pure Applied Sciences, Industrial Safety | e.g. Animal Husbandry, Catering, Fire Services |
| **9.0–7.5** | Acceptable | Acceptable | Acceptable | Acceptable |
| **7.0** | Probably Acceptable | Acceptable | Acceptable | Acceptable |
| **6.5** | English study needed | Probably Acceptable | Acceptable | Acceptable |
| **6.0** | English study needed | English study needed | Probably Acceptable | Acceptable |
| **5.5** | English study needed | English study needed | English study needed | Probably Acceptable |

## Discussion

The IELTS is chiefly used for two main purposes – higher education and immigration – and is thus a high-stakes test. Like the TOEFL and the FCE, the IELTS is administered on a large scale, and therefore efficient scoring is an essential element of the test. Similar to the FCE, the IELTS is used for both academic and non-academic purposes and so needs to address the writing goals of these different populations. Some of the distinctive features of the IELTS writing section are the choice between the General Training Module and the Academic Module, the use of two tasks of different lengths and weightings, the use of analytic scales that differ between the first and second tasks, and the use of double-rating of scripts when there is an uneven profile.

### *Construct*
The published IELTS documentation does not provide an explicit definition of the writing construct being measured in the test, beyond

specifying the types of tasks that test takers will encounter in the test. For example, the description of the General Training Module in the IELTS handbook describes the first task as follows: 'Depending on the task suggested, candidates are assessed on their ability to: engage in personal communication; elicit and provide general factual information; express needs, wants, likes, and dislikes; express opinions (views, complaints, etc.) . . . Part of the task realisation is to respond appropriately in terms of register, rhetorical organisation, style and content' (IELTS 2000a: 13). It is clear from the scoring criteria, however, that the construct includes aspects of organizational competence such as vocabulary, sentence structure, and cohesion as part of what is considered successful execution of the functions elicited by the writing tasks.

Like the FCE, the IELTS requires test takers to complete two different writing tasks, thus sampling the domain of writing ability more broadly than does the TOEFL. The IELTS goes further than the FCE, however, in explicitly distinguishing between general-purpose writing and academic writing by allowing test takers to choose between the two modules. It is interesting to note that, while the tasks differ in complexity across the General Training and Academic Modules, both modules use the same scoring criteria, indicating that the IELTS developers see the same underlying construct at work in both modules. The real difference in criteria is found between those for the shorter informational task and those for the longer argumentative task, which represents a recognition that these different genres call for different strategies on the part of the writer and that different aspects of writing are salient in their evaluation. Finally, the use of an analytic scale reflects the fact that writing involves a complex interaction between several different dimensions of language and cognition, which may not always develop at the same rate within individuals.

### Authenticity

Like the FCE, the IELTS is taken by test takers for a variety of purposes, making it a challenge to find writing tasks that are authentic for the test-taker population. While the FCE offers a range of tasks from which test takers can choose, the developers of the IELTS have taken a different approach to this issue: allowing test takers to choose either the General or the Academic Module, but with no choice of task within modules. This approach recognizes the differences in the domains of writing between academic and non-academic writers but avoids some of the difficulties associated with a large range of possible test tasks that were discussed with reference to the FCE above.

### Other aspects of test usefulness

Like the FCE, scoring the IELTS requires a substantial commitment of resources, due to the use of analytic scales and multiple writing tasks. Adequate reliability is still a concern, however, as the IELTS is a high-stakes test and can have serious consequences for individual test takers. Rather than having every script double rated, the IELTS is similar to the FCE in that other means of ensuring consistency of scoring are in place, including double-rating when the overall profile of the test taker is uneven. This procedure is useful for identifying the most likely instances of rater error without having to double rate every script.

It should be noted that IELTS is developing a computer-based variant of the test, in which test takers will have the option of writing their essays by hand or on the computer (IELTS 2000b). It is likely that IELTS will face some of the same issues of computer-based writing assessment that are discussed with reference to the TOEFL above (see p. 141ff.).

## Basic English Skills Test (BEST)

### Test purpose

The BEST is intended for use with limited-English-speaking adults for whom information on the attainment of basic functional language skills is needed (Center for Applied Linguistics, 1989: 2). The test is designed to be used for placement into ESL courses, progress testing for development of 'survival' skills, diagnostic testing, screening for vocational training, and program evaluation.

### Test content

The test consists of an Oral Interview Section, administered individually, and a Literacy Skills Section, which can be group-administered. The Literacy Skills Section contains a number of basic functional literacy tasks. Reading tasks include reading calendars, food and clothing labels, telephone directories, train schedules, ads and notices, and short informational passages. Writing tasks include filling out personal information (name and address) on a form, writing a check, addressing an envelope, and writing notes. For the purposes of this discussion, I will concentrate only on Part 11:Writing Notes, which is the only section of the test that involves writing connected discourse. This section of the test consists of two items, each of which asks the test taker to write three to four sentences on a given topic. The items are intended to represent genuine communicative tasks that would be relevant to the test-taker population, such as a note to a landlord. Example test items and responses are found in Figures 7.11 and 7.12 (p. 164).

## Scoring

Since the BEST is intended to be administered and scored locally, the BEST Test Manual (CAL, 1989) provides detailed information about how to score the writing tasks. Unlike the other tests considered so far in this chapter, no provisions are made for double-rating or monitoring rater reliability. The writing samples are scored strictly on the basis of the amount of communicative information appropriate to the task conveyed in the writing. The scale that is used is found in Figure 7.13. The test manual makes it clear that writing must be on-task to be scored; if a test taker writes on the wrong topic the score will be 0 even if the writing effectively addresses a task other than the assigned one. Accuracy of grammar and vocabulary are not considerations except insofar as they contribute to the communicative effectiveness of the writing. The scores on the note-writing tasks are added to the scores on the other reading and writing tasks in the Literacy Skills Section of the BEST, and information is given in the BEST Test Manual about how to use the scores for placement and diagnosis.

## Discussion

The BEST Literacy Skills Test is a relatively low-stakes test, as it is intended for placement and diagnostic purposes. Unlike the other tests considered so far, the BEST is primarily intended for adult English language learners at the beginning stages of language learning, and thus both the writing needs of this population and the

---

**Write a note to your English teacher telling him or her why you can't go to class tomorrow. Write 3–4 sentences.**

*Jan. 4. 2000*

*Dear GARY*

*good morning.   I will absent tomorrow because I have*

*appointment with the Public Aid Caseworker.   so I'm*

*very sorry to you. I will come back class on Jan. 6. 2000*

*Thank you*

---

Figure 7.11 Sample BEST writing task (CAL, 1989)

---

**Write a note to your landlord explaining why the rent is late. Write 3–4 sentences.**

Dear Mr George Tom

My name is IAN. I love at your apartment in room 3. I can't

pay the rent of this month now, but I'd pay the rent. This

month for you on next week.

I am very sorry, because this month I have to pay a new

washmachine. I hope you understand for me.

---

Figure 7.12 Sample BEST writing task (CAL, 1989)

criteria by which the writing is scored are quite different from those of the TOEFL, the FCE, and the IELTS. Some of the distinctive features of the BEST are the short, functional writing tasks and the simple rating scale based on communicative effectiveness and task completion rather than linguistic accuracy.

### *Construct*

The construct being measured by the BEST Literacy Skills Section stands in clear contrast to that measured by the other tests considered up to this point. For the population of test takers targeted by the BEST, writing is defined strictly as communicating a simple message

---

**Writing Notes**

This part consists of 2 items. Each item asks the examinee to write 3 to 4 sentences on the topic given. Responses, **as a whole**, should be scored as follows:

5 = An extensive amount of **relevant**, comprehensible information is conveyed. Accuracy in grammar or spelling is not required. If a letter was requested, letter form is **NOT** required.

3 = A reasonable amount of **relevant**, comprehensible information is conveyed; examinee shows an attempt at elaboration.

1 = Only "bare bones" information is given in response to the question. This score should be awarded if any amount of relevant, comprehensible writing is present.

0 = Some writing is present, but it is either irrelevant to the question or completely incomprehensible; no writing at all is present.

   Note that in-between scores, i.e., 2 or 4, **cannot** be awarded. Responses that clearly demonstrate writing proficiency but are irrelevant or off-topic should be given special consideration. In such cases the examinee may have prepared a response beforehand or may have misinterpreted the question. In the latter case, the test score may underestimate the true writing proficiency of the examinee. Other available information on the examinee may indicate whether this is the case.

---

Figure 7.13 BEST scoring guide

through the medium of writing rather than generating and developing ideas, using accurate standard language, or the other aspects of writing tested by the TOEFL, FCE, and IELTS. Communicative effectiveness receives much greater attention on the BEST than does linguistic accuracy; in fact, linguistic accuracy is not a consideration in the scoring criteria at all, except insofar as a lack of accuracy obscures the intended meaning.

### *Authenticity*

Similarly, what is an authentic writing task for the BEST test-taker population is quite different from what we have seen so far with the other three tests. The writing tasks are authentic for low-proficiency immigrants, in that they represent tasks that test takers could plausibly have reason to engage in, such as notes to a landlord or to a friend. The scoring guide – focusing strictly on completion of the task in a comprehensible way – enhances the test's authenticity, as communicative functioning rather than grammatical accuracy is how such tasks would be judged in a non-test situation.

*Other aspects of test usefulness*

One strength of the BEST for the targeted population is its practicality: the test is easy to administer and score, making it feasible for programs with limited resources. Since the BEST is a low-stakes test, reliability is less of a concern than it is for the other tests considered so far in this chapter. As the BEST is scored locally rather than centrally, there is no standard procedure for double-rating the writing tasks. A study of inter-rater reliability reported in the BEST Test Manual suggests that raters following the instructions presented in the Manual can rate with a high degree of consistency (inter-rater reliability for the writing portions of the Literacy Skills Section was reported at .98 to .99, depending on the form of the test (CAL, 1989).

## Contextualized Writing Assessment (CoWA)

### Test purpose

The Contextualized Writing Assessment (CoWA) is part of the Minnesota Language Proficiency Assessments (MLPA) battery of instruments developed for the purpose of certifying the second-language proficiency of secondary and post-secondary students. The battery consists of tests of listening, speaking, writing, and reading in French, German, and Spanish. The CoWA is a test of written proficiency at the Intermediate–Low level of the ACTFL Proficiency Guidelines (American Council on the Teaching of Foreign Languages, 1983). The CoWA is intended for use in situations where a writer's performance in a second language meets a minimal criterion, such as for fulfilling a graduation requirement or as a criterion for placement in post-secondary intermediate level course sequences (CARLA, 2001).

### Test content

The CoWA consists of five tasks, organized around a single theme. Each task is preceded by contextual information that relates the task to the theme. The contextualized tasks engage the test taker in a logical sequence of events with realistic writing tasks to accomplish in the target language. Each task also includes an optional brainstorming task that can be used as a warm-up. The brainstorming task allows students to organize and focus their ideas before writing. According to the CoWA website, 'All tasks in the CoWA target language functions, topics, and discourse within situations appropriate to the Intermediate level. Together the tasks represent the domain of Intermediate–Low performance.' Students are required to write at least seven sentences for each task. Figure 7.14 shows a sample theme with two related tasks.

## Scoring

The CoWA is scored on a pass/fail basis, using the criteria shown in Figure 7.5. As the figure shows, the criteria include task fulfillment, vocabulary, discourse, and correct formation of present time/immediate future. All criteria must be met on at least four of five tasks for a passing grade. Currently scoring is done centrally by trained raters at CARLA, but training materials are being prepared so that scoring can be done locally (Cheryl Alcaya, personal communication, March 29, 2001). Only non-passing performances are double-rated; passing performances are only double-rated if the rater has uncertainties about the score.

## Discussion

The CoWA is a moderately low-stakes test compared to the TOEFL, FCE, or IELTS, and it is used for relatively homogenous groups of test takers. The test is targeted at a higher level of proficiency than the BEST, but at a lower one than the other three tests under consideration. Some of the distinguishing features of the CoWA are the five thematically related tasks with optional pre-writing tasks; a simple, pass/fail scoring rubric, and double-rating only for non-passing scores.

### *Construct*
The CoWA is designed to measure writing performance at a level consistent with the intermediate–low level of the ACTFL Proficiency Guidelines, as noted above. While these descriptions have sometimes been criticized for lacking an empirical basis (see Alderson, 1991, and Valdéz *et al.*, 1992 for summaries of some of the problematic aspects of the ACTFL guidelines), they nevertheless represent a commonly

**Theme**: Keeping a journal

Your teacher has given you a chance to earn extra credit in your French/German/Spanish class by keeping a journal in French/German/Spanish. You decide to take advantage of the offer. After looking at the assignment, you decide to start right away.

**Write legibly**
**Write as much as you can**
**Show what you can do**

**Segment 1:** A great day

**Situation:** Your teacher tells you to think about what a really great day is like for you, and to write about it in your journal.

**Warm-up:** Think about your idea of a great day, then take a minute to fill in the following chart in French/German/Spanish or English.

- Your surroundings (location, sights, sounds, smells, etc.):
- What you do:
- Whom you are with, if anyone:

**Task:** Describe, in French/German/Spanish, your idea of a great day. You might want to include: 1) a description of your surroundings; 2) what you do; 3) whom you are with, if anyone; 4) how you feel.

**Describe your great day in seven to ten sentences in French/German/Spanish.**

---

**Segment 2:** A visitor

**Situation:** For your final entry, your teacher would like you to write some questions for a student from a French/German/Spanish-speaking area who will be coming to visit your class soon. The class has an opportunity for a question-and-answer session with the visitor and your teacher wants the class to be well prepared with questions.

**Warm-up:** Think about what you want to ask the French/German/Spanish-speaking visitor then respond below in French/German/ Spanish or English. You may want to ask about the climate, interesting places to visit, about what young people do for work and entertainment (i.e. music, food, going out, etc.).

Things you want to know:

**Task:** In your journal write at least five questions for the French/German/Spanish-speaking student who is coming to your class. You might want to include questions about: 1) the climate; 2) what young people do for work and entertainment; 3) interesting places to visit, etc.

**Write at least five questions for the visiting student in French/German/Spanish.**

---

Figure 7.14 Sample CoWA writing tasls

### Intermediate–Low Level Writing Test Scoring Criteria

The criteria below are all considered **necessary** conditions for a **minimally** acceptable performance at the Intermediate–Low level.

Consider each task holistically. If the overall performance on a task meets the criteria illustrated below, assign a score of 'Pass'.

| Task Fulfillment | Vocabulary |
|---|---|
| Discourse | Present Time |

**Task Fulfillment**
The format and content of the response generally meet the task requirements. (The task requirements are specified in bold.)

**Vocabulary**
- The response demonstrates ability to use an adequately broad vocabulary in response to topic.
- Writer does not have to resort to excessive repetition of words or phrases.
- Errors in word choice and/or rare lapses into English do not substantially obscure the message.

**Discourse**
- The response demonstrates ability to write basic sentence-level discourse. Simple sentences (S-V-C) are sufficient to meet the Intermediate–Low criteria; students **may** write complex sentences, but not always successfully.
- Writer is able to use more than one sentence pattern.
- Occasional direct translations from English are characteristic of this level.
- Intended meaning is not substantially obscured by grammatical errors.

**Present Time and Immediate Future**
- The response demonstrates student's ability to express present time, as called for by the task (i.e. there are few errors when conjugating **common** verbs in the present tense).
- The response may demonstrate student's ability to express the immediate future (to go + infinitive), and/or to use adverbs of time to express future actions.

**Assign a 'Non-pass' to responses that are unratable because they are:**
- Too short (fewer than 5 sentences / independent clauses, or fewer than 4 questions)
- Generally incomprehensible

Figure 7.15  CoWA scoring criteria

used framework for organizing and planning foreign-language study in the United States. Since the CoWA is intended to make pass/fail decisions at one level of proficiency only, the test developers can be explicit in the scoring rubric about the specific linguistic features of the written product that characterize this level, such as the use of the present tense and basic sentence-level discourse. The writing tasks, in turn, are designed to elicit the structures and discourse types of interest at this level of proficiency. In this sense, then, the CoWA has the most precisely defined construct of any of the tests considered in this chapter.

### Authenticity

Unlike the other tests that have been considered so far, the CoWA is primarily intended for students learning a language that they may never actually need outside the language classroom. One of the challenges in this situation is therefore determining what an authentic writing task is for these students. The developers of the CoWA have resolved this issue by explicitly targeting the language classroom itself as the TLU situation; the authenticity of the tasks thus derives from their plausibility as classroom writing tasks rather than as 'real-world' tasks. This authenticity is enhanced by the provision of optional brainstorming and pre-writing tasks, which simulate classroom writing conditions as well.

### Other aspects of test usefulness

As the CoWA is a relatively low-stakes test and is currently only given to small numbers of students, elaborate measures to ensure reliability are not as important as they are in tests such as the TOEFL, FCE, and IELTS, where many raters and test takers are involved. Double-rating of writing samples is thus only standard in cases where a failing score is given and negative consequences for an individual test taker are possible. This procedure allows the test to be scored with a minimum of resources while providing a mechanism to safeguard against errors that would lead to negative consequences. If the CoWA were to be adopted on a wider level with the potential for more serious consequences for test takers, it is likely that procedures to ensure adequate reliability would need to be developed, thus requiring additional resources to be committed to test scoring.

## Summary

In this chapter I have discussed five different tests of writing for second-language learners at various stages of language development and for several distinct purposes. For each context, the test developers have had to come up with answers to many of the questions raised in Chapters 5 and 6; for example, how many writing tasks to include, how wide a variety of tasks, what effect a variety of tasks will have on scoring, how to ensure sufficient reliability within the constraints of practicality, and so on. For each test, the developers have answered these questions differently for the purposes of their own test. This chapter has illustrated the choices that are made and the implications that these choices have for the various aspects of test usefulness.

# CHAPTER EIGHT

......................................................................................................

# Beyond the timed impromptu test: Classroom writing assessment

## Introduction

The format for writing tests that has been emphasized up to this point – specifically, the timed impromptu test – has a solid research base and has become widely accepted as a means for assessing writing in many situations. Cohen (1994) notes that assessments can be classified under three main uses: administrative, instructional, and research. Most of the situations in which such tests have been researched have been administrative tests – i.e. placement, general proficiency assessments, and the like. Timed impromptu writing tests are also frequently used in research, for example, to collect samples of productive language use for studies of second-language development under a variety of conditions. However, for most instructional test uses (i.e. diagnosis, evidence of progress, feedback to students, and evaluation of teaching or curriculum) the timed impromptu test has several limitations as a test of writing ability. The next two chapters of the book deal with classroom writing assessment and show how, while the model of writing assessment that has been developed and researched for large-scale testing does have benefits for classroom assessment, it is not the most appropriate model for most classroom test uses. This chapter discusses the role of writing in the L2 classroom and goes on to discuss how assessment models for large-scale testing can be applied and adapted for classroom testing. Chapter 9 discusses an assessment model that goes beyond consideration of single texts to consideration of a collection of written texts that show a student's depth of knowledge about writing, flexibility in using strategies for different audiences and writing purposes, and progress over a period of time – that is, portfolio assessment.

It should be noted that, while the alternatives to the timed impromptu writing test that are discussed in this chapter and Chapter 9 are particularly appropriate for classroom assessment, they are also becoming more widely used in large-scale testing as well. One reason for this shift in large-scale assessment is the influence of classroom teachers, whose concerns for forms of assessment that are more closely related to teaching practices and curricula have been a driving force in the move towards portfolio assessment and other less traditional ways of testing writing. Thus while this chapter focuses specifically on classroom assessment, the discussion of portfolios in Chapter 9 deals with portfolios both for classroom and large-scale use, and the general trend in writing assessment towards alternatives to the timed impromptu writing test will be raised again in Chapter 10, which deals with the future of writing assessment.

## The role of writing in L2 classes

When thinking about writing assessment for instructional purposes, we first need to consider how writing is used in classrooms in which L2 writing is a focus of instruction. As readers will recall from earlier discussions in this volume, there is a wide variety of such classes with different foci and student populations. For example, classes may be geared specifically towards writing or towards language proficiency in general, and may include second-language writers only, or second-language writers along with first-language writers. In all cases, however, we can distinguish first between writing that is evaluated by the teacher (i.e. given a grade or a numerical score) and writing that is not. Examples of the latter category might be journal entries, e-mail communications, lecture notes, and the like, which teachers may provide verbal comments on but do not give numerical scores or letter grades to. Since this type of writing does not fall under the rubric of writing assessment, we will not consider it further. As for writing that is evaluated, a further distinction can be made between out-of-class (untimed) and in-class (timed) writing. An important distinguishing feature between these two categories of writing activities is that out-of-class writing tends to be assigned as a learning activity, while in-class writing is ordinarily a testing activity, although there are certainly exceptions to this general tendency. That is, teachers tend to give out-of-class assignments for practice and consolidation of learning, while they tend to use in-class writing to find out whether students have met learning goals of the class.

To clarify this distinction, let us consider two different L2 teaching scenarios: a beginning-level foreign-language class and an advanced-level English for Academic Purposes (EAP) class. At lower levels of language proficiency, out-of-class writing is frequently assigned as homework to review and provide additional practice of language points that have been covered in class. Students can work at their own pace and use additional resources such as dictionaries and grammars to complete their assignments. In contrast, timed writing generally serves to test what students can write in the language on their own, without the aid of external resources.

In L2 writing classes for academic purposes, on the other hand, out-of-class assignments serve not just as language review and practice but also as a means for students to gain first-hand experience in the various phases of the writing process, from gathering and analyzing sources to generating ideas to drafting and revising essays. In the typical EAP class, students receive feedback from the instructor and/or from classmates on one or more early drafts of their essays before turning them in for a final grade; thus, a single writing assignment may be the product of several weeks' work. The emphasis on this type of writing is clearly on learning and practicing an extended writing process. In-class timed writing in academic settings serves the same testing purpose as discussed above; that is, it is used to test students' ability to plan and write an essay or other extended text without the use of outside assistance or resources. However, there is also another frequently cited rationale for in-class timed writing in these settings: students preparing for university study will need to produce writing under timed conditions in their academic courses, and thus it is essential for them to be able to organize, write, and edit a composition in a relatively short amount of time. In fact, recent research has shown that, for undergraduates in particular, timed writing on examinations is by far the most prevalent form of academic writing, at least in the United States (Carson *et al.*, 1992; Hale *et al.*, 1996).

While in-class and out-of-class writing tend to be used for different instructional purposes and to involve different constraints and resources, both types of writing provide information that teachers use to evaluate their students' progress and abilities in writing, and thus both can be considered under the general rubric of writing assessment. This chapter therefore deals with the assessment of both kinds of classroom writing tasks. Before considering how to approach writing assessment within the language classroom, it may be appropriate first to consider how classroom assessment differs from large-scale assessment.

## Contrasting classroom assessment and large-scale assessment

The model of writing assessment that has been considered so far has as its prototypical form one or at most a few writing tasks on a topic or topics unknown to examinees in advance and general enough to be accessible to virtually all examinees. These writing samples are then scored independently by at least two trained raters who are not aware of the identity of the examinees whose work they are reading. Looking at this model of assessment in terms of the Bachman and Palmer (1996) framework discussed in Chapter 3, one could argue that this model has been primarily driven by two aspects of test usefulness: reliability and practicality. The focus on these aspects of usefulness, as discussed previously in Chapter 4, was a historical necessity so that essay tests could be reasonably competitive with so-called indirect testing, which is highly reliable and highly efficient in terms of both time and resources.

In contrast, classroom teachers tend to be more concerned with other aspects of test usefulness: namely, construct validity, authenticity, interactiveness, and impact. While teachers may not use these terms to describe their concerns, they are usually interested in questions such as: How can I tell whether my students have met the writing goals of the class? How will the results of this test help my students improve their writing? How can I design writing prompts that students will be interested in and thus do their best work on? In other words, teachers are interested in how to make sure that their tests reflect the writing goals of their course (construct validity), whether they are meeting the students' needs for writing outside the classroom (authenticity), whether their students are engaged in the writing process (interactivity), and whether the feedback that their students get on their writing will help them identify and improve upon their weaknesses (impact). Of course, teachers are also interested in whether they are consistent in giving grades (relia-bility) and in providing sufficient feedback without consuming inor-dinate amounts of time (practicality), but these issues are not as prominent in classroom-based assessment as they are in large-scale assessment.

Because the concerns of large-scale and classroom assessment are different, it follows that the most appropriate format for the assess-ment is likely to be different as well. The timed impromptu writing test has been shown to be a useful test of writing ability under at least five conditions, to be presented below. In the following discussion, I will discuss these conditions and show how large-scale assessment and classroom assessment differ with regard to these conditions.

*1. For the decisions that are being made on the basis of a test score, a numerical score is all that is required.* Impromptu tests are most appropriate for large-scale testing, when a common metric must be used to discriminate between a large group of test takers in a short amount of time. The advantage of a timed impromptu test for large groups is that scoring can be done reliably and efficiently, particularly if only one or two prompts are used and raters need only assign a number to each written product rather than giving specific feedback on the strengths and weaknesses of the writing.

In a classroom situation, however, teachers generally want to give such feedback, and students want to receive it. Because smaller numbers of students need to be tested in the classroom, classroom teachers can take the time to comment constructively on their stu-dents' writing rather than simply assigning a number to it.

*2. Examinees are brought together for a short time only, for the sole purpose of the test.* An impromptu writing test can be administered within a short time period, generally from 30 minutes to three hours. This is an advantage for large-scale assessment, when time is limited and it is logistically difficult to bring examinees together on more than one occasion or for longer periods. This fact about impromptu tests means, however, that test takers have little or no opportunity to reflect on the topic either alone or in a group before writing about it, and the writing may thus represent a somewhat superficial considera-tion of the topic and a first draft only.

In the classroom, on the other hand, there is ample opportunity to prepare for writing about a topic, by reading about it, discussing it with other students and the teacher, and doing various pre-writing activities. Thus, the classroom provides much better opportunities to replicate the writing process that is involved with reflective writing outside the classroom, and classroom assessments can and should make use of these opportunities.

3. *Students with a variety of experience need to be tested.* Since an impromptu writing test is not tied to any particular curriculum or content, it is most appropriate for situations where students have come from different programs or schools in which they have studied different subjects and have had different types of writing instruction. For example, an impromptu test is a useful tool for placing students from different high schools into a university foreign language program.

In the classroom, however, particularly when the instructor is interested in achievement testing, this condition does not hold. On the contrary, the classroom teacher is specifically interested in whether the students have learned what was taught in class, regardless of their previous experiences. Thus, a classroom writing test can, and indeed should, be more narrowly focused to reflect the particular goals and curriculum of the classroom.

4. *The assessment will have positive, rather than negative, washback.* In large-scale language proficiency testing, a direct writing test is likely to have positive washback in situations where writing has not traditionally been a focus of instruction, as discussed previously in Chapter 3.

In a classroom, on the other hand, where the instructional focus is on the writing process, an impromptu writing test may have negative washback, particularly if it is a high-stakes test such as a final examination. In this case, students may perceive that the instruction in drafting, revising, and editing writing they have received is irrelevant to their immediate goal, which is to pass the test.

5. *The definition of the construct emphasizes the individual rather than the social aspects of writing.* As discussed in Chapter 2, we are ordinarily used to describing writing ability as something that resides within the individual, even though writing in the real world is frequently accomplished with the aid of interactions with other people. For example, in writing this chapter, I have relied on feedback from colleagues, graduate students, and the series editors, and even though I can say that I wrote this chapter, I have incorporated innumerable suggestions from other people, and I am certain that the final product

is much better because of these suggestions. In a test of writing, however, because we are making decisions about individuals, the definition of writing ability has traditionally been restricted to the cognitive and linguistic abilities of the individual test taker. This is particularly the case for large-scale assessment, in part because of the psychometric tradition from which large-scale writing assessment draws many of its procedures. A timed impromptu writing test is perhaps the best way to ensure that the examinee has in fact done the writing without outside assistance, as steps can be taken to keep the topic from becoming known before the test and to keep test takers from giving and receiving help to each other during the test.

For many classroom teachers, the individual view of writing ability is important as well, even in classrooms where students are encouraged to receive feedback on their writing from classmates, the instructor, and/or tutors before turning it in for a final grade. Since the teacher cannot always control or monitor the kind and extent of help that students are receiving on out-of-class writing, many teachers feel it is important to give in-class timed writing tests so that they can evaluate what the students are able to accomplish on their own.

On the other hand, for many teachers, particularly in academic contexts, the social aspects of writing are increasingly being recognized, and an evaluation of writing may also include consideration of the degree to which students have incorporated instructor and/or peer feedback in their writing. In evaluating a final written product, thus, it is no longer strictly the ability of the writer to use his or her own linguistic and cognitive resources to generate appropriate texts independently that is of issue, but rather the ability of the writer to make use of all available resources – including social interactions – to create a text that appropriately meets the needs of the audiences and fulfills a communicative goal. While this view of writing complicates the definition and measurement of the construct enormously, it is perhaps a more accurate view of writing in the real world and one that many contemporary writing teachers want to promote among their students. Clearly an impromptu writing test does not begin to measure the social aspects of writing that are being discussed here, and thus other forms of assessment are required when the construct is defined in this way.

## Applying aspects of the large-scale assessment model to classroom testing

The discussion above has demonstrated that the typical large-scale writing test – in which students write on a previously unknown topic for a set period of time – is inappropriate in several respects for classroom testing. As noted above, of all the potential virtues of timed impromptu tests for large-scale assessment, the most compelling for classroom assessment is the fact that a timed test can ensure that the writing produced is the work of the students themselves. Even this rationale, however, as we have seen, may not be convincing for many teachers who believe in process approaches to writing instruction, and that assessment and curriculum should be as closely integrated as possible.

However, we should not dismiss timed impromptu tests entirely as an assessment tool for the classroom. In some situations it is impractical to ask students to write outside of class – for example, with adult immigrant students who are learning a language for survival reasons and come to class in the evening after a full day's work – and in other situations there are good reasons for using in-class writing as a testing tool, as mentioned above. Rather, we should consider the lessons that have been learned from large-scale testing and apply them to the classroom where appropriate, and where they are not, modify them to take advantage of the benefits that the classroom provides.

As in large-scale assessment, designing classroom assessment procedures involves two main considerations: task design and scoring procedures. For both of these considerations there exists a considerable body of knowledge and experience gained from research on large-scale testing that we can apply to classroom testing. I will discuss these briefly before going on to discuss alternatives to the timed impromptu writing task for classroom assessment.

### Task design

The classroom teacher has many advantages over the designer of large-scale writing tests in terms of being able to design writing tasks that are specifically geared towards the goals of the course and the background and needs of the students. Classroom writing tasks will be geared towards a relatively narrow target language use (TLU) domain (Bachman and Palmer, 1996): that is, writing tasks that reflect the specific language-learning goals of the class or, in the case of academic or professional writing courses, writing outside the language or writing classroom. In contrast, large-scale writing test tasks must be targeted at a potentially much broader TLU domain of 'real-world' writing tasks and thus there is a much wider range of possible test tasks to draw from. In this sense, then, task design for teachers is easier than it is for large-scale test writers, as teachers do not need to consider the needs of large heterogeneous groups of students. However, two important lessons in task design can be drawn from the research on large-scale testing for classroom teachers.

The first lesson is that research has highlighted the importance of carefully considering various elements of the task, from the discourse mode to the specificity of the instructions to whether or not to offer a choice of prompts. These factors will remain the same for classroom assessment as for large-scale assessment, except that the classroom teacher can focus the task more narrowly on the features of writing that are important in class rather than attempting to make tasks as general as possible. In other words, classroom teachers need to consider the same four minimum requirements for designing writing tasks that were put forward by White (1994) and discussed at greater length in Chapter 5: clarity, validity, reliability, and interest. That is, the prompt must be written clearly so that test takers know what is expected of them; the task must be valid, in that it represents the skill of interest and elicits writing that accurately represents test takers' abilities; scoring procedures must be consistent, so as to yield reliable scores; and the test task should be interesting to both the writer and the reader.

The other important lesson in task design from large-scale testing that can be applied to classroom testing is the process of test development. In Chapter 5, a process of test development for writing tests was described, which includes designing the test, operationalizing it, and administering it. This process is essentially the same for designing classroom-based tests as it is for large-scale tests: one first needs to define the ability being tested, decide how best to test it, design appropriate tasks, and administer them to students. For two reasons, however, the process for classroom teachers may be somewhat simplified. First, classroom teachers rarely have the time and resources to devote to a full-scale test development effort, particularly if the test will only be administered one time to a single group of students. Second, there is generally less at stake in a classroom test than in a large-scale test, and therefore the consequences are less serious if the test does not meet rigorous standards of usefulness, such as reliability, for example.

One important aspect of the test development process that should not be neglected by classroom teachers, however, is the development of test specifications. While specifications that are to be used by an individual teacher do not need to be as detailed as those that will be used by several different people in test development, there are several ways in which test specifications can be beneficial to classroom teachers. First, the process of developing specifications ensures that the teacher has carefully considered both the specific aspects of writing that he or she is attempting to test and how those aspects of writing are operationalized in test tasks and scoring procedures. Clear specifications can help teachers be more consistent in developing test tasks, and, when shared by other teachers in the same program, can help maintain similar evaluation standards across different sections of the same course. Another advantage of having written specifications for classroom tests is that they can be shared with students, thus giving students a clear idea of what will be assessed and on what criteria their writing will be evaluated.

Another important aspect of the test development process described in Chapter 5 that can be valuable in the classroom is the pre-testing of prompts before actually administering them to students. While a full-scale pre-testing may not always be feasible, it is a fairly easy matter at least to have one or two colleagues look at potential test tasks to make sure that they are clear and feasible for the time allotted, and to make sure that they cover the content domain of the course. The issue of pre-testing may be somewhat less of an issue for out-of-class writing assignments, as an out-of-class assignment can be negotiated and clarifications made when necessary. On the other hand, if students are going to put a great deal of time and effort into an out-of-class paper, it behooves the teacher to make sure that students are given adequate guidance from the start to avoid confusion and the need for repeated clarification or modifications of instructions. Of course, teachers can learn from one term's experience and modify writing assignments for the next time they teach the same course.

Reid and Kroll (1995) suggest that teachers of different classes or even at different institutions can help each other out by pilot testing each other's writing tasks in their classrooms. They point out that pre-testing of classroom writing assignments involves scrutiny of the prompt itself as well as the written responses to the prompt. According to Reid and Kroll, pre-tested prompts can be considered successful if they fulfill three criteria. First, the prompt needs to discriminate well among the pre-test population: that is, those who have mastered the course content (perhaps as measured by the teacher's knowledge of the students' work thus far) should perform better on the whole than students who have not done so. Second, the written products must be easy to read and to evaluate. Finally, students should be able to write to their potential: that is, the prompt should challenge more able students without being so challenging that less able students cannot find something to write about.

For prompts that seem to be problematic, Reid and Kroll provide a list of questions that can be used to diagnose specific problems with prompts. These questions are summarized in Table 8.1. While the questions are written with academic writing in mind, they are for the most part relevant to non-academic writing as well.

## Scoring procedures

Scoring is perhaps the area where experience from large-scale testing can most benefit classroom teachers. Specifically, the use of explicit scoring rubrics and training to score both in-class and out-of-class writing samples has a number of benefits for the classroom teacher. First, students can be given the rubric in advance and are thus made aware of what the criteria are on which their writing will be judged. In this sense, the rubric becomes a teaching tool as well as a testing tool, as Hamp-Lyons (1991c) and Ferris and Hedgcock (1998) have pointed out. By applying the rubric in class to their own writing and the writing of others, students can come to a better understanding of their teacher's expectations for writing and whether their own writing meets those expectations.

Second, use of a scoring rubric provides the instructor with a standard by which to score papers consistently. As discussed previously, scoring rubrics for large-scale assessment have been shown to be an important factor in increasing inter-rater reliability, and the same is true for classroom assessment. As Ferris and Hedgcock state:

Table 8.1. *Questions to guide an analysis of pre-tested prompts (Reid and Kroll, 1995)*

Is the context of the prompt
- irrelevant to the course or to the students?
- unreasonable, considering the students' capabilities and learning objectives?

Is the content
- too broad to be accomplished within the assignment parameters?
- outside the expertise, experience, or researchability of the student-writers?

Is the language of the instructions or the prompt
- too simple or too complex?
- culturally biased?
- too abstract or philosophical?
- unacademic or otherwise inappropriate?

Are the responses
- trite?
- highly emotional?
- similar?
- misleading or confusing?

> the systematic application of level-appropriate, clear, and specific scoring criteria can contribute to an instructor's reliability in evaluating student work by focusing his or her attention on specific features of student writing as reflected in course objectives and task goals. Consistent use of such criteria and tools can likewise provide an instructor with practice that, over time, will enable him or her to assign scores and offer feedback with confidence.
>
> (Ferris and Hedgcock, 1998: 230)

Rubrics are also valuable for maintaining consistency of standards across different instructors of the same class within the same program. This is especially important in language programs that have several proficiency levels, as it reduces the likelihood that students will be promoted or held back in error. Instructors at the same level of proficiency can grade each other's papers, providing an additional check on scoring reliability. Furthermore, if instructors have been involved in the development of the rubric, they are more likely to be invested in it and thus to use it consistently.

A fourth advantage of using a scoring rubric is that it can simplify the grading process, as teachers can use checklists or numerical scores rather than writing lengthy comments or correcting every stylistic or grammatical infelicity. This is a particularly important point both in terms of saving time for the teacher and in providing useful feedback to students. While many writing teachers feel it is their obligation to point out every error in their students' writing, and students claim to want every error pointed out, this approach to error correction is problematic for a number of reasons. First, as Truscott (1996) has noted, there exists little empirical evidence that grammar correction in writing is effective (i.e. leads to improvements in grammar in subsequent writing assignments). Truscott goes so far as to maintain that grammar correction may indeed be harmful, as it is discouraging to students, teachers are not always able to correctly diagnose and explain errors, and excessive attention to error correction takes time away from focusing on more important aspects of writing. Rather than attempting to correct every error, therefore, a writing teacher may be better off choosing a few error types to concentrate on (see Ferris and Hedgcock, 1998, and Reid, 1998, for useful discussions of how to prioritize error types). A scoring rubric that gives students an overall sense of their performance, and that is easy for instructors to use and for students to understand, is a helpful tool for the writing teacher and may be preferable to other less systematic forms of feedback. Examples of specific classroom scoring rubrics that include reference to various error patterns are presented in the following section.

It should be emphasized that scoring rubrics developed for large-scale testing are not necessarily the most appropriate for classroom use and should not be adopted wholesale, without a serious consideration of the goals of the class and the specifics of the assessment context. For example, the Jacobs et al. (1981) scale, discussed in Chapter 6, gives the most weight to content, followed by language use (grammar), with organization and vocabulary given slightly less weight. However, in an academic writing class that focuses principally on content development and appropriate organization for academic writing, these priorities should be reflected in the scoring rubric, with organization more heavily weighted than language use. Examples of scoring rubrics that were developed for specific classroom situations are presented in the next section of this chapter.

To summarize, many of the considerations in large-scale assessment are also important for classroom assessment. In particular, the classroom teacher should be careful to assign writing tasks – whether for in-class or out-of-class writing – that are relevant to the appropriate TLU domain, clearly written, accessible to all students, engaging, and feasible within the constraints of time and available resources, and to have clear, consistent criteria for scoring the written product. On the other hand, the classroom teacher has the advantage of smaller numbers of students, knowing the students personally, extended time with the students, and less heterogeneity of experience, and can use these advantages to create more authentic, richer forms of assessment, in terms of both the tasks and the scoring rubrics, than are possible in large-scale assessments. We will now look at how classroom teachers can take advantage of these factors to modify the impromptu writing test model for classroom assessment purposes.

## Modifying the large-scale assessment model for classroom testing

As noted earlier in this chapter, in the classroom as opposed to large-scale testing, there is less pressure to privilege reliability and practicality as it relates to large-scale testing – that is, scoring large numbers of student writing samples efficiently – and the classroom teacher is thus able to focus more on other aspects of test usefulness: construct validity, authenticity, interactiveness, and impact. In order to maximize these aspects, a number of alternatives and modifications to the standard timed impromptu writing test can be made. In this section of the chapter, I will outline some of these modifications.

  1. *Evaluate not just in-class but out-of-class writing.* In previous chapters, it was stated that a timed writing test lacks a certain amount of authenticity because the vast majority of writing that is done outside of a testing situation is not done under strict time limits. The first principle in classroom writing assessment, then, is that teachers should not rely solely on in-class writing as evidence of writing ability. While there are frequently good reasons for using in-class writing, and while in some teaching situations it may not be feasible or appropriate to ask students to write outside of class, wherever possible teachers should include both in-class and out-of-class writing in their assessments.

  2. *Evaluate more than one writing sample.* The point has been made in numerous places in this volume that writing ability is not a simple

construct but involves numerous processes, and that a single writing sample written for a specific audience and purpose is extremely limited in its ability to represent the writer's ability to write for other situations, audiences, and purposes. This realization has given rise to the increased popularity of portfolio assessment for classroom use (and for large-scale assessments as well, incidentally), which will be discussed in detail in the next chapter. Short of collecting full-fledged writing portfolios, however, teachers can include multiple writing tasks on classroom tests and use multiple samples of out-of-class writing in their assessments.

*3. Build authenticity and interactiveness into timed writing tasks.* In large-scale testing, as was discussed in Chapter 5, one of the challenges is coming up with writing tasks that are accessible to a wide variety of students but that are not so general as to be trite or banal. Again, classroom teachers have a tremendous advantage in this area, as they are able to tailor writing tasks to the interests and needs of their own students. In addition to ensuring that the writing task is relevant to out-of-class writing needs and interesting and motivating to students, both authenticity and interactivity can be addressed by building in two key components of the writing process: the cycle of schema building through reading, reflecting, and discussing a topic before it is written about, and the process of reflecting on a draft and revising it, either independently or taking into account feedback from others. We generally think of these two components as belonging to out-of-class writing assignments only; however, with some imagination it is possible to build them into timed writing tests as well, thus combining the benefits of the timed writing test with elements of authenticity that are often missing from such tests.

The easiest way to prepare students for a topic is to do some preliminary pre-writing work as a class before the actual writing is done. For example, on a diagnostic writing task at the beginning of a course where no time has been spent discussing or reading about a topic, a teacher can still help the class come up with ideas for a timed writing assignment by conducting a brainstorming session – that is, eliciting ideas from the class and listing them on the board, coming up with a conceptual map of the topic, or other strategies to get students thinking about the topic. In this way, students can devote more time to actual writing and editing rather than spending too much time trying to generate ideas for their writing.

When students have been in class together over a period of days or weeks, preparing students for a timed writing test is even easier. In many language classrooms, instruction is geared around specific content over a period of weeks or even months. In content-based language teaching, a major writing assignment is frequently the culmination of several weeks of study of a content area, comprising readings, listening texts, discussions, and short writing tasks such as summaries or journal entries. Many teachers find it useful to have students write a first draft of a major assignment in class as a graded timed writing assignment, and then allow them to revise the paper in their own time as a separate graded activity.

Another option for modifying the timed impromptu writing test format for classroom use that gives students an opportunity to reflect on their topic before writing is to provide the topic in advance and allow students to write an outline of what they intend to write before the test date. The outline can be handed in to the instructor before the test, and then returned to the student at the test itself. In this way, students can do much of the preliminary organizing and thinking about the topic but the actual writing is done in class.

Weigle and Jensen (1997) provide an example of a final examination in a university-level content-based ESL course that allows students to build up their knowledge of a topic before writing about it. In the final week of class, students view a videotaped lecture, take notes, and write a summary of the lecture. The lecture notes and summaries are collected by the teacher and kept until the day of the test. Students are also given a reading passage on the same topic, which they read at home and in their study groups but do not discuss in class. On the day of the test, the teacher returns the lecture notes and summaries, and gives students a clean copy of the reading passage along with comprehension questions on both the lecture and the reading. Finally, students are asked to write an essay in which they must take a position on the issue discussed in the lecture and reading, using information from their lecture notes and the reading to support their argument. Weigle and Jensen note that this format for the examination reflects more accurately the kind of writing that is expected of university students, in that they must synthesize information which has been gleaned from different sources and use this information to support their point of view.

While this format for an examination deals with one aspect of the writing process (i.e. using sources to gain information on a topic), it does not deal with another important aspect: the process of revision.

This, too, can be built into an examination, by spreading the test out over a period of one or more days. On the first day the topic can be given out to students, who are then given a set time to draft a response. The response is collected by the teacher, and then given back to the students at a later date, at which time students have another period of time to revise their papers. Teachers may even build a cycle of peer revision into this process, with students being allowed to review and comment on each other's papers – but with no intervening teacher feedback – so that some of the collaborative aspects of classroom writing are present in the test. The increasing popularity of networked classrooms and web-based virtual learning environments may make this process easier, as students are able to comment on each other's papers on-line, a development that is discussed in more depth in Chapter 10.

*4. Use scoring instruments that are specific to the assignment and to the instructional focus of the class, and that provide useful feedback to students.* As discussed above, one of the great contributions of large-scale assessment to classroom assessment is the practice of using well-designed scoring rubrics for enhancing reliability and construct validity. An advantage that classroom testing has over large-scale testing is that scoring rubrics can be more detailed and can also easily be modified to meet the needs of a particular classroom or a particular assignment.

As illustrations of scoring rubrics that meet specific classroom needs (rather than general language proficiency), I will discuss two rubrics that were developed for use in the Intensive English Program (IEP) at Georgia State University. The IEP, a pre-academic program that prepares students primarily for undergraduate work, has two separate writing classes at each of the highest three levels of proficiency. In one class, Academic Writing for University Examinations, the course materials focus on a single content area (e.g. US History) for an entire semester, and the writing focus is on in-class, timed writing analogous to what students will encounter in content-area tests (see Weigle and Nelson, 2001, for a complete description of this course). In the other class, Structure/Composition, students work on out-of-class essays and the writing process. The scoring rubrics used for these two classes are found in Figures 8.1 through 8.3.

These rubrics deal with two separate challenges in writing assessment. In Academic Writing for University Examinations, one of the challenges was developing a rubric for **text-responsible writing** (Leki and Carson, 1997); that is, writing that demonstrates understanding of a specific text or texts, since timed essay tests in content area classes are primarily concerned with this type of writing rather than more personal writing. As Leki and Carson point out, in most English composition and ESL classes, the focus in writing has traditionally been on developing and organizing ideas and using appropriate language. Students are frequently asked to use their own experience and opinions as content for their writing, and if a source text is used as input for the writing prompt, it is used primarily as a springboard for student writing rather than as content for which students are held accountable. Scoring rubrics such as those presented in Chapter 6, that have been developed by language rather than content specialists, reflect this priority, and frequently do not address the accuracy of content as an important criterion for grading.

However, accuracy of content is primary in text-responsible writing, and a good deal of research has shown that content area faculty are predominantly concerned with content accuracy rather than linguistic control (e.g. Santos, 1988; Mendelsohn and Cumming, 1987; Boldt *et al.*, 2001). The rubric developed for the Academic Writing course, excerpted in Figure 8.1, specifically targets thoroughness and accuracy of content. In addition, the weighting of the various scales reflects this prioritization, with content and organization worth 10 points each and language use 5 points. This rubric was developed jointly by instructors teaching the courses, and had an additional beneficial effect: because the rubric specifically addresses the accuracy of content, instructors needed to delineate explicitly what counts for accurate content on each test item, rather than grading them impressionistically. This in turn has led to instructors being more careful about the essay prompts that they write, to make sure that the expectations for each essay are clear and that the prompt elicits the appropriate information from the source texts. Thus, the development and use of the scoring rubric has led to improvements in test writing as well as scoring.

It should be noted that this scoring rubric was developed for a narrow TLU domain – essay examinations in content areas – and thus is similar in spirit to primary trait scoring discussed in Chapter 6. Scoring rubrics for other types of academic writing tasks, such as chemistry laboratory reports or literary analyses, would need to reflect the content and organization concerns of tasks in those TLU domains. While it may not always be feasible to develop a different

| **Content**<br>The essay: | **Organization**<br>The essay: | **Language Use**<br>The essay: |
|---|---|---|
| 9–10 | 9–10 | 5 |
| • is complete, accurate, and thorough.<br>• includes all important ideas and demonstrates an understanding of important relationships.<br>• is fully developed and includes specific facts or examples.<br>• contains no irrelevant information. | • is logically organized around major ideas, concepts or principles.<br>• restates the question accurately.<br>• develops ideas from general to specific.<br>• achieves coherence through the appropriate and varied use of academic language structures and other cohesive devices. | • is clearly written with few errors; errors do not interfere with comprehension.<br>• includes academic vocabulary that is rarely inaccurate or repetitive.<br>• includes generally accurate word forms and verb tenses.<br>• uses a variety of sentence types accurately.<br>• contains source text language that is well integrated with student-generated language. |
| 7–8 | 7–8 | 4 |
| • demonstrates a good understanding of the topic.<br>• includes most of the important ideas and shows a good understanding of important relationships.<br>• demonstrates good development of ideas and includes adequate supporting facts or examples.<br>• may contain some irrelevant information. | • is generally well organized around important ideas, concepts, or principles.<br>• includes a restatement of the question.<br>• develops most ideas from general to specific.<br>• achieves some coherence through the use of academic language structures and other cohesive devices. | • is clearly written with few errors; errors do not interfere with comprehension.<br>• uses generally accurate academic vocabulary.<br>• may include inaccurate word forms and verb tenses.<br>• uses simple and compound sentences accurately and attempts to use complex sentences.<br>• contains source text language that is adequately integrated with student-generated language. |

| 5–6 | 5–6 | 3 |
|---|---|---|
| • demonstrates some knowledge and understanding of the topic but may show gaps in the student's knowledge.<br>• includes some of the important ideas related to the topic and shows some but limited understanding of the relationships.<br>• develops ideas adequately and includes some supporting facts or examples.<br>• may be vague, repetitive, or not well developed, and may include misconceptions or some inaccurate information. | • is loosely organized around important ideas, concepts, or principles.<br>• attempts to restate the question.<br>• develops some ideas from general to specific while others are not sufficiently developed.<br>• uses some appropriate academic language and cohesive devices, though these may be repetitious. | • is generally clearly written with few errors; at most a few errors interfere with comprehension.<br>• demonstrates occasional problems with word choice.<br>• includes some inaccurate word forms and verb tenses.<br>• uses simple and compound sentences with occasional errors and may attempt complex sentences.<br>• demonstrates some reliance on source text language, not always integrated with student-generated text. |

Figure 8.1 Scoring rubric for academic writing course (excerpt)

scoring rubric for every writing assignment, instructors should make sure that there is an appropriate match between the writing task and the scoring rubric, and that both are reflective of the TLU domain.

The other course, Structure/Composition, highlights a different challenge for writing teachers. In this case, instructors are concerned with evaluating the writing process itself, rather than just the written product. This poses a dilemma for teachers who are genuinely concerned with teaching the writing process and with emphasizing pre-writing, writing, revising, and editing rather than producing a single draft of a text in a short period of time. Instructors frequently give feedback on intermediate drafts of writing, and often ask students to comment on each other's papers. Yet, unless students are held accountable for incorporating feedback into their final essays, some students may resist doing so. The approach to this dilemma that is being explored in the IEP at Georgia State University is to incorporate revising and editing into the final grade. The rubrics discussed here were developed on a trial basis and will certainly be revised before they are officially adopted; however, for the purposes of this discussion they can serve as models of how to one might be able to incorporate revision into a final grade. Figure 8.2 shows the rubric that was developed for use in the Structure/Composition classes, while Figure 8.3 shows the feedback sheet that is given to students. As Figure 8.2 indicates, students are given a numerical score for their content/ organization and language use based on the written product. On the first draft of a paper, students receive a tentative numerical score based on the two scales shown in Figure 8.2. On the final draft, however, students are also given a grade of excellent, very good, good, fair, or poor on revision and editing, as shown in the rightmost column of Figure 8.3. If students receive a low score for their revision and editing, their letter grade on the paper may be reduced. In this way, students are held responsible not only for the written product, but for aspects of the writing process as well. These examples have shown some ways in which classroom teachers can apply scoring rubrics for specific teaching situations. Especially in a program where several teachers are teaching the same course and students are promoted from one level to the next at least in part on the basis of their writing, whether on in-class or out-of-class writing tasks, scoring rubrics such as these can be important in maintaining consistency across and between levels and across instructors. They can be useful training tools for new teachers to help incorporate them into the culture of the program, and the process of developing rubrics can be beneficial to teachers as it provides them with opportunities to discuss and clarify the aspects of writing that they feel are most important.

## Summary

In this chapter, I have contrasted large-scale testing and classroom-based assessment of both in-class, timed writing and out-of-class, untimed writing. I have argued that the timed impromptu writing test, while it has many benefits for large-scale testing, is not always appropriate for classroom use. Much has been learned from the research on large-scale writing tests, however, that can be of use to classroom teachers as they design their own tests and evaluate their

| Content/Organization | Language Use<br>The essay: |
|---|---|
| **9-10** | **9-10** |
| • The treatment of the assignment completely fulfills the task expectations and the topic is addressed thoroughly.<br>• The introduction orients the reader effectively to the topic and to the author's thesis (purpose, plan, and focus).<br>• The conclusion effectively reinforces and comments on the thesis, providing closure to the essay.<br>• Fully developed evidence for generalizations and supporting ideas/arguments is provided in a relevant and credible way.<br>• Paragraphs are separate and logical units, fully developed, clearly related to the thesis and effectively connected to each other by appropriate, well-chosen, and varied transitions.<br>• Sentences within paragraphs form a well-connected series, using appropriate transition words and other cohesion devices. | • is clearly written with few errors; errors do not interfere with comprehension.<br>• includes accurate and diverse academic vocabulary.<br>• includes accurate word forms and verb tenses.<br>• uses a variety of sentence types accurately.<br>• incorporates ideas from assigned readings and/or outside sources without plagiarism; sources are cited correctly and paraphrased using a variety of techniques. |
| **7-8** | **7-8** |
| • The treatment of the assignment fulfills the task expectations competently and the topic is addressed clearly.<br>• The introduction orients the reader sufficiently to the topic and to the author's thesis.<br>• The conclusion competently reinforces and comments on the thesis.<br>• Strong evidence for generalizations and supporting ideas/arguments is provided in a relevant and credible way.<br>• Paragraphs are separate and logical units, well developed, clearly related to the thesis and well connected to each other by appropriate and varied transitions.<br>• Sentences within paragraphs form a well-connected series, using appropriate transition words and other cohesion devices. | • is clearly written with few errors; errors do not interfere with comprehension.<br>• includes academic vocabulary that is rarely inaccurate or repetitive.<br>• may include inaccurate word forms and verb tenses.<br>• uses a variety of sentence types.<br>• incorporates ideas from assigned readings and/or outside sources without plagiarism; most sources are cited correctly and paraphrased using a variety of techniques. |
| **5-6** | **5-6** |
| • The treatment of the assignment adequately fulfills the task expectations and the topic is addressed clearly.<br>• The introduction orients the reader sufficiently to the topic and to the author's thesis, though it may be brief and/or undeveloped.<br>• The conclusion reinforces and comments on the thesis. | • is generally clearly written with few errors; at most a few errors interfere with comprehension.<br>• demonstrates occasional problems with word choice.<br>• includes some inaccurate word forms and verb tenses. |

*(contd)*

| 5-6 | 5-6 |
|---|---|
| • Sufficient evidence for generalizations and supporting ideas/arguments is provided in a relevant and credible way.<br>• Paragraphs are separate and logical units, related to the thesis and connected to each other by appropriate transitions.<br>• Sentences within paragraphs form a connected series, using appropriate transition words and other cohesion devices. | • uses a variety of sentence types with occasional errors.<br>• incorporates ideas from assigned readings and/or outside sources; most sources are cited correctly and paraphrased. |
| **3-4** | **3-4** |
| • The treatment of the assignment only partially fulfills the task expectations and the topic is not always addressed clearly.<br>• The introduction may not orient the reader sufficiently to the topic or to the author's thesis.<br>• The conclusion may neither reinforce nor comment on the thesis.<br>• Evidence for generalizations and supporting ideas/arguments is insufficient and/or irrelevant.<br>• Paragraphs may not be separate and logical units, related to the thesis or connected to each other by appropriate transitions.<br>• Sentences within paragraphs may not form a connected series; transition words and other cohesion devices may be missing or used inappropriately. | • contains many errors; some errors may interfere with comprehension.<br>• includes limited vocabulary or examples of inappropriate word choice.<br>• includes a number of inaccurate word forms.<br>• contains some problems with verb tenses.<br>• uses a limited number of sentence types.<br>• may not incorporate ideas from assigned readings and/or outside sources without plagiarism; sources may not be cited or paraphrased. |
| **1-2** | **1-2** |
| • The treatment of the assignment fails to fulfill the task expectations and the paper lacks focus and development.<br>• The introduction does not orient the reader sufficiently to the topic or to the author's thesis.<br>• The conclusion neither reinforces nor comments on the thesis.<br>• Evidence for generalizations and supporting ideas/arguments is insufficient and/or irrelevant.<br>• Paragraphs are not separate and logical units, clearly related to the thesis or connected to each other by appropriate transitions.<br>• Sentences within paragraphs do not form a connected series; transition words and other cohesion devices are missing or used inappropriately. | • contains numerous errors.<br>• contains errors that often interfere with comprehension.<br>• uses simple and repetitive vocabulary that may not be appropriate for academic writing.<br>• uses inappropriate word forms and verb tenses.<br>• does not vary sentence types sufficiently.<br>• does not incorporate ideas from assigned readings and/or outside sources without plagiarism; sources are not cited or paraphrased. |

Figure 8.2 Scoring rubric for structure/composition course

ESL 0640/0350 Writing Feedback Form

Name: _____

Assignment: _____
□ First Draft □ Final Draft

Total: _____ /20    Revision/Editing: _____    Grade: _____

| CONTENT/ORGANIZATION _____ /10 (See Scoring Rubric for Descriptions of Point Values) | LANGUAGE USE _____ /10 (See Scoring Rubric for Descriptions of Point Values) | REVISION/EDITING (Final Version Only) | | | | |
|---|---|---|---|---|---|---|
| | | E | VG | G | F | P |

**CONTENT/ORGANIZATION _____ /10**
(See Scoring Rubric for Descriptions of Point Values)

— Your paper addresses the content of all parts of the task with little or no off-topic material.
— Your introduction effectively orients the reader to the topic and your thesis.
— Evidence to support main idea (examples, illustrations, details) is well chosen, clearly explained, and sufficient enough to support the main idea.
— Your conclusion provides effective closure to the paper.
— Each paragraph has one main idea, developed logically and completely through examples and details.
— A variety of transitions (words, phrases, or entire sentences) is used effectively to connect sentences and paragraphs.
— **You reached the following special goals for this assignment:**

_____
_____
_____

**LANGUAGE USE _____ /10**
(See Scoring Rubric for Descriptions of Point Values)

— Your paper is clearly written with few errors.
— Your paper includes accurate and diverse academic vocabulary.
— You use a variety of sentence types accurately.
— Ideas from assigned readings and/or outside sources are cited correctly and paraphrased using a variety of techniques.
**Your paper has a pattern of errors in the following areas:**
— fragments
— verbs
— agreement
— run-on/comma splice
— word order
— word choice
— word form
— **assignment specific goals:**

**REVISION/EDITING**
(Final Version Only)

— You have incorporated feedback from your instructor and/or classmates to improve the content of your paper.
— You have incorporated feedback from your instructor and/or classmates to improve the organization of your paper.
— Your paper has been edited carefully for the language features that have been discussed in class.
— Your paper is formatted appropriately (margins, double spaced, indented paragraphs, headings, references, title page).
— Your paper has been edited carefully for spelling, punctuation, and capitalization.
*****************************
— Few revisions were necessary because your first draft was outstanding.

E = Excellent
VG = Very Good
G = Good
F = Fair
P = Poor

Figure 8.3  Student feedback form, adapted from a form developed by the ESL Services Courses, Department of Applied Linguistics and TESL, UCLA

students' writing. However, classroom teachers can go beyond the timed impromptu test in numerous ways to create assessment tools that more accurately reflect the writing process and allow for feedback that is more useful to students, and several of these ways have been discussed here. In this chapter, however, I have been concerned primarily with the teacher's evaluation of single writing samples, whether written in class or out of class. In the next chapter, I will turn to portfolio assessment, in which not just individual pieces of writing are evaluated, but a collection of writing samples produced over time.

# CHAPTER NINE

····································································································

# Portfolio assessment

## Introduction

Up to this point, we have been considering writing assessment primarily in terms of collecting and evaluating individual writing samples as single performances, and making inferences from these performances about the writing ability of the test takers. However, as has been noted earlier, this approach to writing assessment is limited in several ways. Two of the most serious limitations are: (1) the fact that writing done under timed conditions on an unfamiliar topic does not accurately reflect the conditions under which most writing is done in non-testing situations or writing as it is taught and practiced in the classroom, and (2) the fact that it is difficult to generalize from a single writing sample to a much broader universe of writing in different genres and for different purposes and audiences. Chapter 8 deals to some extent with the first limitation, in that classroom evaluation of writing can be accomplished through untimed as well as timed writing, but a different approach is needed to deal with the second limitation. Portfolio assessment is seen by many as an alternative approach to writing assessment that can allow broader inferences about writing ability than are possible with single-shot approaches to evaluating writing, both in the individual classroom and on a larger scale.

Portfolios have long been a standard form of assessment in fields related to the visual arts such as architecture, design, and photography. In first-language writing as well, portfolios have a fairly long history, although they have only recently become used in large-scale assessment. As Hamp-Lyons and Condon (2000) note in their history of writing assessment, instructors have used writing folders in the British educational system for over 50 years, and individual instructors in the US began using portfolios in their classes in the early 1970s. Portfolio assessment as a tool for program-wide assessment began to be popular only in the mid-1980s when Belanoff and Elbow (1986) demonstrated that program-wide portfolio assessment was not only feasible, but also offered benefits to students, teachers, and program administrators. Currently portfolio assessment is being used in a wide variety of first-language settings, at all levels of education from primary school through university studies, to assess students' progress and achievement in writing. Like other movements in writing assessment, portfolio assessment has spread from L1 settings to second-language writing, particularly in academic contexts. However, most of the available literature on portfolio assessment comes from first-language contexts, and the discussion below derives largely from the first-language literature, with applications for second-language writing assessment where appropriate.

This chapter is organized as follows. First, portfolio assessment is defined, and the most important elements of portfolio assessment are introduced. Next, strengths and weaknesses of portfolio assessment are discussed with reference to Bachman and Palmer's model of test usefulness, introduced earlier in this volume. Finally, practical and logistical issues in portfolio implementation are discussed.

## Definition of portfolio assessment

What is portfolio assessment? A portfolio can be defined as 'a purposeful collection of student works that exhibits to the student (and/ or others) the student's efforts, progress, or achievement in a given area' (Northwest Evaluation Association, 1991: 4, cited in Wolcott, 1998). More specifically in terms of writing assessment, a portfolio is a collection of written texts written for different purposes over a period of time. Because portfolio assessment is used in so many settings, there is wide variation in terms of how portfolios are assembled, evaluated, and used; however, certain common characteristics in these points can be found in many, if not most, portfolio assessment programs.

Hamp-Lyons and Condon (2000) give nine characteristics that are present to a greater or lesser degree in portfolios:

1 A portfolio is a **collection** of written works, rather than a single writing sample.

2 It enables the writer to display a **range** of writing performances, in different genres and for different audiences and purposes.

3 A portfolio possesses **context richness** insofar as it reflects closely the learning situation and demonstrates what the writer has accomplished within that context.

4 An important characteristic of most portfolio programs is **delayed evaluation**, giving students both the opportunity and the motivation to revise written products before a final evaluation is given.

5 Portfolios generally involve **selection** of the pieces to be included in the portfolio, usually by the student with some guidance from the instructor.

6 Delayed evaluation and selection offer opportunities for **student-centered control**, in that students can select which pieces best fulfill the established evaluation criteria and can revise them before putting them into their portfolios.

7 A portfolio usually involves **reflection and self-assessment**, in that students must reflect on their work in deciding how to arrange the portfolio, and are frequently asked to write a reflective essay about their development as writers and how the pieces in the portfolio represent that development.

8 Portfolios can provide a means for measuring **growth along specific parameters**, such as linguistic accuracy or the ability to organize and develop an argument.

9 Portfolios provide a means for measuring **development over time** in ways that neither the teacher nor the student may have anticipated.

Of these nine characteristics, the most important components of a portfolio are collection, reflection, and selection, according to Hamp-Lyons and Condon. By definition a portfolio must include a collection of writing samples, rather than a single piece of writing, since the goal of portfolio assessment is to provide more evidence of a student's ability in writing than a single piece of writing can provide. The collection can vary along a number of parameters – it can include finished products only, or earlier drafts of finished products, to reflect the writer's process of writing and revision; it can be assembled under very strict guidelines or be left to the student's discretion; it can contain just a few writing samples or a large number – but the essential point is that a portfolio is not a portfolio unless it contains more than one piece of writing.

However, simply collecting writing samples is not enough to make a portfolio useful for evaluation: reflection and selection are necessary as well. As Hamp-Lyons and Condon state, 'everything that we have read about how and why portfolios work successfully, as pedagogical tools, teacher development tools, and as assessment tools, teaches that without reflection all we have is simply a pile, or a large folder' (p. 119); in other words, selection of specific contents and their arrangement, made through deliberate reflection, are what turn a collection of writing samples into a portfolio. The process of reflection is frequently explicitly included in the portfolio in the form of a reflective essay that introduces the reader to the portfolio, describes the contents and why they were chosen, and discusses how the writing reflects the writer's strengths and progress in writing.

The basic characteristics of a portfolio are shown in Figure 9.1, taken from Hamp-Lyons and Condon (2000). The figure shows the relationship between collection, reflection, and selection, and the other characteristics of portfolios as mentioned above, with a continual process of feedback to the student at every stage of the process, with final evaluation delayed until the portfolio is turned in. Hamp-Lyons and Condon note that, without delayed evaluation, in which students are given opportunities to reflect on, revise, and select their writing, there is little motivation for the student to assemble a portfolio and it becomes, for the student, a meaningless exercise.

## Portfolios and test usefulness

As with any other form of assessment, the decision to use portfolios needs to be based on a consideration of the qualities of test usefulness. It may be helpful, therefore, to look at portfolios through the lens of Bachman and Palmer's (1996) model of the six qualities of test usefulness – construct validity, reliability, authenticity, interactiveness, impact, and practicality – especially in comparison with timed essay tests. The discussion is organized beginning with the aspects of usefulness that give portfolios advantages over timed writing tests,

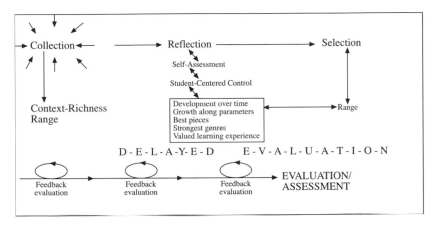

Figure 9.1. Basic portfolio characteristics (Hamp-Lyons, L. and Condon, W., 2000: 122)

particularly for academic writing – construct validity, authenticity, interactivity, and impact – followed by those aspects in which timed writing tests have advantages over portfolios, particularly for large-scale testing – reliability and practicality.

Before discussing the aspects of test usefulness, it is important to note that portfolios can be used for both internal and external assessment (Wolcott, 1998); that is, they can be used by individual teachers to assess students' growth and achievement in writing, or on a larger scale, where people other than the classroom teacher will evaluate the portfolios for various purposes, such as certifying individual student achievement or evaluating a curriculum. In external evaluation of portfolios, the stakes may be quite high for students; for example, in some states in the US portfolios are required for graduation from high school, and at some colleges portfolios are used to place students into composition courses. As with more traditional writing tests, the purpose of the assessment and the stakes for the individual student have important implications for achieving an appropriate balance among the qualities of test usefulness.

## Construct validity

Perhaps the most important benefit of portfolio assessment is its potential for demonstrating the validity of inferences about a broader construct or definition of writing than is possible with timed writing tests. The construct of writing that is tapped in portfolio assessments can potentially be broadened in two ways. First, the inclusion of a variety of writing samples in different genres, written for different purposes and addressing different audiences, allows us to feel more confident in generalizing from the results of a portfolio assessment to a broader domain of writing. Second, including multi-draft essays in a portfolio allows us to make inferences about students' ability to apply aspects of the writing process such as revising for content and organization and editing for sentence-level errors and mechanics. These aspects of the writing construct are particularly important for academic writing, where multi-draft, process-oriented writing and writing for different audiences and purposes are important focuses of instruction.

Another aspect of construct validity that is important for second-language writers has to do with the advantages that additional time gives to these writers. Speeded tests such as timed writing examinations frequently put non-native writers at a disadvantage (Silva, 1993; Hamp-Lyons and Condon, 2000), and allowing students extra time to revise and edit their writing before turning it in for evaluation may give a truer picture of how students will write in non-test situations than a timed essay can provide.

Portfolio assessment clearly has the potential for greater construct validity for school-based writing assessment at all levels of education, where learning to write is a central curricular goal. However, it is a different matter for non-academic L2 writing contexts, such as foreign-language education or adult education, where students' proficiency in the L2 may be minimal and writing has a minor emphasis in the curriculum. In such settings the goal of writing instruction is not ordinarily to teach students to use a process-oriented approach to writing or to write for a wide variety of audiences and purposes. Rather, writing is frequently seen as an aid to developing oral proficiency, and the definition of writing ability is somewhat narrower than in academic contexts, focusing primarily on the linguistic aspects of writing. In this case the arguments for using portfolios to assess a broader construct of writing are not as compelling.

This is not to say that portfolios cannot or should not be used in non-academic settings or with low-proficiency learners. In fact, portfolio assessment is becoming more popular in business and technical writing courses (see, for example, Elliot et al., 1994; Dillon, 1997; and Hoger, 1998). Portfolio assessment is beginning to be adopted in foreign-language study, as well. Of particular note in this regard is the Council of Europe's European Language Portfolio project (Council of Europe, 2000), which is intended to provide individuals from member states with a record of their language-learning experiences and ac-complishments. In this project, individual member states of the COE have developed their own models for portfolios, but all portfolios are tied to the levels of language proficiency outlined in the 'Common European Framework of Reference: Learning, teaching, assessment' (Council of Europe, 2001). Even though the project involves the as-sessment of language proficiency in general (not just writing ability) this project is noteworthy in its innovative approach to the use of portfolios in second-language education.

## Authenticity

Like construct validity, considerations of authenticity make a compel-ling argument for the use of portfolio assessment in situations where writing in the second language is important in the target language use (TLU) domain (Bachman and Palmer, 1996: 29). Again, for school-based writing in particular, portfolios are clearly superior to timed writing tests in terms of authenticity. Indeed, one of the great strengths of portfolios is that they can be designed to include writing samples that were written for some authentic purpose other than the evaluation of writing *per se* – for example, papers that were written for other academic courses. In many writing programs, where many or all of the essays written in class are included in the final portfolio, the test tasks (the portfolio contents) and the TLU tasks (the classroom writing tasks) are virtually identical, which is of course the ultimate in authenticity.

It is important to bear in mind that out-of-class and multi-draft essays are not the only authentic writing tasks for academic writers, particularly at the secondary school and university levels: on the contrary, timed writing is also an authentic TLU task for these stu-dents, as they are required to take essay examinations in their content courses. It is therefore not the case that only untimed, multi-draft essays should be included in a portfolio. However, as discussed in Chapter 8, essay tests in content courses are virtually always based on material that has been covered in class through readings, lectures, and discussions, and there is every reason to include timed writings of this nature in portfolios. Authenticity is also enhanced when writings based on sources are scored using accuracy of content as one criterion, since content is the principle criterion for evaluating such writing in content area classes, as discussed in Chapter 8.

## Interactiveness

Interactiveness was previously defined as 'the extent and type of involvement of the test taker's individual characteristics in accomplishing a test task' (Bachman and Palmer, 1996: 25). Specifically, an interactive test task engages a test taker's language ability, meta-cognitive strategies, topical knowledge, and affective schemata. By this definition virtually any writing task that involves generating and organizing content is interactive, including timed writing tests. However, compared to timed writing tests, portfolio assessment is clearly on the high end of interactiveness. In particular, the act of collecting, selecting, and arranging the portfolio contents engages the metacognitive strategies to a considerable extent and, ideally, involves personal investment on the part of the student/portfolio author. This level of interactiveness can have many benefits, as the process of putting portfolios together can help students learn a great deal about the writing process and can serve as a motivating factor for students. On the other hand, it is probably most beneficial in contexts where writing is a central focus of instruction and may be less appropriate for students who have limited need for writing in their second language.

## Impact

Apart from construct validity, the most frequently cited benefit of portfolio assessment is the impact that it can have on students, teachers, and programs. Murphy and Camp (1996) discuss three principle benefits of portfolios to students. First, portfolios offer opportunities for reflection and the development of self-awareness, both of which play important roles in learning. According to Hamp-Lyons and Condon (2000) the opportunity for reflection is especially important for second-language writers in academic contexts: the ethos of a well-run portfolio program allows more and better opportunities for reflection and feedback on writing, so that students who are struggling both to learn the language and to understand the writing demands of academic courses will be more successful as they return to and reflect on their own writing. Second, students develop a sense of ownership of their writing through having some control over both the conditions for writing and the selection of portfolio contents, which leads to a sense of agency and responsibility. According to Murphy and Camp, 'in the process of creating portfolios, students learn to exercise judgment about their own work, monitor their own progress, set goals for themselves, and present themselves and their work to others' (pp. 113–114). Finally, students can use portfolios as a basis for self-assessment and development of standards, if they are given clear criteria and opportunities to evaluate and revise their own work in preparing their portfolios.

In addition to these potential benefits, portfolio assessment can promote the process of revision, which is a major focus of much contemporary writing instruction. If students know that they have the opportunity to address weaknesses in their writing before the portfolio is turned in, they may be more willing to revise their writing than they might otherwise be.

Portfolio assessment has benefits for instructors and for writing programs as well. Murphy and Camp (1996) point out two important benefits of portfolios to instructors. The main benefit to instructors is that portfolio assessment becomes an integral part of the instructional process rather than a discrete, separate activity. Teachers can articulate important learning goals for their students and design the parameters for their students' portfolios to promote these goals, whether they be flexibility in writing in different genres or using writing as a process of self-discovery. Portfolios also give instructors more information about their students' writing than do scores on essay tests. The variety of texts within a portfolio can give teachers insights into their students' strengths and weaknesses, and a portfolio can also allow raters to identify students with uneven writing skills, who have strengths in one area and weaknesses in others, as is the case with many ESL writers in academic settings. The inclusion of a reflective essay can help teachers understand the processes that their students are using in writing and the students' perceptions of their own strengths and weaknesses, as well as the impact that instruction has had on these perceptions. Murphy and Camp also note that portfolios can provide important information about how language varies across situations:

> Using portfolios to look explicitly at how language varies with audience and purpose and across situations is particularly helpful for teachers of students who need to learn how English used for academic purposes in school differs from other kinds of writing and from language used at home. Because portfolios contain multiple pieces of writing, they invite teachers to help students take a closer look at how texts differ from one another and to compare and contrast rhetorical strategies used in different language and situations . . . In this respect, they offer a unique teaching opportunity.      (Murphy and Camp, 1996: 122)

In terms of impact at the program level, a portfolio assessment program can have positive effects on curriculum and instruction, both in the program in which the portfolios are assessed and in any preparatory programs. When portfolios are used on a program-wide basis, the process of implementing portfolio assessment can be very valuable in getting instructors to share their understandings of the role of writing in the curriculum and to come up with common grading criteria. The process of developing a portfolio assessment program involves a good deal of discussion among instructors to make decisions about the number and kind of writing samples that will go into the portfolio and how portfolios will be graded. While this kind of discussion may be difficult and time-consuming, it has the advantage of making explicit and comparing one's own grading standards to those of one's colleagues, and it can make the program more unified and cohesive. In addition, discussions of portfolios can stimulate teachers' thinking about the kinds of instructional activities that lead to successful portfolios, and can thus be instrumental in driving curricular improvements (Murphy and Camp, 1996).

Portfolio assessment can also have an impact on programs preparing students for academic work. For example, Hamp-Lyons and Condon (2000) report that when the University of Michigan began requiring portfolios for placement into first-year English courses, one result was that high schools began preparing students for the portfolios and emphasizing writing more, presumably thus preparing students better for college-level writing.

Outside of academic writing, portfolio assessment can lead to positive impact as well. Dillon (1997) describes a technical writing course that involved community business leaders in judging student portfolios, thus increasing the connection between the institution offering the course and the local business community. The COE's European

Language Portfolio project lists three goals, all of which relate to impact: (1) raise awareness of and promote the linguistic heritage of Europe; (2) motivate all European citizens to learn languages, including those less widely used; and (3) support lifelong language learning as a way of responding to economic, social and cultural changes in Europe (Council of Europe, 2000). Since the project is still in its infancy, it remains to be seen whether these potential benefits are realized; the point, however, is that portfolios are being implemented primarily for their promise of positive impact.

In summary, portfolio assessment has the potential for positive impact on students, teachers, and programs. It should be noted, however, that some of these benefits are not restricted to portfolios – for example, the fruitful discussions about writing that tend to take place among instructors when implementing portfolio assessment can just as easily take place during any revision of curriculum or testing. It should also be noted that these potential areas of positive impact are exactly that – potential – and are only likely to happen with serious commitment to portfolios on the part of all stakeholders, including students, teachers, and administrators. A study by Spalding and Cummins (1998) provides a good example of how a well-intentioned portfolio assessment system did not achieve the hoped-for positive impact. Spalding and Cummins surveyed freshmen at the University of Kentucky who had been required by state law to complete a writing portfolio during their senior year of high school as a part of educational reform in that state, and found that nearly two-thirds of their respondents felt that completing the portfolio had not been a useful activity. While the portfolio was intended to help students become better writers and to have 'ownership' of their writing, the students perceived the portfolio as taking too much time away from more important activities, and many saw the portfolio as an imposition from a nebulous outside authority (the state) rather than something that would benefit them personally. Finally, it should be emphasized that empirical research documenting the benefits of portfolio assessment is limited; as Hamp-Lyons and Condon (2000: 166–175) note, proponents of portfolio assessment are convinced through their own experience that portfolios are preferable to other forms of assessment, but lack the empirical research base to back up their convictions in ways that can satisfy a variety of audiences (e.g. measurement specialists, school administrators, and the general public). Messick (1994) makes a similar appeal for empirical validation of portfolio assessment.

Furthermore, there exists the potential for negative impact of port-folios as well, principally in the area of the demands of time and energy on students and teachers. Since this area overlaps with con-cerns of resource allocation and feasibility, it is discussed under 'practicality' below.

## Reliability

Reliability is an area where timed writing tests have an advantage over portfolio assessment, as certain aspects of portfolios make relia-bility of scoring somewhat problematic. Results from large-scale port-folio assessments have frequently been shown to be less reliable than timed writing tests – for example, in a highly publicized statewide assessment of writing in Vermont, inter-rater reliabilities for writing portfolios in 1993 for 4th and 8th graders were reported as .56 and .63, respectively (Koretz *et al.*, 1993; cited in Herman *et al.*, 1996). For the individual classroom teacher using portfolio assessment, reliability may not be a major concern, although conscientious teachers will certainly strive to maintain consistent standards for judging their students' portfolios. Reliability is a much more important concern when portfolios are being read by people other than the classroom teacher, who may not be familiar with students or the curriculum, and when the stakes for the individual student are high.

There are several obstacles to overcome in scoring portfolios reli-ably. As Hamp-Lyons and Condon (2000: 134) note, relying on anchor portfolios – that is, portfolios used in rater training to exemplify specific levels on a scoring rubric – can be problematic. Since portfo-lios by their very nature contain different kinds of writing sample, it is often difficult for the anchor portfolios to be truly representative of particular score levels. As a result, the more varied and open the portfolio is, the more difficult it is to score reliably. When reliability is essential, as in high-stakes assessment, a solution to this dilemma is to limit the range of writing samples included in the portfolio (see section on portfolio contents below), and to include as wide a variety of samples as possible in the portfolios that are used for rater training, to give raters some idea of the possible range of texts found within the portfolios.

A related issue has to do with portfolios in which texts within a single portfolio vary in quality. Just as raters may have difficulty judging a single writing sample of uneven quality, particularly on a holistic score, there are similar problems with scoring portfolios if the individual pieces vary in terms of how they meet the scoring criteria. Raters may not consider each text on its own merit or may have difficulty coming up with a single score for texts of uneven quality. Another danger is that a rater's reaction to the first text in a portfolio may influence how he or she responds to other texts, either positively or negatively, and may thus unfairly bias the score that is ultimately given. While it may be impossible to completely eliminate this so-called 'halo effect,' it can be mitigated by raising raters' awareness in rater training, and by allowing sufficient time for raters to consider each writing sample on its own merits rather than rushing through the portfolio.

Herman *et al.* suggest that reliability in scoring portfolios may be easiest to achieve when one or more of the following conditions are met: the contents of portfolios are relatively uniform; there is a small number of highly trained raters; experienced scorers use well-honed rubrics; criteria are clearly articulated and illustrated with samples of student work; and the community of practitioners and scorers share experiences and values that have evolved over time through close collaboration (1996: 51). When portfolios are used in external assessments that have serious consequences for test takers, trying to meet these conditions is an important component in implementing the assessment.

## Practicality

Perhaps the most important limitation of portfolio assessment has to do with the amounts and types of resources – particularly human resources and time – that are required to implement portfolio assessment, especially beyond the level of the individual classroom. The development of a good program-wide portfolio assessment system requires a number of resources that may not be present in settings outside of universities. Specifically, portfolio assessment on a program-wide level requires a core of faculty members who can meet together regularly for standard setting and discussions about portfolios, and who believe that the effort required to sustain such a system is worth the commitment of time and energy. It also requires students who remain within the program long enough to be able to put together a portfolio.

Based just on these conditions, portfolio assessment would be extremely difficult in settings such as many adult education programs, where there is open enrollment and students may only stay for a few weeks. In addition, instructors in such programs frequently have only part-time contracts and are not paid for meetings or service above and beyond teaching their classes. Finally, in such programs writing is often a minor emphasis, and the development of a full-scale portfolio assessment program might require more time and effort than the curricular emphasis would warrant.

For the individual teacher, implementing portfolio assessment may be somewhat easier, as classroom-based portfolio assessment does not require the same level of coordination with other instructors in terms of standard setting, determining portfolio contents, and achieving inter-rater reliability. However, for both individual teachers and programs, perhaps the single most frequently cited disadvantage of portfolio assessments is the fact that they are time and labor intensive for teachers and students alike. While teachers who have worked with portfolios frequently believe strongly that the time and effort involved in implementing portfolios is well worth the benefits received, they are often the first to admit that portfolio assessment is extremely time-consuming. In fact, Herman *et al.* state that reports on nearly every portfolio project include a discussion of

> the intense and pervasive demands on teachers' time . . . to learn new assessment practices, to understand what should be included in portfolios and how to help students compile them, to develop portfolio tasks, to discern and apply criteria for assessing students' work, to reflect on and fine-tune their instructional and assessment practices, and to work out and manage the logistics.
>
> (Herman *et al.*, 1996: 54)

In addition, as Wolcott (1998) points out, introducing the concept of portfolios to students takes not just a single session, but usually several discussions with students to ensure that everyone understands the purpose of the portfolio, the requirements for assembling the portfolio, and the criteria that will be used for scoring the portfolios. For students, putting together a portfolio often involves a great deal of time and effort, and students do not always see the benefits of revisiting writing that they have done earlier to try to improve upon it for their portfolios.

## Summary of test usefulness

In summary, teachers and administrators contemplating using port-folio assessment for their classrooms or for large-scale assessment must consider the aspects of test usefulness for their particular situa-tion. In academic settings in particular, portfolio assessment has the potential for greater construct validity, authenticity, interactiveness, and impact and thus may be an attractive choice for assessing writing. Portfolio assessment is also especially appropriate for internal assessment where classroom teachers want as close a link as possible between instruction and assessment, and reliability is not a major consideration. For large-scale high-stakes assessment, however, the potential drawbacks of portfolio assessment, particularly in terms of reliability of scoring and resource allocation, must be recognized, so that portfolio assessment can be implemented in a way that allows the many potential benefits of portfolios to be realized.

## Implementing portfolio assessment

Just as in any other form of writing assessment, there are a number of considerations that need to be thought through when designing a portfolio assessment system. These include the purposes, the con-tents, the scoring procedures, and logistical issues.

### Specifying the purpose(s) of the assessment

As in timed writing tests, portfolio assessment involves making deci-sions both about the tasks (what will be evaluated) and the scoring method (how the evaluation will be done). And as we have seen in earlier chapters with timed writing tests, these decisions must be made in light of the purpose of the assessment. However, these deci-sions may be more complicated with portfolio assessments. This is because, by virtue of its intimate relationship to curriculum and instruction, portfolio assessment is often used for many different purposes, some of which may conflict with each other. Herman *et al.* (1996) provide the following list of potential purposes for portfolio assessment, some of which go beyond what is normally expected of school-based tests:

- accountability; evaluating program or curriculum effectiveness.

- evaluating individual student progress; grading; certifying student accomplishment.

- diagnosing students' needs; informing classroom instructional planning; improving instructional effectiveness.

- encouraging teacher efficacy (i.e. helping teachers become more effective); encouraging reflective practice at the school and class-room levels; supporting teachers' professional development.

- encouraging student efficacy (i.e. helping students become better learners); promoting student self-assessment; motivating student performance.

- communicating with parents.                    (Herman *et al.*, 1996: 29)

As Herman *et al.* note, these purposes can be mutually complemen-tary in the abstract but may contradict each other in practice, particu-larly between the purposes of classroom assessment and those of large-scale assessment. For example, if the overriding purpose of the assessment is for accountability within a school district, the portfolio contents may need to be standardized so that portfolios are compar-able across different schools. This in turn may limit the amount of student control and thus student investment in the portfolios and may conflict with the purpose of encouraging student efficacy, as was the case with the Kentucky writing assessment discussed above. It is therefore incumbent upon the assessment designers to be very clear about which purposes have the highest priority and which are sec-ondary, so that the assessment is designed to maximize information and processes that will meet the primary purposes first. If this is not done carefully, there is a very real danger that an assessment that is intended to fulfill several purposes at once may end up fulfilling none of them very well.

### Specifying portfolio contents

Determining what should go into a student's portfolio requires careful thought about a number of questions. These questions include the following:

- Who decides what goes into the portfolio?

- What types of writing should be included in the portfolio? That is, should the portfolio include best work only, a range of work from a variety of genres, both in-class and out-of-class work, and so on?

- How many pieces should go into the portfolio?
- What should be included in the portfolio in addition to students' classroom writing samples?
- How can the authorship of the portfolio contents be authenticated?

Since the contents of the portfolio need to be decided in light of the purpose of the assessment, there is obviously no one correct answer to any of these questions. However, certain general considerations for portfolio contents can be used to help make these decisions. I will discuss each of the above questions in turn.

*Who should decide what goes in the portfolio?* Should students, teachers, or a combination make this decision? Hamp-Lyons and Condon (2000) make a strong case for student control of portfolio contents, as the process of reflection entailed in selecting pieces for the portfolio enhances student learning and student investment in the assessment process. In theory, when students are allowed to choose their best work based on explicit criteria, they will be more intrinsically motivated to revise and improve their writing and take pride in their work. If the primary purpose of the portfolio is enhancing student learning, then student control of portfolio contents is probably the most appropriate option.

However, arguments against student control of portfolio contents have been made as well. One disadvantage with student control is that students may not always make the best choices, and thus may include work that, for example, is on a topic that they are particularly interested in but that does not meet the grading criteria. Student control of portfolio contents may thus in some cases work against the student's best interests. Furthermore, as Herman *et al.* (1996) point out, if the portfolio is serving primarily accountability purposes and will be evaluated by raters who are unfamiliar with the local context, it may be preferable for the teacher to select the portfolio contents, as teachers may be better able to select the writing samples that most closely correspond to the grading criteria. Another advantage of teacher control of contents is that portfolios are more consistent and can be more easily compared to each other, thus increasing the reliability of the assessment. Teacher control of portfolio contents is thus most appropriate when outside evaluators will be scoring the portfolios and when reliability is an important consideration.

*What types of writing should the portfolio include?* Herman *et al.* (1996) discuss three types of portfolios: the showcase portfolio, which contains a student's best pieces only; the progress portfolio, which documents evidence of growth over time; and the working portfolio, which contains all work done for a course, or at least samples that represent the major learning goals or units of a course. Again, the purpose of the portfolio will determine which of these three main types will be most appropriate, although there is not a one-to-one correspondence between the assessment purposes listed on pages 211–212 and portfolio type. For example, if the purpose of the assessment is to evaluate individual student progress, clearly a progress portfolio would be most appropriate. On the other hand, all three kinds of portfolios may be used for accountability purposes or to communicate with parents about their children's work in class. Similarly, all three portfolio types may be useful in motivating student performance: a progress portfolio can document how far a student has come, a working portfolio can show the range of writing assignments that the student has completed, and a showcase port-folio can show off the student's best work. In deciding which type of portfolio to use, then, teachers and administrators need to determine whether documenting growth, range, or achievement will allow the most appropriate inferences for the specific purpose of the assessment.

A related question is whether the portfolio entries should represent samples of work written at different times of the year or semester. If we assume that students are improving as a result of classroom instruction, the argument could be made that work from the beginning of a semester or year does not represent the students' best work. However, Herman *et al.* give three reasons for including samples over time: if the purpose of the portfolio is to assess progress, if the best work happens at different times throughout the year, or if the port-folio needs to be an accurate reflection of what occurred during the course of the year.

*How many pieces should go into the portfolio?* Ideally, since port-folios are intended to demonstrate the depth and breadth of a student's writing performance, the simple answer to this question is the more pieces, the better. However, this concern for adequately sampling the domain (i.e. concerns of construct validity) must be balanced by concerns of practicality, particularly in terms of time – both the student's time in assembling the portfolio, and the teacher/

evaluator's time in reading the portfolio – and efficacy. For example, if a reliable and valid decision about a student's work can be obtained from, say, reading five pieces, then there is little to be gained from including eight in the portfolio. At the current time there is little if any research evidence to support any rule-of-thumb suggestions for how many different writing samples should be included in a portfolio; this may be an area where local context and experience will determine the most appropriate balance between variety and efficiency.

*What should be included in the portfolio in addition to students' classroom writing samples?* The central component of the portfolio is, of course, the students' written products, which in many cases students will have revised before including them in the portfolio. In addition to these products, a number of other types of documentation can be included to guide readers through the portfolio and to provide additional perspectives on the written products. In some cases, this documentation is explicitly scored (see the sample rubrics in the section on scoring below), while in other cases it serves to orient the raters to the portfolio contents and provide additional information that can help raters in the evaluation task. This documentation is principally of three types, described below.

### (1) Reflective essay

Many teachers like to have students include their reflections on the process they went through to create their final works. In many portfolios this takes the form of a reflective essay, which introduces the reader to the contents of the portfolio and frequently provides insights into a student's self-assessment of his or her writing strategies and strengths and weaknesses in writing. As was discussed earlier in this chapter, reflection is one of the key elements of a portfolio, and an essay is clearly the most direct way for evaluators to gain insights into students' reflective processes. Additionally, reflective essays have the advantage of giving students the opportunity to explain to their evaluators what they have learned and why they included certain pieces, which provides them with an opportunity to develop their self-awareness and to practice self-assessment. On the other hand, Murphy and Camp (1996) point out that students may not always take this opportunity for reflection seriously and may either use the reflective essay to butter up their teachers ('I love this class') or simply write what Murphy and Camp call the 'fill-in-the-blanks portfolio letter,' which tends to go something like this: 'I put this piece in because . . . , I put this piece in because . . . Finally, I put this piece in because . . .' (p. 118).

### (2) Background/orienting documentation

Another important component of many portfolios is background or supplementary documentation to make the portfolio more understandable to potential evaluators. This may be particularly important for large-scale assessment, as it can provide important contextual information for evaluators who are not intimately familiar with the local context. This documentation could include a table of contents, the writing assignments that students were given, or a course syllabus.

### (3) Documentation of writing processes

Finally, portfolios frequently contain **documentation** related to the students' writing processes. For example, teachers may want to ask for early drafts of papers in addition to the polished product. Teachers may also ask students to provide documentation of any outside help they have received on their writing, for example from classmates or tutors. Such documentation may be particularly helpful in second-language contexts, where students may seek outside help to proofread and correct sentence-level errors.

*How can the authorship of portfolio contents be authenticated?* As was discussed in Chapter 8, a timed writing test is the best way to ensure that the writing has been done independently and thus represents the ability of the writer him or herself. Portfolios, on the other hand, encourage a writing process that often includes seeking and using feedback from others, particularly instructors. Thus a portfolio may become more of a collaborative work than an individual one. This can be a problem in portfolio assessments beyond the classroom level, as different instructors may offer different amounts and kinds of support, and thus some students may be disadvantaged if their portfolios are compared against those of students who have received less help from their instructors. The problem becomes particularly sticky when results of portfolio assessment are used to evaluate instruction and curriculum: in such cases, there is a danger that teachers may become even more invested in the portfolio and may take on an even more directive role in the portfolio, reducing the students' investment in and ownership of the portfolio. One partial solution to this dilemma is to include both timed and untimed writing in the portfolio to make sure that some independent work is included. Students can also be asked to document the amount and kind of help they have received in their writing, as discussed above. Finally, this issue must be raised in discussions with both teachers in preparing their students for portfolio assessment and raters of portfolios in training sessions, to reduce the possibility that some students will be unfairly advantaged or disadvantaged by different amounts of external support.

To summarize, there are numerous considerations to be made in determining the content of portfolios and how these contents will be selected. These decisions can only be made by taking into consideration the goals of the assessment and factors relevant to the local context. These considerations should be discussed at length by all parties involved, including the students, but particularly the teachers who will be helping their students assemble their portfolios. A checklist such as the one shown in Figure 9.2 (from Mabry, 1999) may be useful as an aid in these discussions.

## Scoring portfolios

As with scoring timed writing tests discussed in Chapter 6, a number of issues must be considered in scoring portfolios. While many of the considerations that apply to scoring timed writing tests also apply to scoring portfolios, the complexity of portfolios and the richness of the information that portfolios can provide bring up additional concerns about how to assess portfolios reliably when they consist of a wide range of text types, and how to communicate the information from this assessment, either numerically or verbally, in ways that are easily understood and useful to students and decision makers. In this section, the following considerations in scoring portfolios will be discussed:

1   establishing the criteria for scoring;
2   determining what sort of rating scale to use; and
3   determining how scores are to be reported.

### *Criteria for scoring portfolios*
Just as with timed essays, an essential first step in designing scoring procedures is to determine the criteria to be used to evaluate portfolios. Since portfolios are more complex than essay tests, comprising a variety of texts and other documentation as outlined above, devel-

**2. <u>Contents</u>. What will go into portfolios? Who will create and select the contents?**

| To be selected or created by | Student | | Teacher | | Other | |
|---|---|---|---|---|---|---|
| | *create* | *select* | *create* | *select* | *create* | *select* |
| — Students' best work (tests, papers, reports) | ____.____ | | ____.____ | | ____.____ | |
| — Unsuccessful products | ____.____ | | ____.____ | | ____.____ | |
| — Drafts as well as completed products | ____.____ | | ____.____ | | ____.____ | |
| — Required entries | ____.____ | | ____.____ | | ____.____ | |
| — Optional or nonrequired entries | ____.____ | | ____.____ | | ____.____ | |
| — Evidence of a range ofaccomplishment | ____.____ | | ____.____ | | ____.____ | |
| — Evidence of group work | ____.____ | | ____.____ | | ____.____ | |
| — Evidence of nonschool accomplishment | ____.____ | | ____.____ | | ____.____ | |
| — Nonacademic accomplishment | ____.____ | | ____.____ | | ____.____ | |
| — Reflections on student work, progress | ____.____ | | ____.____ | | ____.____ | |
| — Suggestions for future work | ____.____ | | ____.____ | | ____.____ | |
| — Critical or evaluative comments | ____.____ | | ____.____ | | ____.____ | |
| — Photos, audiotapes, videotapes | ____.____ | | ____.____ | | ____.____ | |
| — Transcript or grade list | ____.____ | | ____.____ | | ____.____ | |
| — Standardized test scores | ____.____ | | ____.____ | | ____.____ | |
| — Other | ____.____ | | ____.____ | | ____.____ | |
| — Other | ____.____ | | ____.____ | | ____.____ | |
| — Other | ____.____ | | ____.____ | | ____.____ | |

List required portfolio components.


List optional portfolio components.


Will student work entries have evaluative comments attached? _____
Will student work entries have reflective comments attached? _____
Will I create forms to be used for evaluative and/or reflective comments or  not? _____
How often will the contents be reviewed and added or pruned? _____
How many pieces should be in the portfolio by the end of the course or year? _____
If a student and I (or others) disagree, how will the final decision regarding contents be made?

_____

I consider these portfolios/the portfolio process to be (check one): _____

_____ relatively unstructured _____ moderately structured _____ relatively structured

Figure 9.2.  Checklist for portfolio contents (Mabry, 1999)

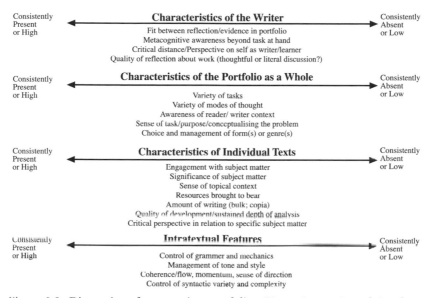

| Consistently Present or High | **Characteristics of the Writer** | Consistently Absent or Low |
|---|---|---|
| | Fit between reflection/evidence in portfolio | |
| | Metacognitive awareness beyond task at hand | |
| | Critical distance/Perspective on self as writer/learner | |
| | Quality of reflection about work (thoughtful or literal discussion?) | |

| Consistently Present or High | **Characteristics of the Portfolio as a Whole** | Consistently Absent or Low |
|---|---|---|
| | Variety of tasks | |
| | Variety of modes of thought | |
| | Awareness of reader/ writer context | |
| | Sense of task/purpose/conceptualising the problem | |
| | Choice and management of form(s) or genre(s) | |

| Consistently Present or High | **Characteristics of Individual Texts** | Consistently Absent or Low |
|---|---|---|
| | Engagement with subject matter | |
| | Significance of subject matter | |
| | Sense of topical context | |
| | Resources brought to bear | |
| | Amount of writing (bulk; copia) | |
| | Quality of development/sustained depth of analysis | |
| | Critical perspective in relation to specific subject matter | |

| Consistently Present or High | **Intratextual Features** | Consistently Absent or Low |
|---|---|---|
| | Control of grammer and mechanics | |
| | Management of tone and style | |
| | Coherence/flow, momentum, sense of direction | |
| | Control of syntactic variety and complexity | |

Figure 9.3. Dimensions for assessing portfolios (Hamp-Lyons, L. and Condon, W., 2000: 144)

oping scoring criteria involves making decisions about how to deal with the various parts of the portfolio in determining an overall score.

Hamp-Lyons and Condon (2000) provide a framework for assessing portfolios that was originally developed at the University of Michigan (see Figure 9.3). As the figure shows, the four dimensions to be considered include characteristics of the writer, characteristics of the portfolio as a whole, characteristics of individual texts, and intra-textual features. While the latter two categories are important for evaluating single samples of writing, the first two (characteristics of the writer and characteristics of the portfolio as a whole) are considerations that are specific to portfolio assessment. These considerations allow instructors and raters to extend the construct of interest beyond the characteristics of individual texts to consideration of the writer's processes and ability to write for different audiences and purposes. Specifically, the category 'characteristics of the writer' encompasses criteria related to evidence of the writer's processes of reflection and self-awareness, while the category 'characteristics of the portfolio as a whole' includes criteria related to the range of writing tasks and the writer's ability to find appropriate strategies for different writing assignments. In this diagram these characteristics are seen on a continuum from consistently present or high to consistently absent or low. Teachers developing criteria for scoring portfolios can use this diagram as a starting point for developing local standards, including which dimensions to emphasize and how to weight each dimension. For example, instructors preparing students to write in university settings may wish to incorporate criteria from all four dimensions, while instructors preparing students to write business correspondence of various types may be less interested in the characteristics of the writer and more interested in the intratextual features.

### Rating scales for portfolio assessment

As in single-sample writing tests, portfolios can be scored on a holistic or an analytic (multi-trait) scale, and the considerations are much the same as those discussed for timed writing tests in Chapter 6. However, it should be kept in mind that for large-scale assessments, scoring a portfolio is more time-consuming than scoring a single writing sample; thus for large-scale assessments a holistic scale may be more feasible than an analytic scale. As Herman *et al.* (1996) point out, even a small saving in time can translate into large monetary savings in district- or state-level assessments.

On the other hand, for classroom assessments, where teachers and students are interested in detailed feedback, an analytic scale may be preferred, as richer information about student performance can be gained from analytic scales that address different aspects of writing or considerations for different parts of the portfolio.

### Score reporting

Herman *et al.* (1996) note the results of portfolio assessment can be expressed in several ways: numerically as scores, as traditional letter grades, or as verbal descriptions (e.g. 'fails to meet expectations, meets minimum expectations, exceeds expectations'). There are advantages and disadvantages to each of these approaches. Herman *et al.* note that the choice between numerical and verbal descriptions depends in part on one's beliefs in the implicit messages that numbers versus descriptions send to students, teachers, and other stakeholders. For example, numerical scores encourage quantitative analyses of the data, such as comparing group means or comparing scores across different scales. While this may be useful for some purposes, there is a danger that inappropriate inferences may be made, since scale scores are generally rank-ordered categories rather than interval-scale scores. That is, a score of 6 on a 6-point scale represents more ability than a score of 5, but it is not necessarily the case that the difference between a 4 and a 5 represents the same increase in ability as the difference between a 5 and a 6. While the same criticism can be leveled against any assessment that uses rating scales, Herman *et al.*'s point here is that the use of numerical scores may encourage a reductionist approach to looking at data from portfolios rather than an approach that encourages a fuller appreciation of the various kinds of information that evaluations of portfolios can provide.

Another concern about numerical scores is that numbers by themselves are oversimplifications of a complex process of evaluation and are not useful in helping students and teachers know where improvement is needed. Verbal descriptions may capture better the complexities of the performances documented in portfolios. However, as Camp (1993) points out, a challenge in portfolio assessment is to communicate this information to non-specialists and to a public 'that has been conditioned to expect numerical representations of achievement whether or not the numbers are understood or used' (p. 208). This is an issue that will be raised again in Chapter 10.

### *Example scoring rubrics*
In many respects, scoring rubrics for portfolio assessment resemble rubrics for essay tests, in that they make reference to one or more dimensions of writing and have descriptors for each level or band within each dimension. As with essay tests, the scoring rubric represents an explicit statement of the construct being measured, and thus different scoring rubrics represent different definitions of the ability of interest. Depending on the focus of the assessment, however, scoring rubrics for portfolio assessment can also address aspects of writing that are more difficult to assess using timed essays, thus allowing for broader definitions of writing ability, as discussed at the beginning of this chapter. For example, a rubric can take into account the degree to which students can sustain a level of competence in various dimensions across a variety of writing tasks, whether students are able to demonstrate range and flexibility in writing for different purposes and audiences, or whether students are able to articulate their writing processes and strategies in a reflective piece. Figures 9.4 through 9.6 exemplify these features of portfolio assessment rubrics

in different contexts. Note that all three rubrics come from L1 contexts; the lack of published rubrics specifically designed for second-language portfolio assessment is indicative that the practice of portfolio assessment in L2 contexts is still in its infancy.

Figure 9.4, from Spalding and Cummins (1998), presents the scoring rubric used for a statewide assessment of the writing of high school seniors. While the descriptors of the levels Novice through Distinguished do not make specific reference to multiple texts and could be easily applied to an individual writing sample, the 'Instructional Analysis' section of the rubric refers explicitly to 'sustained performance' across the texts within the portfolio. Furthermore, the rubric gives specific information about whether a portfolio is complete and scoreable or not. Figure 9.5, from Wolcott (1998), is a holistic rubric used in college-level writing that takes a different approach, with descriptors related to the portfolio as a whole at each level, along with qualities of both out-of-class and in-class writing assignments included in the portfolio. The descriptors explicitly acknowledge the possibility of variability in quality across the different texts in the portfolio. Figure 9.6 presents an analytic portfolio assessment rubric, from Willard-Traub *et al.* (1999). This rubric was used in

| NOVICE | APPRENTICE | PROFICIENT | DISTINGUISHED |
|---|---|---|---|
| • Limited awareness of audience and/or purpose<br>• Minimal idea development; limited and/or unrelated details<br>• Random and/or weak organization<br>• Incorrect and/or ineffective sentence structure<br>• Incorrect and/or ineffective language<br>• Errors in spelling, punctuation, and capitalization are disproportionate to length and complexity | • Some evidence of communicating with an audience for a specific purpose; some lapses in focus<br>• Unelaborated idea development; unelaborated and/or repetitious details<br>• Lapses in organization and/or cohesion  ·<br>• Simplistic and/or awkward sentence structure<br>• Simplistic and/or imprecise language<br>• Some errors in spelling, punctuation, and capitalization that do not interfere with communication | • Focused on a purpose; communicates with an audience; evidence of voice and/or suitable tone<br>• Depth of idea development supported by elaborated, relevant details<br>• Logical, coherent organization<br>• Controlled and varied sentence structure<br>• Acceptable, effective language<br>• Few errors in spelling, punctuation, and capitalization relative to length and complexity | • Establishes a purpose and maintains clear focus; strong awareness of audience; evidence of distinctive voice and/or appropriate tone<br>• Depth and complexity of ideas supported by rich, engaging, and/or pertinent details; evidence of analysis, reflection, insight<br>• Careful and/or subtle organization<br>• Variety of sentence structure and length enhances effect<br>• Precise and/or rich language<br>• Control of spelling, punctuation, and capitalization |

| SCORING CRITERIA | | INSTRUCTIONAL ANALYSIS | COMPLETE/INCOMPLETE PORTFOLIOS |
|---|---|---|---|
| CRITERIA | OVERVIEW | Examining instructional strengths can assist in improving writing and learning in your school. Student portfolios can provide evidence of instructional practices. This section of the Holistic Scoring Guide is provided to assist teachers in identifying sustained evidence of instructional practices through examination of student products. When scoring a student portfolio, scorers may identify any number of the instructional strengths listed below.

The sustained performance in this portfolio demonstrates that the student has applied instruction in the following areas: | A portfolio is incomplete if any of the following apply: |
| PURPOSE/ AUDIENCE | The degree to which the writer <br> • establishes and maintains a purpose <br> • communicates with the audience <br> • employs a suitable voice and/or tone | | • Table of Contents does not contain required information <br> • Table of Contents does not note study areas information (including the letter to the Reviewer) <br> • There are fewer than 7 different entries, including Table of Contents and the Letter to the Reviewer |
| IDEA DEVELOPMENT/ SUPPORT | The degree to which the writer provides thoughtful, detailed support to develop main idea(s) | | • One or more entries are plagiarized (must be proven) <br> • One or more entries are different than those listed in the Table of Contents |
| ORGANIZATION | The degree to which the writer demonstrates <br> • logical order <br> • coherence <br> • transitions/ organizational signals | | • One or more entries are written in a language other than English <br> • One or more entries demonstrate only computational skills, or consist of only diagrams or drawings |
| SENTENCES | The degree to which the writer includes sentences that are <br> • varied in structure and length <br> • constructed effectively <br> • complete and correct | • Establishing focused, authentic **Purposes** <br> • Writing for authentic **Audiences**, situations <br> • Employing a suitable **Voice and/or Tone** <br> • **Developing Ideas** relevant to the purpose <br> • **Supporting** ideas with elaborated, relevant **Details** | • Portfolio contains a group entry <br> • Entries are out of order without clear descriptors on the Table of Contents <br> A portfolio is complete and will be scored according to how well it fulfills the criteria of the Holistic Scoring Guide If one or more entries are: |
| LANGUAGE | The degree to which the writer exhibits correct and effective <br> • word choice <br> • usage | • **Organizing** ideas logically <br> • Using effective **Transitions** <br> • Constructing effective and/or correct **Sentences** | • out of order with clear descriptors on the Table of Contents <br> • questionable concerning fulfillment of the purpose for which it is intended |
| CORRECTNESS | The degree to which the writer demonstrates correct <br> • spelling <br> • punctuation <br> • capitalization | • Using **Language** effectively and/or correctly <br> • **Editing** for correctness | • questionable concerning plagiarism, but the plagiarism cannot be proven |

Figure 9.4. Kentucky writing assessment holistic scoring guide (Spalding and Cummins, 1989)

A 6 portfolio reflects work that is consistently high in quality. The out-of-class work shows care in revising, and the in-class writings – while containing a few errors – are strong as well. There is creativity or depth of content, and the work shows a real engagement on the part of the writer. The overall writing is fluent, and the diction is accurate and sometimes sophisticated. The pieces are, for the most part, well developed, and the organization for most selections is appropriate. The writer has a solid command of grammar and mechanics.

A 5 portfolio reflects work that is generally high in quality. The out-of-class work shows care in revising, although the in-class work may not be quite as strong. There is some depth of content (and/or creativity) throughout, and the development and organization are satisfactory. The writing style is varied, and the diction is accurate. Grammar and mechanics are generally correct. The writer is engaged with most tasks.

A 4 portfolio reflects work that is usually solid in quality. The out-of-class work shows some care in revising, and the in-class writing is adequate. There is some content, as well as some development; the organization is usually adequate. A few errors appear throughout. The portfolio reflects some involvement on the part of the writer.

A 3 portfolio reflects work that is uneven in quality. Some, but not all, out-of-class pieces show care in revising; the in-class writings are often considerably weaker. The content may be shallow, and the organization and development still appear weak. Although the writer has revised the grammar and mechanics, errors continue to exist. The sentence structure and diction are generally pedestrian. The writer's involvement with the tasks often seems mechanical.

A 2 portfolio reflects work that is generally weak. The revisions on out-of-class work are limited, and the in-class writings may be far weaker. The content is often shallow, and the development is often weak. Errors in grammar and mechanics appear throughout, and the sentence structure is usually simplistic. The writer's involvement with the tests is negligible.

A I portfolio reflects work that is very weak. The writer has shown very little, if any, effort in attempting to revise out-of-class work, and in-class writings contain multiple errors. Content development and organization need much improvement. Grammar problems dominate, and the syntax is tangled. The writer seems disengaged from the task.

Figure 9.5. Holistic guide for portfolio scoring (Wolcott, 1998)

large-scale writing portfolio assessment for incoming students at the University of Michigan in the 1995–1996 academic year. While the rubric has undergone revisions since it was used operationally, it is included here as a model, as it comprises several features that distinguish a portfolio rubric from a rubric used for individual writing texts. The rubric has four sections: the reflective piece, portfolio choices,

## 1995 ECB PORTFOLIO RATING MATRIX

### I. REFLECTIVE PIECE

Our primary purpose in asking for the 'reflective piece' is two-fold: to prompt students to reflect about their writing (a process with which most are unfamiliar); and to elicit background information on the contents of the portfolio that will contribute to an informed reading. A strong reflective piece conveys the sense that the writing process is more than simply a sum of its discrete parts.

In our instructions, we asked students to use the reflective piece to contextualize their submissions for us, explaining the assignments and situations to which they were responding. A rating for 'Introduction of writing tasks for reader of the portfolio' will become part of feedback we give to students. While we would also like readers to rate reflections relative to the 'sense of self' a student portrays (e.g. her awareness of her purposes in writing, etc.) we will not be including this rating as part of our feedback to students, and a judgement relative to this 'sense of self' should be taken into account in conjunction with other aspects of the portfolio when deciding on a placement.

|  | 1 | 2 | 3 | 4 |
|---|---|---|---|---|
| *Introduction of writing tasks for reader* | Provides little information about assignments and writing process; weak sense of audience, need to orient reader. May explicitly ask for help. | Provides some information about assignments, and may provide some information about writing process. Awareness of reader/writer context is mechanical. | Provides useful discussion about assignments and writing process. On the whole, successfully addresses readers' needs. | Provides ample, rich discussion of assignments and writing process; clear sense of audience and purpose. Aware of writing as a way to do something beyond fulfilling school assignments. |

### II. PORTFOLIO CHOICES

In our instructions, we asked students to submit four different types of writing: the reflective piece; a piece that responds 'critically or analytically' to a reading; a piece from a class other than English; and a piece they would term their favorite or most representative of their writing. In choosing to substitute for any of these pieces, we told students that we would expect to see (in their reflection) an explanation of why they felt such substitution(s) were appropriate. They did not need to revise their papers before submitting them. In judging the choices students make, it may be appropriate to consider evidence (in individual pieces and in the reflective piece) of the presence or absence of opportunities to make appropriate or creative choices (e.g. in terms of range of tasks assigned, range of subject matter made available, etc.), but it's not appropriate to rely solely on extra-textual information, such as where the student went to high school, etc.

|  | 1 | 2 | 3 |
|---|---|---|---|
| *Adequacy of choices made, and of explanations for substitutions* | All are inappropriate choices, or evidence of limited curriculum/lack of opportunity to make good choices: e.g. very limited range of tasks, evidence of rudimentary assignments, or submissions too brief to allow for assessment of abilities on a variety of writing tasks. | One or two choices may be appropriate, but one or two are poor or questionable; port overall may evidence some limitations of curricular opportunities. | All pieces are good choices: they demonstrate a range of tasks; port overall shows evidence of varied curricular opportunities. |

*(contd)*

## III. COMPLEXITY OF IDEAS

This dimension is at the heart of our assessment because it captures best the nature of the intellectual work students will be expected to do at this university. In our instructions, we told students that 'a critical analysis based on readings you have done is one of the most common assignments at Michigan.'

Analysis can be expressed in the context of a range of tasks or assignments: e.g. 'academic' writing common to the humanities, scientific writing, and creative writing. By 'analysis' we mean evidence of the ability to think abstractly about specific examples, reading, and/or personal experience. Such evidence includes an ability to generate ideas for writing; to make connections between different examples or perspectives; to formulate an explicit statement of a 'theory'; to synthesize different perspectives, or specific examples, in a way which implies a 'theory' or general statement; and/or to experiment with genre or style.

In the course of an analysis, students may draw on various kinds of resources that offer additional perspectives (or voices) on the subject at hand: e.g. written texts, interviews, personal observations and experiences, etc.

|  | 1 | 2 | 3 | 4 |
|---|---|---|---|---|
| a) Analysis | More summarizing of ideas than analysis/ synthesis; over-reliance on generalization, clichés or repetition. | Adequate to strong description and summary, but analysis is simple, fragmented and/ or underdeveloped. | Adequate to strong description and summary, but analysis is unevenly developed, although there is some evidence of synthesizing ideas in a complex way and offering a 'theory'. | Strong analysis; e.g. consistent, substantial, and inventive development of ideas in each piece, along with good sense of how to frame a problem. |
| b) Flow | Lack of continuity between ideas; between and within paragraphs. | One piece may be coherent, but other pieces lack continuity among ideas; paragraphs may seem 'cobbled' together. | Most pieces show continuity among ideas. Continuity may falter in one piece or in a few places. | Strong continuity from one idea to the next in all pieces. |
| c) Use of resources (see above) | Inadequate use of resources, or other perspectives overwhelm student voice. | Awkward or inconsistent use of sources and alternative perspectives. | Overall, in control of resources, although some lapses may occur. | Facility with complex integration of other perspectives including synthesis of personal and text-derived perspectives. |

(contd)

## IV. TEXTUAL CONVENTIONS

| | 1 | 2 | 3 | 4 |
|---|---|---|---|---|
| *Grammar, syntax and mechanics; diction and tone. Para-graphing. Familiarity with essay form when appropriate.* | Grammatical and mechanical problems obscure meaning or fragment text; monotonous syntax; inappropriate or inconsistent use of diction, tone. May exhibit severe paragraphing problems or show lack of familiarity with essay form. | – grammar and syntax: basically in control<br><br>– patterns of mispunctuation or mechanical errors **often** present, but they don't obscure meaning<br><br>– diction/tone: may have **moderate** difficulties<br><br>– paragraphing: **moderate** problems; organization is often formulaic | – grammar and syntax: basically in control; may exhibit some attempt at creativity/syntactic variety<br><br>– patterns of mispunctuation or minor mechanical errors **sometimes** present<br><br>– diction and tone: **minimal** difficulties<br><br>– paragraphing: **minor** problems; organization may be formulaic, although may also show some success in varying formulas such as the 5 paragraph form | Complexity of language (able to play with language and still control it); may or may not exhibit minor mechanical problems; awareness of impact of word choices; dexterity with language: e.g. metaphor or imagery; able to adopt or recreate tone and style of other authors. Transition between paragraphs may help bring out subtle complexities. May show evidence of ability to synthesize creative and academic forms. |

Figure 9.6. Analytic portfolio scoring rubric (Willard-Traub *et al.*, 1999)

complexity of ideas, and textual conventions. In addition to the scale descriptors, the first three of these sections give information to the raters about the context of the assessment and considerations that they should bear in mind when choosing scores. One of the interesting features of this rubric is the fact that it addresses issues specific to portfolio assessment, such as the degree to which the reflective piece discusses writing assignments and processes, the range and appropriateness of the choice of portfolio contents, and variation in effectiveness between different pieces in the portfolio (specifically in the dimension of 'flow').

## Logistical issues in portfolio assessment

In addition to the important decisions about portfolio contents and methods of scoring, a number of logistical issues must be dealt with in implementing portfolio assessment. These issues can be thought of in terms of both time and space. Teachers planning to use portfolios in their classrooms must be prepared to devote sufficient time to introducing the concept of portfolios to their students and to discussing both the rationale for portfolios and the procedures that will be involved in assembling the portfolios. Teachers must also be prepared to spend class time revising work for the portfolio, and, when appropriate, time outside of class working with individual students or providing feedback to students on their writing at various stages. Of course, as mentioned earlier in this chapter, evaluating portfolios can be time-consuming as well. While many writing teachers already do much of this work as a matter of course in their teaching, the amount of time needed to implement portfolios in the classroom is not to be underestimated.

Implementing portfolios on a program-wide basis requires a large investment of time and human resources. In any program, there are likely to be teachers who are initially enthusiastic about the idea of portfolios, and others who have well-founded reservations. If portfolio assessment is to be successfully implemented, the concerns of all teachers must be taken very seriously, and enough time must be devoted to reaching a consensus about both the purpose and the procedures so that teachers are comfortable with the idea and do not feel it is being imposed upon them against their wishes. Hamp-Lyons and Condon (2000) discuss this issue at length, stating that 'the importance of a reflective and participatory system for working with teachers in the program to ensure that they are able to assess portfolios fairly and meaningfully, and for teachers to work together to agree on the structure of the portfolio, the criteria for assessment, and the value to be given to the readings of all concerned, cannot be overstated' (p. 128).

Another crucial logistical aspect of a portfolio assessment system that must be worked out has to do with storage and access to portfolios, both during the preparatory stages of developing the portfolios and after they have been evaluated. While portfolios are being prepared there must either be a place inside the classroom for in-progress materials to be stored, or students must take the responsibility to hold on to their drafts and other papers. Decisions must also be made about the storage of completed portfolios – will they be returned to students, or kept at the school, and if so, for how long? Since many schools are chronically short of storage space and portfolios tend to be bulky, this may be a serious issue in some places and must be taken seriously, although improvements in information storage technology may soon make this consideration obsolete, as portfolios can be stored in electronic format. If portfolios are not returned to students, additional decisions must be made about who will have access to them – for example, will other students be able to use completed portfolios as models? Will administrators or researchers be able to use portfolios at a later date for other evaluative purposes? While it is impossible to predict who will want to look at completed portfolios and for what purpose, it may be wise to collect a release signature from students giving or withholding permission to others to use their portfolios for research or instructional purposes.

## Summary

In this chapter, we have looked at the benefits and limitations of portfolio assessment, and have outlined some considerations to bear in mind when designing and implementing portfolio assessment in a classroom or for large-scale assessment. Particularly in academic contexts, where writing is a strong focus of the curriculum, portfolio assessment has a number of strengths in terms of integrating curriculum and assessment and of providing richer information about students' writing ability. At the present time, portfolio assessment may not be relevant or feasible for many second language learners in non-academic settings; however, it is important for those involved in second-language writing assessment at every level to be aware of the potential benefits – as well as the potential drawbacks – of portfolios so that they can decide for themselves whether the benefits of portfolios outweigh the drawbacks.

# CHAPTER TEN

.........................................................................................

# The future of writing assessment

## Introduction

When we look back at writing assessment in the 20th century, we see a number of phenomena. These include the rise of large testing firms and the concomitant rise in the popularity of so-called 'objective tests' that purported to measure writing ability through multiple-choice tests; the subsequent movement – led primarily by writing teachers – to measure writing through actual writing, and the resulting refinement and general acceptance of the impromptu essay test; and another teacher-led movement, this time towards portfolios, as a reaction to the 'one-shot' approach to essay testing. At the same time, rapid advances in technology and increased global communication have been leading to radical changes in the way writing is used and tested, changes we are only just now beginning to appreciate. Furthermore, there is a growing awareness among educators, theorists, and assessment specialists of the sociopolitical aspects of assessment. Thus, rather than viewing writing assessment as neutral, value-free activities, we now clearly understand that decisions about whom to test, what to test, how, when, and where to test it, and how test results are to be used take place in arenas where different groups of stakeholders have different agendas and value systems. As we progress through the 21st century, therefore, there are a number of areas in which we can expect to see changes and challenges in writing assessment. In this chapter I will focus on two of these areas. First, I will look at the impact of technology on writing and writing assessment, and second, I will look at critical stances towards writing assessment and how they may influence the field over the next several decades.

## Technology and writing assessment

There is no doubt that the rapid growth of new technologies is changing writing in ways that we can only begin to imagine. While a complete discussion of the impact of technology on writing is beyond the scope of this volume, I will discuss three implications of the growth of technology for writing assessment. First, new technologies are affecting the nature of writing itself, in terms of the writing process, the norms and standards for written texts, and the development of new genres of writing. Second, advances in technology are being applied to the scoring of writing by computer, a trend that has raised controversy among writing teachers. Finally, technology, particularly the growth of the internet, has increased global access to information and has contributed to the dominance of English as an international language on the one hand, but may also be increasing divisions between those who have access to new technologies and those who do not. There are thus important social and political consequences of new technologies that must be considered.

### The effects of technology on writing

One important effect of technology on writing is the fact that technology is changing the way we think about writing and how we do it. The traditional distinction between speech and writing is becoming increasingly blurred as a result of the pervasiveness of electronic mail in business, schools, and other settings. The increasing practice of offering courses on-line is also a contributor to this process, as chat rooms and on-line discussions become standard components of university courses. In these contexts, writing takes on many of the aspects traditionally associated with speaking, such as shorter, less complex or even incomplete sentences, lack of attention to accuracy, and less formal language. While this shift to more speech-like writing is attributed by many to the expansion of technology, Baron (1998) maintains that the expanding use of e-mail actually serves to reinforce a trend in this direction already present in formal education, particularly in the United States, as a result of the transformation from a product to a process approach to writing. Baron argues that the increasing practice of composing on-line will further reinforce this tendency, making written language in the future even more speech-like. Furthermore, Baron suggests that, because of the dominance of American English on the internet, 'it seems likely that American writing styles, as represented by computer mediated communications, are destined to influence written norms both in other English-speaking and non-English speaking countries as well' (p. 53). This shift in written norms may have implications for writing assessment in terms of the standards by which writing is judged in the future. It will be interesting to look at scoring rubrics used to judge writing in 20 or 30 years – what will be considered the hallmarks of 'good writing' in future generations?

The shift to more speech-like writing is only one aspect of writing that has been influenced by technology. Another change in writing that has been made possible through technology is the use of hyper-text, or texts that are connected by links which the reader can choose or ignore, allowing the reader to construct his or her own exploration of the text in virtually any order. The use of hypertext challenges our perceptions of written texts – particularly academic texts – as linear documents with an inherently logical ordering of ideas and arguments. Parfitt (1997: 8) argues that 'good' hypertext 'satisfies by being rich and suggestive rather than being compellingly persuasive . . . since there can be so many paths for the reader to explore, hypertext design is perhaps analogous to landscaping or park design, with more emphasis on pleasant surprises than on a single, irresistible narrative or argument.' In this sense the genres that are being created through hypertext may be more like poetry or fiction and may never be as relevant for writing assessment as other more traditional genres. Nevertheless, the use of hypertext may become more prevalent over the next few decades as technology expands, and it is impossible to predict how this form of writing may become relevant for assessment in the future.

Technology is also changing the way writing is taught. The use of technology in writing classes ranges from merely requiring final drafts to be word-processed to teaching in networked classrooms, where much of teacher–student and student–student interaction takes place on-line rather than face-to-face. The use of networked classrooms has led to the increase in actual writing time in class for both native speakers (Palmquist *et al.*, 1998) and ESL students (Braine, 1997), and while there is not conclusive evidence that the increase in writing time leads directly to the improvement in writing quality, some research does suggest that this is the case (Palmquist *et al.*, 1998). From a second language acquisition perspective, it can be hypothesized that the increase in student–student interaction that is afforded by networked classrooms promotes language acquisition and thus can facilitate better writing skills (Braine, 1997).

It is clear from the discussion above that technology is affecting writing in numerous ways. For the purposes of this volume, however, the main question is how these changes will be reflected in writing assessment and how they will influence the ways in which writing is both defined and assessed. Again, it is impossible to predict the future, but we can provide some informed speculation based on what has been discussed so far. First, the changing uses of writing are likely to cause us to rethink our definition of the construct. As technology influences the way writing is taught, particularly in terms of networked classrooms, the social aspects of writing may become more salient. It may become more and more difficult to defend the view of writing ability as an underlying characteristic of an individual that can be measured, like height or weight. In a networked classroom where peers are giving each other frequent feedback on their writing, the most successful papers may not be the ones with the most well-formed sentences and felicitous word choices, but the ones whose authors have reflected on their peers' comments and have used this feedback to hone their arguments and ideas to meet the expectations of their audience. This view of writing stresses the metacognitive aspects of writing over the purely linguistic ones, and may lead us to broaden our definitions of writing ability considerably. In defining constructs for testing purposes, test developers will need to consider very carefully to what extent the ability of interest lies in an individual's ability to interact with others, to take into account others' perspectives in writing and revising, or some other factors, in order to design tasks and scoring procedures that take into account these more metacognitive and social factors. As mentioned above, the movement towards more speech-like qualities of writing and the increasing use of writing for functions that were formerly reserved for oral language – for example, the use of e-mail rather than the telephone for obtaining information – point us towards different writing tasks in writing assessment and different standards for judging writing. There may be less of an emphasis on formal persuasive writing and more of an emphasis on the kinds of writing that are becoming more and more relevant to everyday life – particularly electronic mail and other forms of electronic communication. In terms of writing assessment, this shift may lead to a rethinking of the kinds of tasks that we include on writing tests and the criteria by which such tasks are scored. As workplace writing tasks gain importance, it is likely that more research will be done on workplace writing as opposed to academic writing, which may also lead us in unexpected directions as we broaden our notions of the functions and uses of writing.

## Computer scoring of writing

An important aspect of technology in writing assessment is the use of computers in place of or in addition to human raters to score essays. Computer scoring of essays was first proposed in the 1960s by Page and associates (Daigon, 1966; Page, 1966, 1968). Page's approach to computer scoring, called Project Essay Grade (PEG), involves using a statistical procedure, regression analysis, to determine how well a number of variables, such as average sentence length, number of paragraphs, and punctuation, could predict the scores given by human raters to a fairly large set of training essays (approximately 270). The variables used by PEG represent surface features of the essays, and the values obtained from the statistical analysis are then used to predict scores for the rest of the essays. Recent studies with the PEG system have found that essay scores derived from PEG correlate with scores given by single human raters as well as or better than pairs of raters correlate with each other (Page, 1994; Page and Peterson, 1995; Peterson, 1997; all cited in Chung and O'Neil, 1997). While this result is certainly impressive, Chung and O'Neil point out several limitations of the PEG system. First, and foremost from a construct validity point of view, the PEG system does not consider the meaning or content of the essays, since it considers only surface features of the essay. In addition, a PEG system needs to be specifically developed for each set of essays used. Scores derived from PEG are only meaningful with respect to the set of essays being used; that is, they cannot be compared to an external criterion. Finally, an exact description of the variables used by PEG has never been published, so that little is known about the relative effectiveness of different variables in determining the essay scores.

Another approach to computer essay scoring is called Latent Semantic Analysis (LSA), which is 'both a computational model of human knowledge representation and a method for extracting semantic similarity of words and passages from text' (Foltz *et al.*, 1999: 1). In contrast to the PEG system, LSA methods are based on comparing the semantic content of words used in essays rather than surface features of the texts, and thus it is more appropriately used for writing in content-area courses, where writing is used to display students' knowledge in a specific area. To use LSA for a particular essay assignment, LSA is first 'trained' on a range of domain-representative texts so that the system represents the information from these texts as a matrix relating words and documents. Essays are then judged against this matrix to determine how similar they are to the source documents. Like the PEG system, LSA is quite reliable; Foltz *et al.* (1999) report that, in a set of 188 essays on the functioning of the human heart, the average correlation between pairs of human raters was .83, while the correlation of LSA scores with scores given by human raters was .80. One advantage of LSA is that, as a web-based application, it can give students immediate feedback on their essays, including information on how the essays can be improved by adding information about specific subtopics. Another advantage of LSA is that it can use both relative and absolute scoring methods; that is, an essay can be compared to other essays within the same sample, or it can be compared to an outside source document, such as a textbook or an 'expert' essay (Chung and O'Neil, 1997). On the other hand, one disadvantage of LSA is that word order is not taken into account because of the matrix arrangement of information, making every possible combination of words in a sentence equivalent.

A third rating system, developed recently by ETS, called E-rater, is currently being used operationally to rate essays written for the Graduate Management Admissions Test (GMAT), in conjunction with human raters. E-rater is designed to analyze essays according to the characteristics specified in the scoring guides used by human raters (Burstein *et al.*, 1998). E-rater is similar to PEG in that it uses the same statistical analysis (regression) of a large number of variables on scores of training essays to predict scores for the rest of the essay set. However, unlike PEG, E-rater features include syntactic structure, rhetorical structure, and topical analysis. Syntactic structures include complement clauses, subordinate clauses, relative clauses, and modal auxiliaries, and syntactic variety is measured by ratios of syntactic structures per essay and per sentence. Rhetorical structure is dealt with by partitioning the essay into its arguments, using syntactic and paragraph-based distributions of words, phrases, and structures that signal rhetorical organization. Finally, topical analysis compares the vocabulary in essays to vocabulary used in the training essays that represent each level on the rating scale in a manner similar to that used by LSA. Studies at ETS have shown that E-rater's scores are at least as reliable as those of human raters for both GMAT essays and TWE essays (Burstein and Chodorow, 1999; Burstein *et al.*, 1998). Research and development of E-rater and other forms of automated essay scoring are ongoing; see Shermis and Burstein (forthcoming) for a comprehensive overview of computer-scored writing assessment.

Perhaps not surprisingly, the use of computers to score essays has engendered some controversy. Writing teachers in particular have expressed opposition to computer scoring of essays. As Drechsel (1999) states, 'not only does this method of assessment disregard decades of research on the writing process, but it also assumes a theory of reading that goes backward in time to New Criticism – when all there was to a page of writing was a page of writing (p. 384).' The notion that writing can be graded on the basis of linguistic features of the text rather than the message that the text conveys is understandably abhorrent to teachers who see their role as preparing students to write convincingly for genuine purposes and audiences rather than to produce texts that make use of the textual features that are used by computers to score essays.

For the foreseeable future it is unlikely that computers will completely replace human raters in large-scale assessment. As Breland (1996), a strong advocate of the use of technology in writing assessment instruction, points out, 'grading is a high-stakes event that can affect other important events, such as college admission; accordingly, grading seems an unlikely task for the computer' (p. 255). Breland suggests that computers can best be used to help students edit their work and to help teachers see aspects of their students' writing that they may have overlooked. Nevertheless, the exigencies of large-scale writing assessment, in which large numbers of essays must be graded in a relatively short time at a reasonable cost, will make the move towards computer-graded essays on the part of large testing companies, at least to supplement if not replace human raters, almost inevitable.

## The technology gap

One aspect of technology and writing that is a concern is the potential for a gap between those with access to and familiarity with computers and those without. This is particularly a problem for computer-based large-scale assessments such as the TOEFL where using a computer is optional or even mandatory. The so called 'digital divide' is a topic of concern for educators. In a survey of students at a US university, Chisholm et al. (1998) found that minority students were less likely to have computers at home than majority students and that minority students began using computers at a later age than their majority counterparts. Internationally, access to computers varies greatly as well. Chisholm et al. (1999) found that Chinese and Ghanaian students at a US university were far less likely to own computers than their US counterparts. Similarly, researchers at ETS found that computer familiarity varied considerably among TOEFL candidates from different countries (Taylor et al., 1998). While certain types of computer-based assessments involve only rudimentary computer skills such as clicking and dragging with a mouse, writing on the computer is an entirely different matter, involving complex keyboarding skills. Unless such skills are part of the construct (as they might be, for example, in a test for office workers) it is clearly inequitable to require students with weak or non-existent keyboarding skills to use a computer rather than pen and paper on writing tests. ETS recognizes this potential for inequity and allows writers the choice between writing by hand or keying in their essays; however, the potential for inequity still exists, as word-processed essays and handwritten essays may be scored differently, as was discussed in Chapter 6. As technology becomes more sophisticated, particularly in the area of speech and handwriting recognition protocols, this may become a moot point – that is, in a few years, keyboards may become obsolete, and computers may become so inexpensive that virtually everyone will own them – but in the meantime it is important to recognize the potential for inequity that exists with unequal access to technology.

## Writing assessment as politics: critical stances towards assessment

Most specialists in language testing believe that tests, when developed carefully and used properly, can fulfill a useful societal role in helping to allocate societal resources in a fair and equitable way; for example, by identifying students who have a high probability of success in post-secondary education and those who might need extra assistance to be successful. However, many scholars have pointed out that education and educational testing have political aspects as well, in that education can serve to further the interests of certain groups in society at the expense of others. Perhaps the most political aspect of education is educational testing, as tests can be used by one group to wield power over other groups, by serving as gatekeeping mechanisms that allow or prevent people from pursuing their educational, professional or personal goals. This view of testing has recently come to the forefront of discussions about language testing, and is summarized succinctly in an article by Shohamy, who provides the following list of the characteristics of critical language testing:

- Critical language testing views test takers as political subjects in a political context.
- It views language tests as tools directly related to levels of success, deeply embedded in cultural, educational and political arenas where different ideological and social forms struggle for dominance.
- It asks questions about what sort of agendas are delivered through tests and whose agendas they are.
- It challenges psychometric traditions and considers interpretive ones.
- It claims that language testers need to ask themselves what sort of vision of society language tests create and what vision of society tests subserve; are language tests merely intended to fulfill pre-defined curricular or proficiency goals or do they have other agendas?
- It asks questions about whose knowledge the tests are based on. Is what is included in language tests 'truth' to be handed on to test takers, or is it something that can be negotiated, challenged, and appropriated?
- It considers the meaning of language test scores, the degree to

which they are prescriptive, final, or absolute, and the extent to which they are open to discussion and interpretation.

- It perceives language testing as being caught up in an array of questions concerning educational and social systems; the notion of 'just a test' is an impossibility because it is impossible to separate language testing from the many contexts in which it operates.

(Shohamy, 1998: 332–333)

Seen through the lens of critical language testing, the history of writing assessment outlined briefly at the beginning of this chapter can be characterized in terms of conflicts between various stakeholders in the assessment process. White (1996) contrasts the agendas and issues for four different groups of stakeholders: teachers, researchers and theorists, testing firms and government bodies, and students, particularly minorities and other disadvantaged student groups. For example, White notes that testing firms and their clients (administrators in school districts, state boards of education, and colleges and universities) want assessments that produce scores quickly and cheaply, and assessments that lead to 'the sorting of students according to existing social patterns' (p. 20), while teachers want assessments that acknowledge the complexity of writing and that respect teachers' professionalism. The different world views and agendas of these groups lead almost inevitably to conflicts, as each group has a stake in how writing is defined for the purpose of assessment, how it is tested, and how test results are used.

Thus the three main movements in writing assessment in the 20th century – the use of so-called indirect tests of writing (i.e. multiple-choice tests of usage), the renewed acceptability of the timed impromptu writing test, and now the movement towards portfolio assessment – can be seen as directly tied to the agendas of these different groups. Indirect tests of writing represented the domination of the agenda of testing firms and their clients, who wanted fast, reliable, and inexpensive ways of sorting students according to the status quo of existing social patterns.

The first major challenge to this state of affairs was led by teachers who felt that these tests did not meet their needs or those of their students. The impromptu essay test subsequently became the standard approach to testing writing. Different groups of stakeholders had to compromise – teachers had to give up some of what Scharton (1996) refers to as 'home rule,' in which the teacher is the sole arbiter of writing quality, to agree to a set of standards and rating procedures for the sake of reliability, which was an important criterion for testing firms. At the same time, testing firms had to accept the notion that a single essay – in essence, a one-item test – provided sufficient information for decision-making purposes. The impromptu essay test is thus a compromise between the view of teachers, who see writing as a complex, multi-faceted process and assessment as something which must be closely integrated with instruction, and the view of psychometricians, whose equally valid concerns for reliability lead them to a preference for tasks that break writing down into writing ability as the sum of discrete, measurable, component parts.

The move towards portfolio assessment represents a further stage in this tension, with teachers again leading the effort to have their perspectives on writing influence the way writing is assessed, rather than relying so heavily on the views of testing firms and outside authorities in assessment. Scharton (1996) describes the tension between the 'instructional perspective' of teachers, represented in particular by the portfolio movement, and the 'programmatic perspective' of large bodies such as institutions, in terms of the narratives implied by each perspective. The implied narrative in the instructional perspective involves 'right-minded teachers struggl[ing] against ruthless big-company test designers who merely want to sell a test score to administrators interested in a quick fix' (p. 56) while in the narrative implied by the programmatic perspective, 'a skeptical scientist uses sophisticated techniques to test hypotheses generated by observations of a natural phenomenon. In this narrative, science provides the educational enterprise with hard data able to correct the misapprehensions and rebut the anecdotal evidence of naive practitioners' (p. 64). What constitutes validity for these stakeholders varies according to the perspective taken: instructors value assessment methods that faithfully mirror the kinds of writing that occur in their classroom, while psychometricians value assessment methods that can consistently rank-order students and that can be compared with other measures of the same construct. With these radically different perceptions of assessment, conflicts are perhaps inevitable. White (1996) argues that such conflicts can only be solved by including as many perspectives as possible in the debate and laying out the assumptions of all sides in an open forum. A similar argument is made by Hamp-Lyons and Condon (2000).

Whether those who hold firmly to the instructional and programmatic perspectives on writing assessment will ever truly see eye-to-eye is an open question. In the meantime, at least two different solutions to the validity issues raised by portfolios have been put forth. Camp (1993) argues that psychometricians will need to develop new measurement models that will take into account the complexity of the writing process and that will meet the needs of teachers and students in the assessment process. In Camp's words:

> [The] characteristics of the performances represented in writing portfolios put them outside the realm of conventional psychometrics. Yet they are the characteristics that make the portfolios most worthwhile, most compatible with current views of writing and writing instruction, and most consistent with new approaches to assessment – meaningful tasks that are complex, challenging, and inherently valuable to learning; knowledge and skills measured in the context of complex performance; an extended timeframe for the performance; opportunity to demonstrate the use of processes and strategies important to performance; opportunity for collaboration and support in the performance environment. Furthermore, the portfolios whose benefits for learning and instruction appear to have greatest immediate and long-term effect are most at odds with traditional psychometrics. This conflict suggests that the apparent difficulty in balancing the purposes of teaching and learning and those of measurement arise from the limitations of measurement theory and methodology based on assumptions about learning that are inconsistent with current perspectives. That is, the methodology associated with conventional psychometrics may well be incompatible with assessments that directly serve teaching, learning, and accountability as they are currently understood. This is not to say that the issues that motivate the use of conventional psychometric methodology are irrelevant to portfolios; validity, consistency of judgment, and equity, among other considerations, are still important. But it may mean that in using portfolios to answer the need for richer information and more credible performances we have created models for assessment that are beyond the range of current measurement theory. (Camp, 1993: 206–207)

On the other hand, there is another movement in writing assessment away from traditional psychometric approaches to what Moss (1994) proposes as a hermeneutical approach, which involves 'holistic, integrative interpretations of collected performances that seek to understand the whole in light of its parts, that privilege readers who are most knowledgeable about the context in which the assessment occurs, and that ground those interpretations not only in the textual and contextual evidence available, but also in a rational debate among the community of interpreters' (p. 7). Moss contrasts the traditional approach to achieving reliability in writing assessment – rater training, independence of scores, standardization of tasks – with procedures that allow for discussion and debate among raters, taking into account all available evidence. As an example she discusses the procedures for hiring a university faculty member, in which candidates prepare a portfolio, search committee members are appointed based on their expertise, and a great deal of discussion of the candidate's qualifications takes place before a decision is made. This procedure allows for a valid and fair decision to be made without invoking the psychometric concerns of reliability. Moss proposes that hermeneutic approaches to writing assessment allow for validity by taking into account the voices of all stakeholders, by encouraging dialogue and debate, and by utilizing the expertise of those most directly involved with the students being tested; that is, classroom teachers.

Huot (1996) builds upon Moss' ideas with a set of principles for writing assessment, shown in Table 10.1. According to Huot, writing assessment should be site-based, locally controlled, context-sensitive, rhetorically based, and accessible to those whose writing is being evaluated. In other words, these principles of writing assessment explicitly acknowledge the social and contextual factors that writing practices are embedded in. As of this writing it is too early to say whether psychometricians will rise to Camp's challenge of developing new models that can deal with complexities of the writing process or whether a more hermeneutical approach will become more widely accepted. Both Camp and Moss recognize the need to incorporate a broader view of writing ability than can be measured adequately by current models and scoring procedures that emphasize reliability and generalizability at the expense of local contextualized knowledge. The movement towards computer scoring of essays seems to be antithetical to these concerns, and one of the challenges of the next decades may be to attempt to reconcile these perspectives. It may be that the most appropriate middle ground, as suggested by Breland (1996), is to see computer scoring of essays and local expert knowledge as complementary sources of information that can both be used to make informed decisions about test takers.

Table 10.1. *Principles for a new theory and practice of writing (Huot, 1996: 562)*

SITE-BASED
An assessment for writing is developed in response to a need that occurs at a specific site. Procedures are based upon the resources and concerns of an institution, department, program or agency, and its administrators, faculty, students, or other constituents.

LOCALLY-CONTROLLED
The individual institution or agency is responsible for maintaining, revising, updating, and validating the assessment procedures that should be carefully reviewed according to clearly outlined goals and guidelines on a regular basis to safeguard the concerns of those affected by the assessment process.

CONTEXT-SENSITIVE
The procedures should honor the instructional goals and objectives as well as the cultural and social environment or agency and its students, teachers, and other stakeholders. It is important to establish and maintain the cultural integrity necessary for the authentic reading and writing of textual communication.

RHETORICALLY-BASED
All writing assignments, scoring criteria, writing environments, and reading procedures should adhere to recognizable and supportable rhetorical principles integral to the thoughtful expression and reflective interpretation of texts.

ACCESSIBILITY
All procedures and rationales for the creation of writing assignments, scoring criteria, and reading procedures, as well as samples of student work and rater judgement, should be available to those whose work is being evaluated.

## Summary and conclusion

In this chapter we have considered a number of issues that I believe will be relevant to writing assessment in the 21st century. The growth of technology has already changed the nature of writing in important ways that will continue to influence how writing is assessed, both in terms of the writing itself and in terms of how writing tests are created and scored. In addition, the range of issues that assessment specialists need to factor into test development and use has broadened over the past few decades to include a close investigation of the societal and political implications of assessment. While there are still controversies and important issues that must be dealt with, there are also several points on which there is little disagreement. First, it is clear that effective communication in writing will continue to be a crucial skill for academic, professional, and everyday life settings, and may become even more important as technology allows for instantaneous global communication. Second, assessment of writing skills is a valuable social activity that can serve to promote social goals such as increasing access to education, diagnosing areas of strength and weakness, and certifying the writing ability of professionals for whom performance on the job depends on effective communication skills. Third, it is absolutely essential, particularly in high-stakes situations, that any assessment methods be carefully designed with due attention to the aspects of test usefulness outlined in Bachman and Palmer (1996) and in this book. Finally, for a test or assessment method to serve its function well and to be accepted as a useful and equitable social tool, the perspectives of all stakeholders need to be addressed in the process of developing, administering, and communicating about a test. Carried out thoughtfully and conscientiously, writing assessment can be a positive tool for supporting student learning, helping language learners achieve their personal and professional goals, and promoting more effective communication worldwide.

# Bibliography

Adams, R. (1981). The reliability of marking of five June 1980 examinations. Mimeo, Associated Examining Board, Guildford.

Alderson, J. C. (1991). Bands and scores. In Alderson, J. C. and B. North (eds.), *Language testing in the 1990s: The communicative legacy*. London: Modern English Publications/British Council/Macmillan, 71–86.

Alderson, J. C. (2000). *Assessing reading*. Cambridge: Cambridge University Press.

Alderson, J. C., Clapham, C. and Wall, D. (1995). *Language test construction and evaluation*. Cambridge: Cambridge University Press.

Alderson, J. C. and Hamp-Lyons, L. (1996). TOEFL preparation courses: a study of washback. *Language Testing*, 13 (3), 200–97.

American Council for the Teaching of Foreign Languages. (1985). *ACTFL Proficiency Guidelines*. Hastings-on-Hudson, NY: ACTFL Materials Center.

Apodaco, M. (1990). *Proficiency sample project*. Denver, CO: Colorado State Department of Education. (ERIC Document Reproduction Service No. ED 332 507).

Arnold, V., Legas, J., Obler, S., Pacheco, M. A., Russell, C. and Umbdenstock, L. (1990). Do students get higher scores on their word-processed papers? A study of bias in scoring hand-written versus word-processed papers. Unpublished manuscript, Rio Hondo College, Whittier, CA.

Arrington, P. (1988). A dramatistic to understanding and teaching the paraphrase. *College Composition and Communication* 33 (2), 185–197.

Bachman, L. F. (1990). *Fundamental considerations in language testing*. Oxford and New York: Oxford University Press.

Bachman, L. F. (forthcoming). *Statistics for language assessment*. Cambridge: Cambridge University Press.

Bachman, L. F. and Palmer, A. S. (1996). *Language testing in practice*. Oxford: Oxford University Press.

Baddeley, A. D. (1986). *Working memory*. Oxford: Oxford University Press.

Bailey, K. M. (1996). Working for washback: a review of the washback concept in language testing. *Language Testing* 13 (3), 257–79.

Baron, N. S. (1998). Writing in the age of email: the impact of ideology versus technology. *Visible Language* 32, 35–53.

Bauer, B. A. (1981). *A study of the reliabilities and cost-efficiencies of three methods of assessment for writing ability* (ERIC Document Reproduction Service No. ED 216 357).

Belanoff, P. and Elbow, P. (1986). Using portfolios to increase collaboration and community in a writing program. *Writing Program Administration* 9 (3), 27–40.

Bensoussan, M., Sim, D. and Weiss, R. (1981). The effect of dictionary usage on EFL test performance compared with student and teacher attitudes and expectations. *Biannual Conference of the International Association of Applied Linguists* (ERIC Document No. ED 232 436).

Bereiter, C. and Scardamalia, M. (1987). *The psychology of written composition*. Hillsdale, NJ: Lawrence Erlbaum Associates.

Bernhardt, E. (1991). *Reading development in a second language*. Norwood, NJ: Ablex.

Biber, D. (1988). *Variation across speech and writing*. Cambridge: Cambridge University Press.

Bloom, B. S. (1956). *Taxonomy of educational objectives: Classifications of educational goals. Handbook I: Cognitive domain*. New York: McKay.

Boldt, H., Valescchi, M. I. and Weigle, S. C. (2001). Evaluation of ESL student writing on text-responsible and non-text responsible writing tasks. *MEX-TESOL Journal* 24, 13–33.

Braine, G. (1997). Beyond word processing: networked computers in ESL writing classes. *Computers and Composition* 14 (1), 45–58.

Breland, H. M. (1996). Computer-assisted writing assessment: The politics of science versus the humanities. In E. M. White, W. D. Lutz and S. Kamusikiri (eds.), *Assessment of writing: politics, policies, practices*. New York: Modern Language Association of America, pp. 249–256.

Breland, H. M. and Jones, R. J. (1984). Perception of writing skills. *Written Communication* 1 (1), 101–19.

Bridgeman, B. and Carlson, S. (1983). *Survey of academic writing tasks required of graduate and undergraduate foreign students*. Princeton, NJ: Educational Testing Service.

Brossell, G. (1983). Rhetorical specification in essay topics. *College English* 45, 165–73.

Brossell, G. (1986). Current research and unanswered questions in writing assessment. In K. L. Greenberg, H. S. Weinder and R. A. Donovan (eds.), *Writing assessment: Issues and strategies* (pp.168–82). New York: Longman.

Brossell, G. and Ash, B. H. (1984). An experiment with the wording of essay topics. *College and Communication* 35, 423–25.

Brown, H. D. (1994). *Teaching by principles: An interactive approach to language pedagogy*. Englewood Cliffs, NJ: Prentice Hall Regents.

Brown, J. D. (1991). Do English and ESL faculties rate writing samples differently? *TESOL Quarterly* 25, 587–603.

Brown, J. D., Hilgers, T. and Marsella, J. (1991). Essay prompts and topics: minimizing the effects of mean differences. *Written Communication* 8, 533–556.

Burstein, J. and Chodorow, M. (1999). *Automated essay scoring for nonnative English speakers*. Available on-line: www.ets.org/research/erater.html

Burstein, J., Kulkich, K., Wolff, S., Lu, C., Chodorow, M., Braden-Harder, L. and Harris, M. D., (1998). Automated scoring using a hybrid feature identification technique. Available on-line: www.ets.org/research/erater.html

Butler, F. A., Weigle, S. C., Kahn, A. B. and Sato, E. Y. (1996). *Test development plan with specifications for placement instruments anchored to the model standards*. Los Angeles: University of California, Los Angeles, Center for the Study of Evaluation.

Byrd, P. (1998). Grammar FROM context. In P. Byrd and J. Reid (eds.), *Grammar in the composition classroom: Essays on teaching ESL for college-bound students* (pp. 54–68).

CAL (1984). Basic English Skills Test. Washington: Center for Applied Linguistics.

Camp, R., (1993). Changing the model for the direct assessment of writing. In M. M. Williamson and B. A. Huot (eds.), *Validating holistic scoring for writing assessment* (pp. 45–78). Cresskill, NJ: Hampton.

Canale, M. and Swain, M. (1980). Theoretical bases of communicative approaches to second language teaching and testing. *Applied Linguistics* 1, 1–47.

CARLA (2001). Center for Advanced Research on Language Acquisition. *CoWA (Contextualized Writing Assessment)* Available on-line: http://carla.acad.umn.edu/CoWA.html

Carlson, J. G., Bridgeman, B., Camp, R. and Waanders, J. (1985). *Relationship of admission test scores to writing performance of native and nonnative speakers of English* (TOEFL Research Report #19). Princeton, NJ: Educational Testing Service.

Carr, N. (2000). A comparison of the effects of analytic and holistic composition in the context of composition tests. *Issues in Applied Linguistics* 11, 207–41.

Carrell, P. and Eisterhold, J. C. (1983). Schema theory and ESL reading pedagogy. *TESOL Quarterly* 17, 553–573.

Carroll, J. B. (1989). The Carroll model: A twenty-five-year retrospective and prospective view. *Educational Researcher* 18 (1), 26–31.

Carson, J. G. (2000). Reading and writing for academic purposes. In Pally, M. (ed.), Sustained content teaching in academic ESL/EFL, chapter 3, pp. 19–34.

Carson, J. G., Chase, N. D., Gibson, S. U. and Hargrove, M. (1992). Literacy demands of the undergraduate curriculum. *Reading Research and Instruction* 31 (4), 25–50.

Cast, B. M. J. (1939). The efficiency of different methods of marking English compositions. *British Journal of Educational Psychology* 9 (1), 257–69.

Chapelle, C. A. (1998). Construct definition and validity inquiry in SLA research. In L. Bachman and A. Cohen (eds.), *Interfaces between second language acquisition and language testing research* (pp. 32–70). Cambridge: Cambridge University Press.

Chapelle, C. A., Grabe, W. and Berns, M. (1993). *Communicative language proficiency: Definitions and implications for TOEFL 2000.* [ETS Internal Report.] Princeton, NJ: Educational Testing Service.

Charney, D. (1984). The validity of using holistic scoring to evaluate writing. *Research in the Teaching of English* 18, 65–81.

Chase, C. I. (1968). The impact of some obvious variables on essay test scores. *Journal of Educational Measurement* 5, 315–18.

Chisholm, I. M., Irwin, L. and Carey, J. M. (1998). An international comparison of computer perceptions, attitudes and access. *Technology and teacher education annual. Society for Information Technology and Teacher Education International Conference, USA*, 98, 195–198.

Chisholm, I. M., Carey, J. and Hernandez, A. (1999). Access and utilization of computer technology by minority university students. *Technology and teacher education annual. Society for Information Technology and Teacher Education International Conference, USA*, 99.

Chung, Gregory K. W. K. and O'Neil, H. F. Jr. (1997). Methodological approaches to online scoring of essays (Report No. CSE-TR-461) (ERIC Document Reproduction Service No. ED 418 101).

Cohen, A. D. (1994). *Assessing language ability in the classroom.* (2nd ed.). Boston, MA: Heinle and Heinle.

Cole, N. and Moss, P. (1989). Bias in test use. In R. Linn (ed.), *Educational testing* (3rd ed. pp. 201–219). New York: Macmillan.

Collado, A. V. (1981). Using the students' first language: Comparing and contrasting. *TESOL Higher Education Interest Section Newsletter* 3, 9–10.

Connor, U. and Carrell, P. (1993). The interpretation of tasks by writers and readers in holistically rated direct assessment of writing. In J. G. Carson and I. Leki (eds.), *Reading in the composition classroom* (pp. 141–160). Boston, MA: Heinle and Heinle.

Council of Europe (2001). Common European framework of reference: Learning, teaching, assessment. Cambridge: Cambridge University Press.

Council of Europe (2000). European Language Portfolio. Available on-line: http://culture2.coe.int/portfolio/

Crowhurst, M. (1980). Syntactic complexity and teachers' ratings of narrations and arguments. *Research in the Teaching of English* 13, 223–31.

Cumming, A. (1989). Writing expertise and second language proficiency. *Language Learning* 39, 81–141.

Cumming, A. (1990). Expertise in evaluating second language composition. *Language Testing* 7, 31–51.

Daigon, A. (1966). Computer grading of English composition. *English Journal* 55, 46–52.

Daly, J. A. and Dickson-Markman, F. (1982). Contrast effects in evaluating essays. *Journal of Educational Measurement* 19 (4), 309–16.

Daly, J. A. and Miller, M. D. (1975). Further studies in writing apprehension: SAT scores, success, expectations, willingness to take advanced courses, and sex differences. *Research in the Teaching of English* 9, 549–253.

Davidson, F. and Lynch, B. K. (2002). *Testcraft: A teacher's guide to writing and using language test specifications.* New Haven, CT: Yale University Press.

Diederich, P. B. (1974). Measuring growth in English. Urbana: NCTE.

Dillon, W. T. (1997). Corporate advisory boards, portfolio assessment, and business and technical writing program development. *Business Communication Quarterly* 60 (1), 41–58.

Douglas, D. (2000). *Assessing languages for specific purposes.* Cambridge. Cambridge University Press.

Drechsel, J. (1999). Writing into silence: Losing voice with writing assessment technology. *Teaching English in the Two-Year College* 26 (4), 380–387.

Dweck, C. (1986). Motivational processes affecting learning. *American Psychologist* 41, 1040–1048.

Ericsson, K. A. and Simon, H. (1980). Verbal reports as data. *Psychological Review* 87, 215 51.

Elliot, N., Kilduff, M. and Lynch, R. (1994). The assessment of technical writing: A case study. *Journal of Technical Writing and Communication* 24 (1) 19–36.

ETS (1989). *TOEFL Test of Written English Guide.* Princeton, NJ: Educational Testing Service.

ETS (1998). *TOEFL* 1998–99 Information Bulletin for Computer-Based Testing.

ETS (2000). *Test of English as a Foreign Language (TOEFL).* Princeton, NJ: Educational Testing Service.

Faigley, L., Daly, J. A. and Witte, S. (1981). The role of writing apprehension in writing performance and writing competence. *Journal of Educational Research* 75, 16–21.

Feak, C. and Dobson, B. (1996). Building on the impromptu: A source-based academic writing assessment. *College ESL* 6, (1), 73–84.

Ferris, D. and Hedgcock, J. S. (1998). *Teaching ESL composition: Purpose, process and practice.* Mahwah, NJ: Lawrence Erlbaum Associates.

Flower, L. and Hayes, J. (1980). The dynamics of composing: Making plans and juggling constraints. In L. W. Gregg and E. R. Steinberg (eds.), *Cognitive processes in writing*. Hillsdale, NJ: Lawrence Erlbaum Associates.

Flower, L. and Hayes, J. (1980a). The cognition of discovery: Defining a rhetorical problem. *College Composition and Communication* 31, 21–32.

Foltz, P. W., Laham, D. and Landauer, T. K. (1999). Automated essay scoring: Applications to educational technology. In Proceedings of EdMedia '99. Available on-line: http//www-psych.nmsu.edu/~pfoltz/reprints/Edmedia99.html

Francis,J. C. (1977). Impression and analytic marking methods. Mimeo, MS Aldershot: Associated Examining Board.

Fredrickson, J. R. and Collins, A. (1989). A systems approach to educational testing. *Educational Research* 18, 27–32.

Freedman, S. W. (1979). How characteristics of student essays influence teachers' evaluations. *Journal of Educational Psychology* 71, 328–381.

Freedman, S. W. (1981). Influences on evaluators of expository essays: Beyond the text. *Research in the Teaching of English* 15 (3), 245–55.

Gardner, H. (1985). *The mind's new science: A history of the cognitive revolution*. New York: Basic Books.

Gardner, R. and Lambert, W. (1972). *Attitudes and motivation in second language learning*. Rowley, MA: Newbury House.

Gathercole, S. E. and Baddeley, A. (1993). *Working memory and language*. Hillsdale, NJ: Lawrence Erlbaum Associates.

Gould, J. D. and Grischkowsky, N. (1984). Doing the same work hard copy and with CRT terminals. *Human Factors* 26, 323–337.

Grabe, W. and Kaplan, R. B. (1989). Writing in a second language: Contrastive rhetoric. In D. M. Johnson and D. H. Roen (eds.), *Richness in writing* (pp. 263–284). New York and London: Longman.

Grabe, W. and Kaplan, R. B. (1996). *Theory and practice of writing*. New York: Longman.

Grabowski, J. (1996). Writing and speaking: Common grounds and differences toward a regulation theory of written language production. In C. M. Levy and S. Ransdell (eds.), *The science of writing*. NJ: Lawrence Erlbaum Associates.

Grice, H. P. Logic and conversation. In P. Cole and J. L. Morgan (eds.), *Syntax and semantics: Speech acts*. New York, NY: Academic Press.

Grobe, C. (1981). Syntactic maturity, mechanics, and vocabulary as predictors of writing quality. *Research in the Teaching of English* 15, 75–85.

Haas, C. (1987). How the writing medium shapes the writing process: Studies of writers composing with pen and paper and with word processing. Unpublished doctoral dissertation. Carnegie Mellon University.

Hake, R. (1986). How do we judge what they write? In K. L. Greenberg, H. S.

Weinder and R. A. Donovan (eds.), *Writing assessment: Issues and strategies* (pp. 153–67). New York: Longman.

Hale, G., Taylor, C., Bridgeman, B., Carson, J., Kroll, B. and Kantor, R. (1996). *A study of writing tasks assigned in academic degree programs.* (TOEFL Research Report No. 54). Princeton, NJ: Educational Testing Service.

Hales, L. W. and Tokar, E. (1975). The effects of the quality of preceding responses on the grades assigned to subsequent responses to an essay question. *Journal of Educational Measurement* 12, 115–17.

Hamp-Lyons, L. (1986). Testing second language writing in academic settings. Unpublished doctoral dissertation, University of Edinburgh.

Hamp-Lyons, L. (1990). Second language writing: Assessment issues. In B. Kroll (ed.), *Second language writing: Research insights for the classroom.* New York: Cambridge University Press.

Hamp-Lyons, L. (1991a). Basic Concepts. In L. Hamp-Lyons (ed.), *Assessing second language writing in academic contexts.* Norwood, NJ: Ablex.

Hamp-Lyons, L. (1991b). Pre-text: Task-related influences on the writer. In L. Hamp-Lyons (ed.), *Assessing second language writing in academic contexts.* Norwood, NJ: Ablex.

Hamp-Lyons, L., (1991c). Scoring procedures for ESL contexts. In L. Hamp-Lyons (ed.), *Assessing second language writing in academic contexts.* Norwood, NJ: Ablex.

Hamp-Lyons, L. (1991d). The writer's knowledge and our knowledge of the writer. In L. Hamp-Lyons (ed.), *Assessing second language writing in academic contexts.* NJ: Ablex Publishing Corporation.

Hamp-Lyons, L. and Condon, W. (2000). *Assessing the portfolio: Principles for practice theory and research.* Cresskill, NJ: Hampton Press.

Hamp-Lyons, L. and Kroll, B. (1997). *TOEFL 2000 – writing: Composition, community, and assessment.* (TOEFL Monograph Series Report No. 5). Princeton, NJ: Educational Testing Service.

Hamp-Lyons, L. and Matthias, S. P. (1994). Examining expert judgments of task difficulty on essay tests. *Journal of Second Language Writing* 3 (1), 49–68.

Hatch, E. and Lazaraton, A. (1991). *The research manual: Design and statistics for applied linguistics.* Boston: Heinle and Heinle.

Hartog, P. J., Rhodes, E. C. and Burt, C. (1936). *The marks of examiners.* London: Macmillan.

Hayes, J. R. (1996). A new framework for understanding cognition and affect in writing. In C. M. Levy and S. Ransdell (eds.), *The science of writing.* NJ: Lawrence Erlbaum Associates.

Hayes, J. R. and Flower, L. S. (1980). Identifying the organization of writing processes. In L. W. Gregg and E. R. Steinberg (eds.), *Cognitive processes in writing* (pp. 31–50). Hillsdale, NJ: Lawrence Erlbaum Associates.

Herman, J. L., Gearhart, M. and Aschbacher, P. R. (1996). Portfolios for class-room assessment: Design and implementation issues. In R. Calfee and P. Perfumo (eds.), *Writing portfolios in the classroom: Policy and practice, promise and peril.* Mahwah, NJ: Lawrence Erlbaum Associates.

Hinds, J. (1987). Reader vs writer responsibility: A new typology. In U. Connor and R. Kaplan (eds.), *Writing across languages: Analysis of L2 text.* Reading, MA: Addison-Wesley.

Hinkel, E. (1994). Native and nonnative speakers' pragmatic interpretations of English texts. *TESOL Quarterly* 28 353–376.

Hoetker, J. (1982). Essay examination topics and students' writing. *College Composition and Communication* 133, 377–392.

Hoetker, J. and Brossell, G. (1989). The effects of systematic variations in essay topics on the writing performance of college freshmen. *College Composition and Communication* 33, 377–92.

Hoger, Elizabeth A. (1998). A portfolio assignment for analyzing business communications. *Business Communication Quarterly* 61 (3), 64–66.

Homburg, T. J. (1984). Holistic evaluation of ESL composition: Can it be validated objectively? *TESOL Quarterly* 18, 1, 87–107.

Horowitz, D. (1991). ESL writing assessments: Contradictions and resolutions. In L. Hamp-Lyons (ed.), *Assessing second language writing in academic contexts.* Norwood, NJ: Ablex.

Hughes, A. (1989). *Testing for language teachers.* Cambridge: Cambridge University Press.

Hughes, D. E. and Keeling, B. (1984). The use of models to reduce context effects in essay scoring. *Journal of Educational Measurement* 21 (3), 277–81.

Hughes, D. E., Keeling, B. and Tuck, B. F. (1980). The influence of context position and scoring method on essay scoring. *Journal of Educational Measurement* 17, 131–35.

Hughes, D. E., Keeling, B. and Tuck, B. F. (1983). Affects of achievement and handwriting quality on scoring essays. *Journal of Educational Measurement* 20, 65–70.

Huot, B. (1988). The validity of holistic scoring: A comparison of talk-aloud protocols of expert and novice holistic raters. Unpublished doctoral dissertation, Indian University of Pennsylvania.

Huot, B. (1990a) Reliability, validity, and holistic scoring: What we know and what we need to know. *College Composition and Communication* 41 (2), 201–213.

Huot, B. (1990b). The literature of direct writing assessment: Major concerns and prevailing trends. *Review of Educational Research* 60 (2), 237–263.

Huot, B. (1996). Toward a new theory of writing assessment. *College Composition and Communication* 47, 549–66.

Hymes, D. (1972). On communicative competence. In J. Pride and A. Holmes (eds.), *Sociolinguistics.* NY: Penguin. 269–93.

Jacobs, H., Zinkgraf, S., Wormuth, D., Hartfiel, V. and Hughey, J. (1981). *Testing ESL composition: A practical approach*. Rowley, MA: Newbury House.

Jakobson, R. (1960). Linguistics and poetics. In T. A. Sebeok (ed.), *Style in language*. New York: John Wiley.

Janopolous, M. (1992). University faculty tolerance of NS and NNS writing errors: A comparison. *Journal of Second Language Writing* 1 (2), 109–121.

Johns, A. M. (1990). L1 composition theories: implications for developing theories of L2 composition. In B. Kroll (ed.), *Second language writing: Research insights for the classroom*. Cambridge, England and New York: Cambridge University Press.

Kaplan, R. B. (1966). Cultural thought patterns in intercultural education. *Language Learning* 16, 1–20.

Kean, D., Gylnn, S. and Britton, B. (1987). Writing persuasive documents: The role of students' verbal aptitude and evaluation anxiety. *Journal of Experimental Education* 55, 95–102.

Keech, C. L. (1982). Practices in designing writing prompts: Analysis and recommendations. In J. R. Gray and L. P. Ruth (eds.), *Properties of writing tasks: A study of alternative procedures for holistic writing assessment* (pp. 132–214) Berkeley: University of California, Graduate School of Education, Bay Area Writing Project (ERIC Document No. ED 320 576).

Keech, C. L. and McNelly, M. E. (1982). Comparison and analysis of rate responses to the anchor papers in the writing prompt variation study. In J. R. Gray and L. P. Ruth (eds.), *Properties of writing tasks: A study of alternative procedures for holistic writing assessment*. Berkeley: University of California, Graduate School of Education, Bay Area Writing Project.

Kenyon, D. (1992). Introductory remarks at symposium on development and use of rating scales in language testing, 14th Language Testing Research Colloquium, Vancouver, 27 February–1 March.

Kobayashi, H. and Rinnert, C. (1999). Factors affecting composition evaluation in an EFL context: Cultural rhetorical pattern and readers' background. *Language Learning* 46 (3), 397–437.

Koretz, D., McCaffrey, D., Klein, S., Bell, R. and Stecher, B. (1993). The reliability of scores from the 1992 Vermont portfolio assessment program. Washington, DC: RAND Institute on Education and Teaching.

Krapels, A. R. (1990). An overview of second language writing process research. In B. Kroll (ed.), *Second language writing: Research insights for the classroom*. New York: Cambridge University Press.

Kroll, B. (1990). *Second language writing: Research insights for the classroom*. New York: Cambridge University Press.

Kroll, B. and Reid, J. (1994). Guidelines for designing writing prompts: Clarifications, caveats, and cautions. *Journal of Second Language Writing* 3 (3), 231–255.

Land, R. E. and Whitley, C. (1989). Evaluating second language essays in regular composition classes: Towards a pluralistic U.S. In D. M. Johnson and D. H. Roen (eds.), *Richness in writing: Empowering ESL students* (pp. 284–293). New York: Longman.

Leki, I. (1992). *Understanding ESL writers*. NH: Heinemann Educational Books.

Leki, I. and Carson, J. (1997). Completely different worlds: EAP and the writing experiences of ESL students in university courses. *TESOL Quarterly* 31 (1), 39–70.

Lewkowicz, J. (1997). Investigating authenticity in language testing. Unpublished doctoral dissertation, University of Lancaster.

Lloyd-Jones, R. (1977). Primary trait scoring. In C. R. Cooper and L. Odell (eds.), *Evaluating writing* 33–69. NY: National Council of Teachers of English.

Lumley, T. (forthcoming). Assessment criteria in a large-scale writing test: What do they really mean to the raters? Language Testing.

Lynch, B. K. and Davidson, F. (1994). Criterion-referenced language test development: Linking curricula, teachers and tests. *TESOL Quarterly* 28 (4), 727–43.

Mabry, L. (1999). *Portfolios plus: A critical guide to alternative assessment*. Thousand Oaks, CA: Corwin.

Madigan, R., Linton, P., and Johnson, S. The paradox of writing apprehension. In Levy, C. M. and S. Ransdell (eds.), *The science of writing*. Hillsdale, NJ: Lawrence Erlbaum Associates.

Markham, L. R. (1976). Influence of handwriting quality on teacher evaluation of written work. *American Educational Research Journal* 13, (4), 277–283.

Matalene, C. (1985). Contrastive rhetoric: An American writing teacher in China. *College English* 47, 789–807.

McNamara, T. F. (1996). *Measuring second language performance*. London and New York: Longman.

*MELAB Technical Manual* (1996). Ann Arbor, MI: University of Michigan Press.

Mendelsohn, D. and Cumming, A. (1987). Professors' ratings of language use and rhetorical organizations in ESL compositions. *TESL Canada Journal* 5 (1), 9–26.

Messick, S. (1989). Meaning and values in test validation: The science and ethics of assessment. *Educational Researcher* 18 (2) 5–11.

Messick, S. (1994). The interplay of evidence and consequences in the validation of performance assessments. *Educational Researcher* 23, 2, 13–23.

Moss, P. A. (1994). Can there be validity without reliability? *Educational Research* 23 (2), 5–12.

Murphy, S. and Camp, R. (1996). Moving towards systematic coherence: A discussion of conflicting perspectives in portfolio assessment. In R. Calfee and P. Perfumo (eds.), *Writing portfolios in the classroom: Policy and practice, promise and peril*. Mahwah, NJ: Lawrence Erlbaum Associates.

Murphy, S. and Ruth, L. (1993). The field testing of writing prompts reconsidered. In M. W. Williamson and B. A. Huot (eds.), *Validating holistic scoring for writing assessment: Theoretical and empirical foundations*. Cresskill, NJ: Hampton Press.

Nesi, H. and Meara, P. (1991). How using dictionaries affects performance in multiple-choice EFL tests. *Reading in a Foreign Language* 8 (1), 631–643.

Nold, E. W. and Freedman, S. W. (1977). An analysis of readers' responses to essays. *Research in the Teaching of English* 11, 164–174.

Norris, J., Brown, J. D., Hudson, T. and Yoshioka, J. (1998). Designing second language performance assessments. University of Hawai'i at Manoa: Second Language Teaching and Curriculum Center.

North, B. and Schneider, G. (1998). Scaling descriptors for language proficiency scales. *Language Testing* 15 (2) 217–263.

Northwest Evaluation Association. (1991). Portfolios. *Portfolio News* 2 (3), 4

Ostler, S. (1987). English in parallels: A comparison of English and Arabic prose. In U. Connor and R. Kaplan (eds.), *Writing across languages: Analysis of L2 text*, Reading, MA: Addison-Wesley.

Page, E. (1966). The imminence of grading essays by computer. *Phi Delta Kappan*, 46, 238–243.

Page, E. (1968). The use of computers in analyzing student essays. *International Review of Education* 14, 127–142.

Page, E. (1994). Computer grading of student prose: Using modern concepts and software. *Journal of Experimental Education* 62 (2), 127–142.

Page, E. and Peterson, N. S. (1995). The computer moves into essay grading: Updating the ancient text. *Phi Delta Kappan* March, 561–565.

Palmquist, M., Kiefer, K., Hartvigsen, J. and Goodlew, B. (1998). *Transitions: Teaching in computer-supported and traditional classrooms*. Greenwich, CT: Ablex.

Palmquist, M. and Young, R. (1992). The notion of giftedness and student expectations about writing. *Written communication* 9 (1), 137–168.

Parfitt, M. (1997). What kind of discourse? Thinking it through. *Annual Meeting of the Conference on College Composition and Communication*. (ERIC Document No. ED 418 406).

Peirce, B. N. (1995). Social identity, investment, and language learning. *TESOL Quarterly* 29 (1), 9–31.

Pennington, M. (1996). *The computer and the non-native writer*. Creskill, NJ: Hampton Press, Inc.

Perl, S. (1979). The composing process of unskilled college writers. *Research in the Teaching of English* 13 (4), 317–336.

Peterson, N. S. (1997) Automated scoring of written essays: Can such scores be valid? Paper presented at NCME in Chicago, 26 March.

Polio, C. and Glew, M. (1996). ESL Writing assessment prompts: How students choose. *Journal of Second Language Writing* 5 (1), 35–49 (ERIC Document Reproduction Service No. EJ 527 730).

Pollitt, A. (1990). Response to Charles Alderson's paper: 'Bands and scores.' Alderson, J. C. (1991). In J. C. Alderson and B. North (eds.), *Language testing in the 1990s: The communicative legacy.* London: Modern English Publications/British Council/Macmillan, 87–91.

Popham, W. J. (1978). *Criterion-referenced measurement.* Englewood Cliffs, NJ: Prentice Hall.

Powers, D. E., Fowles, M. E., Farnum, M. and Ramsey, P. (1994). Will they think less of my handwritten essay if others words process theirs? Effects on essay scores of intermingling handwritten and word-processed essays. *Journal of Educational Measurement* 31 (3), 220–233.

Powers, D. E. and Fowles, M. E. (1996). Effects of applying different time limits to a proposed GRE writing test. *Journal of Educational Measurement* 33 (4) 433–452.

Purves, A. (1992). Reflection on research and assessment in written composition. *Research in the Teaching of English* 26, 108–122.

Purves, A. C., Soter, A., Takala, S. and Vähäpässi, A. (1984). Towards a domain-referenced system for classifying assignments. *Research in the Teaching of English* 18 (4), 385–416.

Quellmalz, E. S., Capell, F. J. and Chou, C. P. (1982). Effects of discourse and response mode on the measurement of writing competence. *Journal of Educational Measurement* 19 (4), 242–258.

Raimes, A. (1985). What unskilled ESL students do as they write: A classroom study of composing. *TESOL Quarterly* 19 (2) 229–258.

Raimes, A. (1991). Out of the woods: Emerging traditions in the teaching of writing. *TESOL Quarterly* 25 (3) 407–430.

Ransdell, S. and Levy, M. (1996). Working memory constraints on writing quality and fluency. In C. Levy and S. Ransdell (eds.), *The science of writing.* NJ: Lawrence Erlbaum Associates.

Reid, J. (1990). Responding to different topic types: A quantitative analysis from a contrastive rhetoric perspective. In B. Kroll (ed.), *Second language writing: Research insights for the classroom.* New York: Cambridge University Press.

Reid, J. (1998). Responding to ESL student language problems: Error analysis and revision plans. In P. Byrd and J. Reid (eds.), *Grammar in the composition classroom: Essays on teaching ESL for college-bound students* (pp. 118–137).

Reid, J. and Byrd, P. (1998). Writing to persuade and the language of persuasion. In P. Byrd and J. Reid (eds.), *Grammar in the composition classroom: Essays on teaching ESL for college-bound students* (pp. 101–117).

Reid, J. and Kroll, B. (1995). Designing and assessing effective classroom writing assignments for NES and ESL students. *Journal of Second Language Writing* 4 (1), 17–41.

Ruth, L. and Murphy, S. (1984). Designing topics for writing assessment: Problems of meaning. *College Composition* 35 (4) 410–421.

Ruth, L. and Murphy, S. (1988). *Designing writing tasks for the assessment of writing.* Norwood, NJ: Ablex.

Saari, H. and Purves. A. C. (1992). The curriculum in mother-tongue and written composition. In A. C. Purves (ed.), *The IEA study of written composition II: Education and performance in fourteen countries.* Oxford: Pergamon (37–86).

Sacks, H., Schegloff, E. and Jefferson, G. (1974). A simplest semantics for the organization of turn-taking conversation. *Language* 50, 696–735.

Santos, T. (1988). Professors' reactions to the academic writing of nonnative-speaking students. *TESOL Quarterly* 22 (1), 69–90.

Scharton, M. (1996). The politics of validity. In E. M. White, W. D. Lutz and S. Kamusikiri (eds.), *Assessment of writing: Politics, policies, practices.* New York: The Modern Language Association of America.

Schumann, J. H. (1978). *The pidginization process: A model for second language acquisition.* Rowley, MA: Newbury House Publishers.

Scott, V. M. (1996). *Rethinking foreign language writing.* Boston: Heinle and Heinle.

Shen, F. (1988). The classroom and the wider culture: Identity as a key to learning English composition (Staffroom Interchange). *College Composition and Communication* 40, 4, 459–66.

Shermis, M. and Burstein, J. (forthcoming). *Automated essay scoring: A cross disciplinary perspective.* Hillsdale, NJ: Lawrence Erlbaum Associated.

Shohamy, E. (1998). Critical language testing and beyond. *Studies in Educational Evaluation* 24 (4), 331–345.

Shohamy, E., Denitsa-Schmidt, S. and Ferman, I. (1996). Test impact revisited: Washback effect over time. *Language Testing* 13 (3), 298–317.

Shohamy, E., Gordon, C. and Kraemer, R. (1992). The effect of raters' background and training on the reliability of direct writing tests. *Modern Language Journal* 76(4), 513–521.

Silva, T. (1993). Toward an understanding of the distinct nature of L2 writing: The ESL research and its implications. *TESOL Quarterly* 27, 657–77.

Sloan, C. and McGinnis, I. (1982). The effect of handwriting on teachers' grading of high school essays. *Journal of the Association for the Study of Perception* 17 (2), 15–21.

Smith W. L., Hull, G. A., Land, R. E., Moore, M. T., Ball, C., Dunham, D. E., Hickey, L. S., and Ruzich, C. W. (1985). Some effects of varying the structure of the topic on college students' writing. *Written Communication* 2, 73–89.

Sommer, N. (1980). Revision strategies of student writers and experienced adult writers. *College Composition and Communication* 31, 378–88.

Spaan, M. (1993). The effect of prompt on essay examinations. In D. Douglas and C. Chapelle (eds.), *A new decade of language testing research* (pp. 98–122). Alexandria, VA: TESOL.

Spack, R. F. (1988). Initiating ESL students into the academic discourse community: How far should we go? *TESOL Quarterly* 22 (1), 29–52.

Spalding, E. and Cummins, G. (1998). It was the best of times. It was a waste of time: University of Kentucky students' view of writing under KERA. *Assessing Writing* 5 (2), 167–199.

Sperling, M. (1991). *High school English and the teacher–student writing conference: Fine tuned duets in the ensemble of the classroom.* (Occasional Paper No. #26). Berkeley, CA: Center for the Study of Writing.

Sperling, M. (1996). Revisiting the writing–speaking connection: Challenges for research on writing and writing instruction. *Review of Educational Research* 66, 53–86.

Sproull, L. and Kiesler, S. (1986). Reducing social context cues: Electronic mail in organization communication. *Management Science* 32, 1492–1512.

Stewart, M. and Grobe, C. (1979). Syntactic maturity, mechanics of writing, and teachers' quality ratings. *Research in the Teaching of English* 13 (3) 207–15.

Stock, P. L. and Robinson, J. L. (1987). Taking on testing. *English Education* 19, 93–121.

Sullivan, F. J. (1987). Negotiating expectations: Writing and reading placement tests. Paper presented at the meeting of the Conference of College Composition and Communication, Atlanta, GA.

Swales, J. (1990). *Genre analysis: English in academic and research settings.* Cambridge: Cambridge University Press.

Sweedler-Brown, C. O. (1985). The influence of training and experience on holistic essay evaluation. *English Journal* 74 (5) 49–55.

Sweedler-Brown, C. O. (1993). ESL essay evaluation: The influence of sentence-level and rhetorical features. *Journal of Second Language Writing* 2 (1), 3–17.

Taylor, C., Jamieson, J., Eignor, D. and Kirsch, I. (1998). *The relationship between computer familiarity and performance on computer-based TOEFL test tasks.* (TOEFL Research Report No. 61). Princeton, NJ: Educational Testing Service.

Tedick, D. (1990). ESL writing assessment: Subject-matter knowledge and its impact on performance. *English for Specific Purposes* 9, 123–43.

Tedick, D. and Mathison, M. (1995). Holistic scoring in ESL writing assessment: What does an analysis of rhetorical features reveal? In D. Belcher and G. Braine (eds.), *Academic writing in a second language: Essays on research and pedagogy* (pp. 205–230). Norwood, NJ: Ablex.

Truscott, J. (1996). The case against grammar correction in L2 writing classes. *Language Learning* 46 (2), 327–369.

UCLES (1997). *First Certificate in English: a handbook.* Cambridge: UCLES.

UCLES (2002). *International English Language Testing System.* Cambridge: UCLES, The British Council, IDP Education, Australia.

Valdéz, G., Haro, P. and Echevarriarza, M. (1992). The development of writing abilities in a foreign language: Contributions toward a general theory of L2 writing. *Modern Language Journal*, 76, 3, 333–52.

Vaughan, C. (1992). Holistic assessment: What goes on in the rater's mind? In L. Hamp-Lyons (ed.), *Assessing second language writing in academic contexts* (pp. 111–26). Norwood, NJ: Ablex.

Vähäpässi, A. (1982). On the specification of the domain of school writing. In A. C. Purves and S. Takala (eds.), *An international perspective on the evaluation of written composition* (pp. 265–289). Oxford: Pergamon.

Wall, D. (1996). Introducing new tests into traditional systems: Insights from general education and from innovation theory. *Language Testing* 13 (3), 334–354.

Weaver, F. (1973). The composing process of English teacher candidates: Responding to freedom and constraint. Unpublished doctoral dissertation, University of Illinois, Champaign-Urbana, IL.

Weigle, S. C. (1994). Effects of training on raters of ESL compositions. *Language Testing* 11, 197–223.

Weigle, S. C. (1998). Using facets to model rater training effects. *Language Testing* 15 (2), 263–87.

Weigle, S. C. (1999). Investigating rater/prompt interactions in writing assessment: Quantitative and qualitative approaches. *Assessing Writing* 6 (2), 145–178.

Weigle, S. C. and Jensen, L. (1997). Assessment issues for content-based instruction. In M. A. Snow and D. Brinton (eds.), *The content-based classroom: Perspectives on integrating language and content* (pp. 201–212). White Plains, NY: Addison Wesley Longman.

Weigle, S. C. and Nelson, G. (2001). Academic writing for university examinations. In I. Leki (ed.), *Academic writing programs* (pp. 121–135). Alexandria, VA: TESOL.

Weigle, S. C., Lamison, B. and Peters, K. (2000). Topic selection on a standardized writing assessment. Paper presented at Southeast Regional TESOL, Miami, FL, October.

Weir, C. J. (1988). Construct validity. In A. Hughes, D. Porter and C. J. Weir (eds.), *ELTS Validation project report (ELTS Research reports 1 (ii)).* London: The British Council/UCLES.

Weir, C. J. (1990). *Communicative language testing.* NJ: Prentice Hall Regents.

White, E. M. (1984). Holisticism. *College Composition and Communication* 35 (4), 400–409.

White, E. M. (1985). *Teaching and assessing writing.* San Francisco, CA: Jossey-Bass.

White, E. M. (1994). *Teaching and assessing writing: Recent advances in understanding, evaluating and improving student performance.* (2nd ed.). San Francisco: Jossey-Bass.

White, E. M. (1995). An apologia for the timed impromptu essay test. *College Composition and Communication* 46, 30–45.

White, E. M. (1996). Power and agenda setting in writing assessment. In E. M. White, W. D. Lutz and S. Kamusikiri (eds.), *Assessment of writing: Politics, policies, practices.* New York: The Modern Language Association of America.

Willard-Traub, M., Decker, E., Reed, R. and Johnston, J. (1999). The development of large-scale portfolio placement assessment at the University of Michigan: 1992–1998. *Assessing Writing* 6 (1), 41–84.

Wolcott, W. (with Legg, S. M.) (1998). *An overview of writing assessment: Theory, research and practice.* Urbana, IL: National Council of Teachers of English.

Yorkey, R. (1977). Practical EFL techniques for teaching Arabic-speaking students. In J. Alatis and R. Crymes (eds.), *The human factors in ESL.* Washington: TESOL.

Zamel, V. (1983). The composing processes of advanced ESL students: Six case studies. *TESOL Quarterly* 17, 165–187.

# Index